# ORTHO'S GUIDE TO HERBS

Created and Designed by
the Editorial Staff of Ortho Books

Author
**Monica Brandies**

Illustrator
**Cyndie C.H. Wooley**

# ORTHO BOOKS

**Publisher**
Robert B. Loperena

**Editorial Director**
Christine L. Jordan

**Editors**
Robert J. Beckstrom
Michael D. Smith

**Managing Editor**
Sally W. Smith

**Prepress Supervisor**
Linda M. Bouchard

**Sales & Marketing Manager**
David C. José

**Publisher's Assistant**
Joni Christiansen

**Graphics Coordinator**
Sally J. French

**Editorial Coordinator**
Cass Dempsey

Address all inquiries to:
Ortho Books
Box 5006
San Ramon, CA 94583-0906

| 1 | 2 | 3 | 4 | 5 | 6 | |
|---|---|---|---|---|---|---|
| 97 | 98 | 99 | 2000 | 01 | 02 | Softcover |

| 1 | 2 | 3 | 4 | 5 | 6 | |
|---|---|---|---|---|---|---|
| 97 | 98 | 99 | 2000 | 01 | 02 | Hardcover |

ISBN 0-89721-313-0 Softcover
ISBN 0-89721-316-5 Hardcover

Library of Congress Catalog Card Number 96-67629

**THE SOLARIS GROUP**
2527 Camino Ramon
San Ramon, CA 94583

**Consultant**
Paula Ann Winchester

**Proofreader**
David Sweet

**Indexer**
Frances Bowles

**Thanks to**
Gail and Hank Biddle
Myra Bonhage-Hale,
  La Paix Farm, Alum Bridge,
  West Virginia
Nick Cohon
Deborah Cowder
Suzie Eglin
Kathy and Joe Jolson
Tyvan Pulis
David Van Ness

**Separations by**
Color Tech. Corp.

**Lithographed in the USA by**
Banta Book Group

**Photo Stylist**
Stevie Bass

**Assistant Stylist**
Rose Hansen

**Front Cover**

Herbs enter and enhance our lives in many ways—through their beauty, their scent, and their many uses. This backyard garden includes lavender, santolina, Russian chamomile, and bergamot.

**Title Page**

Welcome to the Herb Garden!

**Back Cover**

**Left:** Herb flowers and leaves in aspic dress up a cheese spread. See page 91.

**Center:** Purple coneflower, like many herbs, is a beautiful flower as well as an herb. This is the source of the herbal remedy echinacea. See page 256.

**Right:** Even in a small space you can grow a generous supply of fresh herbs for kitchen and crafts.

**Photographers**

Names of photographers are followed by the page numbers on which their work appears.

Liz Ball: Photo/Nats: 187B

Laurie Black: 259T

Patricia J. Bruno/Positive Images: 19, 40L, 64

Gay Bumgarner: 15, 77, 249, 283B, back cover R

Gay Bumgarner: Photo/Nats: 199

Karen Bussolini/Positive Images: Front cover, 7, 32

Christi Carter: 45, 195T, 201, 203, 209, 222L, 243, 246, 250, 253, 279B

Priscilla Connell: Photo/Nats: 8, 262T, back cover C

Crandall & Crandall: 207, 232R

R. Todd Davis Photography, Inc.: 40R, 121, 221R, 236, 252, 256, 273

Alan & Linda Detrick: 3B, 20, 168-169, 178, 192, 247, 258, 265, 276, 284

Michael A. Dirr: 14, 143, 171, 179B, 180, 185, 186, 191, 197, 221L, 226, 230, 280, 283T

Wally Eberhart: Photo/Nats: 285

Elemental Images: 198, 210

Thomas E. Eltzroth: 216, 260, 274

Derek Fell: 1, 3TL, 3TC, 4-5, 12, 22, 24, 27, 33, 38-39, 51, 118, 138, 172L, 175, 177T, 177B, 181, 182, 189B, 200T, 202, 205B, 211, 212, 213, 214, 217, 232L, 234, 237B, 238, 245B, 251T, 255B, 262B, 263, 277T, 282

Betsy Fuchs: Photo/Nats: 205T

Harry Haralambou/Positive Images: 29, 114, 170, 239, 240, 241

Saxon Holt: 10, 25, 28, 36, 55, 57TR, 57B, 78, 133, 173, 208, 223, 225, 228L, 235B

Jerry Howard/Positive Images: 65, 75, 172R, 189T, 190, 206, 271

Sydney Karp: Photo/Nats: 49

John A. Lynch: Photo/Nats: 101, 219

Robert E. Lyons: Photo/Nats: 204, 267T, 286

J. Napton: 139, 184R

John Neubauer: 61

Geoffrey Nilsen: 3BC, 11, 70-71, 76, 80, 85, 89, 91, 93, 94, 96, 98, 99, 100, 103, 104, 105, 107, 108-109, 111, 117, 122, 124, 126, 128-129, 130, 132, 134, 135, 140, 141, 146, 147, 148, 150, 153, 154-155, 157, 160, 161, 163, 166, back cover L

Jo-Ann Ordano: Photo/Nats: 242

Ortho Photo Library: 59, 60, 73, 127, 179T, 184L, 215

Pam Peirce: 21

Ben Phillips: Photo/Nats: 193

Ann Reilly: 259B

Laura C. Scheibel: Photo/Nats: 224

Richard Shiell: 136, 144, 183L, 200B, 218, 231, 272, 278, 279T

John J. Smith: Photo/Nats: 255T

Pam Spaulding/Positive Images: 3T, 16-17, 57TL

David M. Stone: Photo/Nats: 266, 270

Joseph G. Strauch, Jr.: 34, 46, 53, 87, 90, 174, 183R, 195B, 196, 222R, 227, 229, 235T, 237T, 244, 248, 254, 257, 261, 267B, 275, 277B, 281

Kim Todd: Photo/Nats: 106

Tom Tracy: 58, 66, 68, 72, 79, 188, 194, 228R

John N. Trager: 187T, 245T, 251B, 269

Mark Turner: 63

Lee Anne White/Positive Images: 9

# CONTENTS

# LIVING WITH HERBS

*Stacked logs make attractive raised beds for an informal herb garden. Among the herbs in this garden are lamb's-ears, basil, lavender, and wormwood. Butterflies are sipping at the lavender flowers.*

Herbs are among the easiest plants to grow and know. Enjoying them can be as simple as rubbing a sprig of rosemary between your fingers or brushing against a drift of mint to release its fragrance. Or you can use herbs in the kitchen to appreciate their culinary virtues. Or herbs can be crafted into wreaths and potpourris to make their fragrance and subtle blooms everlasting.

Awareness of herbs is the first step to acquaintance. Many common plants that we see every day are herbs. Learning about herbs is an adventure, one that starts easily with commonly known herbs and can progress to more unusual herbs that are a challenge to find. Knowing how various cultures throughout history have made practical use of herbs bonds us with those who had many of the same needs we have today.

# HERBS IN EVERYDAY LIFE

There is at least one herb in almost every dish of every meal, from rosemary in a pizza topping to oregano in an omelet to tarragon in fine French cooking. Herbs flavor liqueurs and root beer. They may be unobtrusive or proclaimed ingredients in soaps, shampoos, perfumes, bath powders, and skin moisturizers. Almost half of all modern medicines include herbs as a significant ingredient, whether extracted from the actual plant or synthesized to imitate it.

In sidewalk restaurants in France, it is customary to set a potted basil plant on each table, not only for decoration but also to keep away flies. Nicandra (*Nicandra physaloides*), also called shooflyplant, was commonly grown in the days before windows were screened. Many people are rediscovering today that nicandra reduces fly problems on modern farms, drastically lowering the number of flies in the farm kitchen. A few osage-oranges (*Maclura pomifera*) tucked under sinks and in the back of closets can help keep a house free of roaches and waterbugs.

Hair rinses made with parsley, sage, rosemary, nasturtium, or watercress can give hair luster. Crushed leaves of comfrey, violet, or mullein help take the itch out of mosquito bites. The juice of an aloe vera leaf can soothe diaper rash and minor burns. Many delicious herbal teas help ease the discomfort of the common cold.

## EASY WAYS TO USE HERBS

Here are some quick and practical uses for herbs.

▪ Refresh the breath with parsley. Chew it after a meal for its chlorophyll, which takes away garlic and onion odors.

▪ Garnish with herbs. Restaurants and food photographers use fresh herbs lavishly. Home cooks tend to forget how important eye appeal can be. Keep parsley and chives on the kitchen windowsill or close to the back door for quick snips. Try sprigs of rosemary, scented geranium, lemon balm, or mint leaves. Use flowers of chives or daylilies.

▪ Enjoy an herbal bath. Put leaves of lemon balm or mint in a mesh bag and suspend it from the faucet. Or use herbal tea bags. Some herbs will soothe and relax, others will refresh and invigorate, so use different herbs for morning or evening.

▪ Dress up party drinks with herbs frozen in ice cubes. Use rose petals, sprigs of mint or lemon balm, or flowers of borage, violet, johnny-jump-up, or pineapple sage. Use distilled water to make them absolutely clear. Arrange borage blossoms upside down in the water so that the black stamen tips will not float to the top.

▪ Debug the garden with chiles. Liquify several small hot chiles or one large one in a blender with plenty of water. Let the debris settle to the bottom, then strain off the liquid, transfer it to a spray bottle, and spray the tops and undersides of plant leaves.

▪ Debug the pantry. Especially in warm climates, one or two dried bay leaves or one or two whole nutmegs placed in a flour canister, cracker box, or rice or cereal packages will deter bugs.

▪ Replace mustiness with fragrance. Place a few sprigs of fresh or dried leaves of your favorite fragrant herb—lavender or rosemary are excellent—in a sofa bed when guests leave, in empty suitcases between trips, in out-of-season clothes, or in the cooler between picnics.

▪ Plant mint around clothesline posts or the trash can storage area. Stepping on the mint releases the fragrance and helps make a dull chore delightful.

▪ Drift off to sleep smelling lavender. A few drops of essential oil of lavender, available in small vials, on the pillow will smell wonderful and lull you to relaxing sleep.

▪ Scent fires with herbs. Save woody prunings and stems from herbs in a special container beside the indoor fireplace or outdoor grill and add them to the fire a little at a time for fragrance.

▪ Neutralize smoking odors. Instead of ashtrays, use attractive bowls of white sand with a bit of baking soda mixed in as a deodorizer. Add a few drops of your favorite essential oil for a pleasant scent.

*Beautiful in the gar-
den, lavender can
also bring its scent
indoors in countless
ways. Place sprigs of
lavender in guest
beds to dispel musty
odors, place them
in linen drawers, or
hang lavender
wands (see page
120) in your closet.*

*Purple coneflower, a flower-garden favorite that qualifies as an herb because of its medicinal uses, attracts butterflies to the garden.*

## WHAT IS AN HERB?

The pronunciation and definition of the word *herb* have long been the subject of debate. Some say "herb," pronouncing the *h*. In the United States the word is usually pronounced "erb," with the *h* silent. Both pronunciations are correct.

One dictionary definition of the word *herb* is "a seed-producing annual, biennial, or perennial that does not develop persistent woody tissue but dies down at the end of the growing season." Unfortunately, this definition disqualifies rosemary and bay laurel, for example, as herbs, since both develop woody tissue. A second dictionary definition is "a plant or plant part valued for its medicinal, savory, or aromatic qualities." But this definition does not distinguish *herb* from *spice*.

For the purpose of this book, herb is defined as any part of a plant with culinary, aromatic, cosmetic, insecticidal, insect-attracting, or dye-making uses—beyond the usual uses of plants for landscaping or producing food. An herb is easily grown in temperate climate gardens, is usually an herbaceous plant, and has as its most useful part the leaf or flower.

What is the difference between an herb and a spice? A spice is a strongly flavored, aromatic substance, primarily from bark, root, berry, or pod, and most often from a vine, shrub, or tree grown in tropical regions of the Eastern Hemisphere. Most spices are not easily grown in temperate-climate home gardens, although some, such as allspice (*Pimenta dioica*), can be grown as a potted houseplant.

## ENJOYING HERBS

The importance and delight of herbs are based partly on their ability to comfort and uplift. Although herbs often have small, even inconspicuous, flowers, the plants are fragrant and alive with bees, butterflies, and hummingbirds. Herb foliage comes in a great variety of textures and colors, forms and fragrances. Some herbs need to be brushed against or rubbed between the fingers to release the aroma. Others will do it at the kiss of a breeze.

Herbs can be planted almost anywhere, but they will be enjoyed most where they are frequently touched, trodden upon, sat on, or met at eye or nose level. Herbs don't have to be consumed to be enjoyed. They can simply be looked at, sniffed, or observed as they grow, bloom, and bear seed.

Suggestions for easy ways of using herbs are given on page 6. Ideas for introducing herbs to

*Locate herb gardens near a favorite sitting area or grow them beside a walk where their scent will waft to you as you pass. You can enjoy a scented plant without damaging it by rubbing a leaf gently between two fingers, then sniffing your fingers.*

*This tiny, informal herb garden, simple to make, is an attractive way to supply fresh herbs for the kitchen. Square and circular designs have been traditional in herb gardens for centuries.*

children of preschool age through grade 8 are suggested on page 13. Using herbs to dye Easter eggs is fun for adults and children; instructions are given on page 14.

## Planting and Tending Herbs

Chances are that most gardeners have grown herbs among their flowers or shrubs. Nasturtiums, calendula, scented geraniums, and vinca are commonly grown plants that are not always recognized as herbs. Some herbs are considered weeds; many others, such as mint, are taken for granted. If you are intimidated by the thought of carefully planning a formal herb garden, you can start with a small, informal plot, or incorporate herbs into your existing plantings.

Most herbs are easy to grow and widely available. Potted chives, basil, sage, and thyme can often be found in the supermarket. Common herbs are found in almost every seed catalog. Most herbs start readily from seed or cuttings. Well-stocked nurseries usually carry a wide variety of herbs, including unusual ones.

Even gardeners with limited space can grow herbs. Whereas a 2- by 4-foot vegetable garden would scarcely provide for a small family, fresh and dried herbs from the same-size herb garden could enhance an entire year's worth of meals. Herbs can also be grown in pots on a sunny windowsill—an enjoyable and satisfying year-round diversion for children as well as adults.

## Cooking With Herbs

Herbs added to food and drink can make the difference between dull and delicious. Parsley sprigs on a meat platter, a few nasturtium blooms atop a salad, and a leafy celery stalk in a tall glass of tomato juice make the plainest of fare look festive. Even a reluctant child may be enticed to eat an unfamiliar vegetable when it smells and looks inviting.

By growing only the four herbs made memorable by the song "Scarborough Fair"—parsley, sage, rosemary, and thyme—you can enhance many dishes. Parsley modifies the strong flavors of the onion family and helps blend the flavors of other herbs. Sage leaves can be chopped and added to biscuit or bread dough, dumplings, or apple fritter batter. Sprigs of sage laid on top of hot coals give grilled food a special flavor and the yard a wonderful aroma. Sage is a traditional ingredient in poultry stuffing. Rosemary leaves add zest to chicken, pasta, potatoes, pizza, and bread.

Thyme comes in a variety of flavors: caraway, coconut, nutmeg, lemon, and oregano, to name a few. Delicious with other herbs or by itself, thyme is essential to bouquet garni and is used in French, Creole, and Cajun cooking.

*Sage adds fragrance and flavor to grilled chicken. Place the leaves on the coals as well as on the chicken.*

## Sharing Herbs

One of the most delightful ways to use herbs is to share them with friends. A sprig of germander or thyme pressed between the folds of a letter adds both scent and sentiment. So does a sprig of rosemary (for remembrance) or juniper or spruce when tied in the bow of a gift package.

A vase of fresh herbs will pleasantly perfume a sickroom. Mint will probably root before the speediest recovery; the patient's "therapy" could include potting the rooted sprigs or planting them in the garden. Freshly cut herbs that can be dried and will last for months or years are any of the artemisias, yarrow, bergamot, goldenrod, joe-pye-weed, or tansy.

Herbal wreaths can be used for decoration as well as providing clippings to be used in cooking. Dried herbs can be tucked into a wire backing; living sprigs can be secured in damp sphagnum moss. Dried and fresh combinations will decorate and scent a room all winter long.

Sachets and potpourris can add fragrance to rooms and wardrobes. You can make them from rose petals, the zest from oranges, and even the skins and seeds left from canning apples and peaches. Longevity can be added with fixatives and essential oils, which are readily available from mail-order herbal suppliers (see page 287).

Even pets enjoy herbs. Plant some catnip for a kitten or anise for a puppy and watch their antics as they roll in it. Pet toys or bedding stuffed with dried catnip, anise, pennyroyal, or tansy can make a pet more contented, comfortable, and pest free. Pennyroyal planted on the lawn helps keep fleas off pets and therefore out of the house.

*Opposite: Herbal wreaths and other herb crafts make wonderful presents. You can use many types of dried herbs to make almost any shape by tying the herbs to a wire armature or gluing them to a Styrofoam base. The fragrance of the herbs will scent the room for weeks.*

### HERB PROJECTS FOR CHILDREN

These projects will familiarize children of all ages with the delights of herbs, whether for a school science project, for entertainment that has a hidden core of education on a rainy day, or just for the fun of it.

### PRESCHOOL CHILDREN

■ Give them bits of edible leaves and flowers to feel, smell, and taste.
■ Share the joy of gardening with your children. Begin naming plants early and continue as long as the child seems interested.
■ Mark family celebrations by planting trees or perennial herbs.
■ Let a plant or a garden plot be known and labeled as the child's from toddler days on. Select plants with fragrance and quick and sure results, such as mint, chives, or catnip.
■ Make crowns of red clover by weaving the entire plant—stem with leaves and flowers—into a circle.
■ Encourage children to pick dandelions and other flowers in your yard or garden; at the same time teach them what they should not pick or touch or eat.

### GRADES 1–4

■ Identify, collect specimens of, and make notes on several herbs according to color of leaf, color of flower, fragrance, size and shape of plant, and time of bloom.
■ Observe the effect of catnip on a cat and of anise on a dog.
■ Presprout seeds on moist paper towels to check their viability and get a head start on growth.
■ Start plants using cuttings, layering, and offshoots.

### GRADES 5–8

■ Grow edible herbs in rich and poor soil; compare the difference in the fragrance and flavor of the foliage.
■ Experiment with natural dyes to show what colors result from which plants and plant parts. Dye reeds or fabric with nutshells or onion skins for brown; use red cabbage leaves, Indian corn, or sage for red and green.
■ Make dyed cornhusk dolls from husks soaked overnight in grape juice. (Or make a dye by adding water to the grape skins strained off after making juice or jelly.)
■ Enhance food with natural colors. Soak shelled hard-cooked eggs in pickled beet juice to make them red. Blend calendula petals into cooked noodles to make them gold or orange; use any kind of edible greens to make green noodles.
■ Prepare potpourri (see page 110) with and without fixative to illustrate its effect on herbal fragrance.

*Correct identification ensures that you get the plant you expect. A good way to become familiar with different herbs is to visit a public garden, where signs like this not only give the correct name, but add other information about the plant.*

## DYEING EASTER EGGS

Using natural dyes to color Easter eggs is a way to teach children new uses for plants without relying on the supermarket for commercial products. It is also a practical way to color large batches of eggs, perhaps for the village Easter egg hunt.

▌ For blues and purples use blueberry juice, cranberry juice and purple grapes, or blackberry juice.

▌ For reds use the water from cooking beets. The color will be stronger if the beets are peeled after cooking and the skins returned to the cooking water and then steeped for several hours. Shades of red can also be made from combining raspberries, cranberries, and blackberries.

▌ For greens and yellows use spinach or carrot tops, calendula flowers, or yellow or brown onion skins. Ground turmeric from your spice shelf can also be used.

▌ For browns use coffee grounds, tea bags or loose leaves, walnut hulls, or cayenne pepper. Other herbs that produce brown dye are walnut or maple bark or alkanet root.

To prepare the dye, place the cut-up plant parts in a stainless steel or an enamel pot with enough water to cover. Bring the water to a boil, boil for 2 minutes, then simmer for 20 to 30 minutes. Strain the colored water into teacups. Add 1 teaspoon vinegar to each cup (vinegar isn't necessary when dyeing with onion skins).

To color the eggs, immerse them in the dye. The longer the eggs stay in, the stronger the color, although pastel shades are to be expected.

To boil the eggs directly in the dye, prepare the dye as above but pour it into a clean pot after straining, then let the dye cool somewhat. (The plant parts can be added to the compost pile.) Have the eggs at room temperature, which helps prevent cracking during boiling. Add the eggs carefully; they should be completely immersed. Return the dye to a boil, then immediately reduce the heat and simmer the eggs for 15 minutes. Remove the eggs with a slotted spoon and place them in cold water to stop the cooking.

## NAMING AND IDENTIFYING HERBS

Throughout this book plants are referred to by their common name and the Latin botanical names for their genus and species. Pronunciation of the genus is given in the encyclopedia. Enough disagreement over pronunciation exists even among the experts to make mispronunciation less serious than the mistaken identity of a plant. So to ensure getting the plant you want at a nursery, it's best to refer to it by its botanical name, because many plants have similar or identical common names.

It is important to be sure of a plant's identity before eating it. The chart on page 19 lists look-alike plants that could lead to confusion.

*Butterfly weed* (As-clepias tuberosa), *although beautiful and eaten by butter-flies, is toxic to people. Many common plants are poisonous. Don't eat any plant, wild or domestic, unless you are sure of its identity and know that it is edible.*

Other warnings appear throughout the book about possible plant toxicity.

Plants look different at varying times of the year and in different climates. Also, varieties of the same plant look different. See pages 18 to 20 about identifying plants in general and the encyclopedia starting on page 169 for detailed information on specific plants.

The encyclopedia also discusses how to use and grow more than a hundred of the most commonly used herbs and a good many more that are available to the grower today. It does not include all herbs, which number well over a thousand.

Because most people will use the encyclopedia mainly for reference, some facts will be explained once but not in detail in every entry. If questions arise as a consequence of this, the glossary should give quick and easy-to-find answers.

# HERBS IN THE LANDSCAPE

*Herbs have a place in the ornamental border as well as in the herb garden. Here, bergamot (Monarda didyma), the red flower at the left, doubles as an ornamental in a perennial border. Bergamot makes a lovely, light tea that has been used for centuries to ease the discomfort of colds.*

Clover, tansy, dandelions, and violets are easy to recognize. These plants are so common that they are often considered weeds. But down through the centuries they have been used as herbs. Some of them still are.

Roadsides, meadows, and woodlands are full of wild herbs such as mint, wild strawberry, chicory, blackberry, burdock, marshmallow, wild mustard, and valerian. Close observation will teach you where they grow and when they bloom and bear fruit. Then, by following some common-sense guidelines, you can gather the harvest or even dig up the plant. You should be sure that the plant is not an endangered species and that there are enough plants in the plot that removing some will not deplete the natural supply. Having the landowner's permission is essential. Most important of all, no part of any plant should be used until the plant has been positively identified. That's why it's important to carry—and use—a weed and wildflower book with clear illustrations and thorough descriptions.

## IDENTIFYING PLANTS

There are several ways to identify a plant. A wildflower book written especially for the local region is most helpful. One by one, check off each characteristic of the plant you want to identify. If in bloom, what color and what time of year? How are the individual flowers formed—singly or in clusters? Erect or drooping? Tubular or daisylike?

Examine the leaves. Determine if they're simple—a single leaf arising from each bud—or compound with many leaflets on a stem that arises at each bud. Are the leaf edges lobed, toothed, or smooth? Ovate, heart shaped, round, lance shaped, or finely cut?

Determine the growth habit of the plant. Do the leaves arise in a rosette, such as those of a dandelion? Are they low and mounded

## LEAF SHAPES

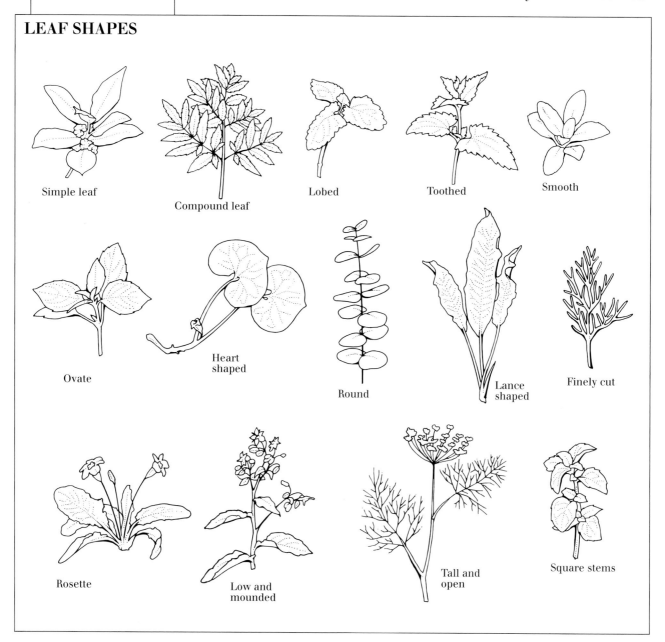

Simple leaf

Compound leaf

Lobed

Toothed

Smooth

Ovate

Heart shaped

Round

Lance shaped

Finely cut

Rosette

Low and mounded

Tall and open

Square stems

## BEWARE OF LOOK-ALIKE HERBS

Do not put any plant in your mouth until you are sure what it is. This is especially true of the plants described below. Many edible plants look much like others that are deadly or toxic to some degree. If you don't remember planting comfrey, angelica, parsley, horehound, or chile peppers in your garden and you find something growing there that looks like them, be sure of their identity before you eat any part. It helps to label the good guys.

■ False-hellebore (*Veratrum viride*), also known as green-hellebore and Indian-poke, can be mistaken for wild onion (*Allium stellatum*). False-hellebore is a cardiac depressant that will make one violently ill. Black-hellebore (*Helleborus niger*), also known as Christmas-rose, is a cardiac stimulant. All the hellebores have leaves that are mostly basal and palmately divided and cause a burning sensation in the mouth. They bloom in early spring in the North, in winter in mild climates. Better to buy onions and label the chives in your garden.

■ Many foxgloves (*Digitalis purpurea*) have the same basal rosette of simple leaves as does comfrey (*Symphytum officinale*), and both have leaves that alternate on the stem. Comfrey leaves are gray-green and hairy; foxgloves have woolly leaves, too, though of a crisper texture. Foxglove has a spire of bell-like flowers that are much larger than those of comfrey, which bloom in hanging clusters. Comfrey leaves are often steeped to make tea. A tea of foxglove leaves can be fatal.

■ Water hemlock (*Cicuta maculata*) can easily be mistaken for angelica (*Angelica archangelica*). Water hemlock has a heavy scent; both grow in the same moist habitat. Both have stout, hollow stems that look ideal for making whistles, but whistles made of water hemlock can poison. If you didn't plant and label it, don't eat it or even blow through the stem. (Angelica can be toxic if eaten in large amounts.)

■ Poison hemlock (*Conium maculatum*), the plant that killed Socrates, has the same finely indented leaves and umbel of flowers as parsley (*Petroselinum crispum*). Poison hemlock can grow 6 feet tall and has a hollow purple-spotted stem, a foul smell, and umbels of white flowers. Edible parsley grows only about 19 inches tall, has a solid stem, a fresh scent, and greenish yellow flowers that bloom in the second growing season. The seeds of hemlock have been mistaken for those of anise (*Pimpinella anisum*) and the roots for parsnip (*Pastinaca sativa*). Whenever using a parsley plant of uncertain origin, roll a leaf between your fingers and check for the pleasant aroma.

■ Black horehound (*Ballota nigra*), also called stinking horehound, grows with a habit and leaf pattern almost exactly like that of useful white horehound (*Marrubium vulgare*), usually called simply horehound. White horehound has white flowers and ovate, woolly white leaves. Black horehound has lavender flowers and ovate to lanceolate hairy leaves; its foliage has a strong, unpleasant odor and may be toxic if taken in large quantities.

■ The bulb of the edible saffron crocus (*Crocus sativus*) looks much like that of the autumn-crocus (*Colchicum autumnale*), also called meadow-saffron, which can be fatal if ingested. Both bloom in fall with similar lovely flowers. The edible part of saffron crocus comes from the 3-branched prominent stigmas, or female flower parts, which protrude between the petals of the flower cup like intense cinnamon red tongues. The poisonous autumn-crocus is a member of the lily family and is distinguished by its 6 stamens, or male flower parts. The leaves of saffron crocus are grasslike; the leaves of autumn-crocus are wider.

■ Jerusalem-cherry (*Solanum pseudocapsicum*), also called Christmas-cherry, looks much like some chile peppers (*Capsicum annuum*) but is used only for decoration. The leaves and unripe fruit are mildly toxic. The leaves of both are dark green, but chile pepper leaves have a longer, more tapered point, and more leaves grow from the same bud. Jerusalem-cherry usually has only 2 leaves, one small and one tiny, per bud. Chile pepper fruits are podlike and hollow; Jerusalem-cherry fruits are more rounded and seed filled, and the seeds are smaller than those of chile peppers.

■ Bulbs of flowering plants may look like onions to young children. Keep flowering bulbs in bags clearly marked as future flowers. Store them well away from the onions and out of the reach of children.

*Comfrey, shown here, and poisonous foxglove are look-alikes.*

*Visit public gardens—such as the New York Botanical Garden, shown here—to learn about herbs. Not only can you learn about individual herbs, but you can gather ideas for creating herb gardens or for combining plants attractively.*

or tall and open? Many herbs belong to the mint family and have square stems.

The fragrance of a plant's foliage can be a giveaway to its identity. Often just rubbing a leaf, then sniffing your fingers will tell what the plant is, or at least to which family it belongs.

Continued observation of a plant and how it changes throughout the growing season increases your familiarity with it. Like people, plants are sometimes easily recognized in one setting but not in another setting, or another season.

Learning is easier and more fun with the aid of someone familiar with the local flora. Participate in wildflower walks led by experts.

If you still have a question about the identity of a plant, take or send samples to the county extension office. A list of easily confused plants that can be toxic if ingested is given on page 19.

## GATHERING INFORMATION FOR YOUR GARDEN

Gardeners who are intimidated by planting an herb garden should look around their own gardens and count how many herbs they already have—probably parsley, mint, chives, violets, and nasturtiums, possibly calendula, tansy, lavender, and yarrow.

If herbs are included in public parks or botanical gardens in your area, visit periodically to browse, observe, and/or shop. Many retail nurseries and mail-order nurseries carry a wide selection of herbs.

Observe neighbors' gardens. If a specific plant looks interesting, notice whether it's growing in sun or shade, in a dry or moist place, in soil that looks rich or poor. Observe how it relates to the plants growing around it.

When observing public and private gardens, you are bound to accumulate ideas for your own garden. Begin to separate the usable ideas from those that are overly ambitious. From the seemingly endless possibilities, make personal adjustments until the ideas fit.

A pocket-sized notebook is an ideal place to record gardening ideas. When you see an interesting plant growing in nature, note the date, place, habitat (meadow, woodland, sunny garden, and so forth), and identifying characteristics (color and texture of the foliage, color and shape of the blossoms if the plant is in bloom, and the plant's overall shape). Note whether the plant is growing alone or in abundance. Periodically check on the development of each plant and note how it looks in early spring, summer, fall, even winter.

You might also collect small samples of each plant and tape them in the notebook alongside the description. At home, you can arrange the specimens on absorbent material, such as paper towels, then press them under a heavy weight, such as a dictionary. The notebook could also include wish lists from plant catalogs.

Your notebook will be helpful for recording the progress of the garden once you have started it. It's important to keep a record of plant

names, because plant labels in the garden often become lost.

Make notes about any special conditions, such as a very hot or wet spring, when the first leaves of each plant were picked, when each plant bloomed, how far it spread, what thrived around it, what looked especially striking with it or was overshadowed or crowded out by it. Such records are an invaluable help in the evolution of a garden.

*Another place to learn about herbs is your local garden center. Visit every couple of weeks; the herbs on display change frequently. Some are available in several varieties. Note their variety names, and smell the leaves to see which you like best.*

# LANDSCAPING WITH HERBS

There are herbs for every landscape, whether or not it includes a garden. Herbal trees and shrubs can be used for framing, foundation plantings, or hedges. Herbs such as chives and marjoram can be used as edging along paths. Low, spreading herbs such as Corsican mint and varieties of thyme can be planted between stepping-stones. Taller spreading herbs such as lamb's-ears and prostrate rosemary make good ground covers. Corsican mint, pennyroyal, some varieties of thyme, and chamomile can be used instead of lawns or among the lawn grasses. Many herbs can be grown in containers in entryways, on steps, on patios, on balconies, and in window gardens by those who have very little or no garden space at all.

*Many herbs can be used as edging. This is basil 'Spicy Globe', which grows into unusually neat rounded forms.*

## Among the Shrubs

Herbs can be planted among and in front of the shrubs that surround the house. This is an ideal place for herbs; they can be seen, passed, and brushed against, and their fragrance can be enjoyed every day.

The focal point of your entranceway and front door should be reserved for herbs that thrive in your particular climate and soil. New plants can be tried out in a less prominent place, then moved to the front when they prove worthy.

## For Screening and Shade

You can screen unpleasant aspects of the landscape from view by planting vines such as passionflower, hops, or climbing nasturtiums. They may be used alone or with other fast-growing annual and perennial climbers. They can be trained up trellises or on fencing

to give a feeling of privacy to an entryway or outdoor living area.

Vines are not only faster growing than trees, they are more economical for those living in rented or temporary housing. Deciduous vines, which lose their leaves in winter, offer the advantage of shade in summer and unblocked sun in winter.

Any vertical frame covered with vines will give shade the first season—much more quickly and in a much narrower space than a tree. Such a screen can make a marked difference in the atmosphere as well as the temperature of a picnic-table nook or spa.

Raised beds around a patio or planting boxes along a deck railing give a measure of privacy for outdoor relaxation. Suitable herbs for such spaces include cascading geraniums, lemon balm, or any of the mints or oreganos. In addition to serving as a screen, they will be readily available to snip and use in the kitchen or bath.

## In Flower and Vegetable Gardens

The flowers of most herbs are subtle rather than showy. Such plants are valued in the flower garden for foliage color, texture, fragrance, or overall shape. The dramatic foliage of 'Dark Opal' basil, bronze fennel, and silver gray lamb's-ears serves as a background for and harmonizes with brighter colors in the garden. Evergreen herbs are valued for giving interest to the garden in winter, except in very cold climates; evergreen herbs include germander, hyssop, rue, sage, santolina, and thyme.

Some herbs have showy flowers. Chives bloom with lovely lavender to pink globes in spring at the same time as tulips and the earliest iris. A drift of perennial blue flax will

### COMPANION PLANTING

Gardeners have come up with many time-honored although not scientifically proven combinations of plants that seem to prove mutually beneficial when they are grown in proximity. Personal experience and local results may be the most important test of the validity of companion planting. You may want to try some of the combinations suggested here, but also notice what seems to work well in your own garden. It's helpful to take notes in a garden notebook, then repeat what succeeds and rearrange what does not. Many combinations that work well in the cooking pot also work well in the garden, which makes them easier to remember.

■ Asparagus grows well near tomatoes and nasturtiums but not onions or leeks.

■ Basil helps asparagus and tomatoes.

■ Beans, cabbage, carrots, and sage grow well near rosemary.

■ Beets grow well near onions or kohlrabi but not pole beans.

■ Bergamot is beneficial to tomatoes.

■ Borage benefits squash, strawberries, and tomatoes.

■ Butterfly weed attracts all sorts of insects but is unscathed by them.

■ Cabbage grows well with potatoes.

■ The entire cabbage family does not grow well with strawberries, tomatoes, or beans.

■ Carrots grow well with tomatoes, lettuce, and chives but not dill.

■ Cauliflower and celery are good companions. Celery grows well with leeks and tomatoes.

■ Chives benefit roses but not peas.

■ Corn grows well near potatoes or interplanted with beans, peas, pumpkins, melons, squash, and cucumbers.

■ Cucumbers grow well with nasturtiums but no other herb.

■ Dill, sage, mint, and chamomile ward insects off cabbage.

■ Eggplant and green beans are good companions.

■ Horseradish helps potatoes.

■ Lettuce grows well with strawberries, carrots, and radishes.

■ Marigolds benefit virtually every other plant, especially when worked into the soil as a mulch.

■ Peas and carrots go well together in the garden and on the table. They also grow well with turnips but not onions or garlic.

■ Radishes grow well with peas, lettuce, and chervil.

■ Rosemary is beneficial to beans, carrots, cabbage, and sage.

■ Spinach grows well with strawberries.

■ Summer savory and beans go well together in the garden and in cooking. Summer savory, garlic, and onions are also good companions in the garden.

■ Tansy benefits raspberries, roses, grapes, and fruit trees, but it should not be planted where cattle will graze.

■ Tomatoes grow well with parsley, cabbage, asparagus, potatoes, cucumbers, and elephant garlic.

■ Wormwood sometimes deters small animals and dogs when planted as a border.

*Many herbs provide attractive foils for flowers in the garden. This fresh, attractive green is 'Dwarf Curled' parsley.*

brighten the garden from early spring well into summer. Annuals such as nasturtiums bloom from midsummer until frost. Among the herbs grown especially for their flowers are calendula, with orange and yellow blooms; bergamot, in many shades of red, pink, and white; and yarrow, in shades of yellow, white, pink, salmon, and red.

Fragrant herbs are valued in all seasons in all types of gardens. Thyme releases its scent when scuffed on the coldest winter day. In warm weather, fragrant herbs swarm delightfully with bees, butterflies, and hummingbirds.

A long-standing practice in the vegetable garden is companion planting—growing in proximity two or more plants that prove mutually beneficial. For unknown reasons, some plants seem to grow better when planted next to others. Advocates of companion planting say that selective combinations can result in fewer insect pests. The aromatic qualities of herbs make them excellent candidates for companion planting. Some seem to draw harmful insects away from the vegetables and onto themselves and to sustain injury with less damage. See page 23 for a list of herbs thought beneficial to vegetables.

Some fragrant herbs attract beneficial insects to the garden, such as bees, which are necessary for pollination. Herbs also offer shade, moisture, and shelter for such garden helpers as lacewings, parasitic wasps, spiders, butterflies, and birds.

## In Wild and Woodland Gardens

Most herbs are sun lovers, so they are not often thought of for woodland plantings. Yet violets carpet the woodland floor, thriving in the cool shade and moist, rich soil.

*Sweet woodruff, with its small white flowers, thrives in the shade, making it an excellent ground cover for a woodland garden. This is the herb that adds its distinctive sweet flavor to May wine, a traditional spring drink in Germany.*

## HERBS FOR LAWN SUBSTITUTES
Certain varieties of chamomile, mint, and thyme are ideal lawn substitutes.

### Chamomile
This fragrant plant can be started from seed and needs only occasional mowing, which releases its wonderful scent. 'Treneague' is a nonflowering variety that needs no mowing and is tolerant of dry conditions; it must be started from plants.

### Mints
Corsican mint has tiny leaves, a strong minty aroma, and pale purple flowers in midsummer. It might not survive harsh winters even if mulched, but it may reseed. It prefers moisture. Pennyroyal has bright green leaves with a pungent peppermint scent, and spikes of lavender flowers. It spreads well in moist areas.

Wild mint can be invasive, but it tolerates dry conditions.

### Thyme
All varieties of thyme prefer dry, sandy soil.

Mother-of-thyme, also called wild thyme, is the original uncultivated variety of thyme; it is an excellent bee plant and a beautiful ground cover, is very hardy, and has mauve flowers. Variety 'Minus' has the smallest leaves of any thyme; they are a vivid shade of green. Variety 'Elfin' forms a mat or dome.

White creeping thyme grows 2 inches tall with light green leaves and nonfragrant white flowers; it is a rapid spreader.

Woolly thyme makes an excellent 3-inch-tall ground cover; it has pink to purple flowers over a mat of woolly gray foliage. Variety 'Longwood' has larger leaves than any other woolly thyme and has relatively long spikes of lilac to purple flowers.

Herbs that include *wood* in their name, such as sweet woodruff, wood anemone, and wood betony, will do well in these types of gardens. See also "Herbs for Shade" on page 42.

## In the Cutting Garden
Many gardeners who grow flowers and foliage especially for bouquets plant a special cutting garden, perhaps a few rows beside the vegetables or in an inconspicuous part of the backyard. Because this garden is not intended as a focal point, flowers can be cut freely without detracting from the overall effect.

Herbs will not necessarily be the stars of a cutting garden, simply because so many of them do not have showy flowers. But several of them do (see the list on page 42), and many with less conspicuous blooms make long-lasting fillers. Many are also excellent for drying, such as the artemisias. The fragrant fresh foliage of mint and lemon balm is attractive when arranged alone in a vase or mixed with other foliage and flowers. If there is a choice of varieties, those with the longest stems should be selected so that they can be used in tall as well as small bouquets.

## In Rock and Wall Gardens
Low, spreading herbs are ideal choices for rock gardens and walls. The natural setting creates a pleasing background for the garden.

Any of the creeping or prostrate herbs are excellent choices for this type of garden. Moisture often collects at the base of the shady side of a wall, which creates an ideal environment for violets, lamb's-ears, thyme, and sweet woodruff.

## Along Paths
Paths are ideal places to line with herbs that release their fragrance when brushed against. Some low-growing herbs such as thyme can even be occasionally trod upon without damage, and they will scent the garden as they are disturbed.

## As a Ground Cover and Lawn Substitute
Water conservation has increased in priority from a common-sense practice to a matter of law in many areas. Because lawns take a lot of water, fertilizer, and energy—both human and fossil fuel—reducing the area devoted to grass is one of the most important modern garden trends.

One way to do this is by planting a ground cover. Any existing grass must be tilled in or covered with mulch, then the ground cover planted. Once established, it will take much less work and water than does grass. A ground cover

also adds variety to the landscape with the many species, colors, and textures that are available. Herbs suitable for use as ground covers are given on page 42.

A shade-tolerant ground cover, such as sweet woodruff, is useful around trees to keep the lawn mower and weed cutter away from fragile bark. The ground cover also acts as a mulch to retain moisture and uses less water itself than would lawn grasses.

Planting mint and other rampant-growing herbs in a mowed lawn is a good way to keep the herbs under control. They will spread into the grass and not take over, although they should not be mowed too often or too low.

Whereas most ground covers are not able to withstand foot traffic, making them unsuitable as a lawn, herbs are an exception. Low-growing varieties of thyme and chamomile, for example, can be grown in large patches as a lawn substitute or in smaller patches as a "welcome mat" at entryways, in front of a garden seat, and between the beds of an herb garden. These herbs have periods of subtle bloom and take little if any mowing.

*Chamomile has been used as a ground cover since classical times. It tolerates foot traffic better than almost any other non-grass plant. Indeed, an old folk saying is that chamomile will not grow well unless it is trod upon.*

## PLANNING AND INSTALLING THE GARDEN

Herb gardens can be planned in one of two ways—spontaneously or by design. The first is the most common way—planning as you go along. Plants are acquired by ac-cident or impulse. From several potential planting spots, the most likely one is selected. Plant height, color, texture, and time of bloom may not be taken into considera-tion because there is usually some pressure to get the plant in the ground as soon as possible.

The spontaneous method is not all bad. It is much better than not planting anything at all or putting off gardening for weeks, months, or years until a proper plan is drawn.

There will be indecision at every planting, and mistakes will be not only made but multiplied. But as the plant collection increases, so eventually will knowledge from trial and error. On-the-spot garden-ers have plenty of company— probably a good 80 percent of the gardening population.

Planning an herb garden on paper will, however, yield better results in the long run and require less moving of plants. The garden can be designed and planted all at once or one step at a time over sev-eral seasons or years. It could begin with one bed, then another could be added each year as time, plants, or money become available. It's helpful to make the original plan a five-year one, so that you'll be working toward a definite goal and not just planting haphazardly.

*This elegant herb garden was made to be seen from an up-stairs window. A garden as formal as this must be care-fully planned in ad-vance. Spontaneous planting works best with casual, infor-mal gardens.*

## Selecting the Site

Whether your herb garden is planned spontaneously or by design, it is more likely to succeed if the site is selected with the following considerations in mind.

The choice of site may be influenced by the size of the garden, so it is wise to decide in advance how much time you can spend gardening. It is better to start small and expand with enthusiasm than to start too big and lose plants to weeds or lack of water.

Most herbs need five to six hours of direct sun a day at the very least. Morning sun is preferable to afternoon sun. Herbs that need shade can be tucked into the shadows of taller, bushier plants.

In very warm climates some shade, especially in the afternoon, helps herbs endure the hottest part of summer. Some herbs either tolerate or do better with partial shade (see pages 42 and 43). Only a few herbs need a good bit of shade. Planting them in the shade of trees can create a pleasing effect.

Culinary plants should be handy to the kitchen. Locate a fragrance garden under windows or near a patio where breezes waft the scent inside; use in raised beds or containers for convenient sniffing. Decorative gardens are best placed in view of windows or near frequently used entries. A cutting garden or dye garden can be on the edge of the vegetable garden or in an out-of-the-way place, where it won't be noticed when every bloom has been picked or the foliage has been cut back to the ground.

Most herbs need some protection from strong or constant winds. If there isn't an appropriate wall, fence, bush, or tree to shield herbs, you can install a screen or fence or arrange the sturdier plants to protect the more delicate ones.

Herbs require good drainage. They prefer soil that is slightly acid to neutral (pH 6 to 7). Most herbs are adaptable to a wide range of soil types, from very sandy soil to heavy clay. Although most herbs do not need rich soil, they do best if ample humus is added to the soil.

*The knot garden is one type of formal herb garden. This knot garden is at Agecroft Hall in Richmond, Virginia.*

## MAKING HERB-ETCHED PAVING STONES

Concrete paving stones with etched impressions of herb foliage are especially attractive in an herb garden. The best effects are achieved by using plants whose leaves are not too finely cut. Leaves of angelica, borage, burdock, comfrey, elecampane, lovage, and scented geraniums have bold shapes that are strong enough to work well.

Make a frame of 1×2s. A 20-inch square works well. Bevel the edges, then attach the frame to a base of hardboard.

Select herb leaves of appropriate sizes to fill the square. Place the leaves face down in the form and make them lie flat either with masking tape or by weighting them down under newspapers for a few hours.

To make enough concrete to fill a 20-inch form, use a half-gallon bucket of sand and half as much portland cement. Add enough water to form a batter-like gruel.

Remove the tape or newspapers from the herb leaves, then spread a thin layer of the concrete carefully over the leaves. Be sure that no concrete gets under the leaves. Add more concrete until the form is about half full.

Cut a piece of 1-inch-mesh chicken wire the size of the square. Place it on top of the wet concrete as reinforcing, then fill the form with the remaining concrete and smooth the top so that it is level.

When the concrete seems dry, in 12 to 24 hours, place a sheet of plywood over the form and carefully invert it. Test each corner to be sure that no concrete has adhered to the form. Then raise the form gently, and carefully remove the herb leaves. The surface should still be soft enough to etch the name of each herb into the concrete with a large nail.

Fill in any voids with fresh concrete. Cure the block under damp burlap for a few days so that it won't dry out too rapidly and crack.

## Drawing a Plan

Once you have selected the site for the herb garden, it's time to draw a garden plan. Graph paper makes it easier because each block on the paper can represent a certain measure, say 1 foot, of the yard.

First, measure the area of the site and mark it on the paper. Locate the north point, and indicate any nearby walls, trees, or structures that will cast shade. Also indicate important windows, walkways, and other viewing areas of the house.

Decide whether the garden should be formal or informal in style. This decision usually depends on the style of the house and the rest of the landscape, but it also depends on the preferences of the people who live there.

Herbs lend themselves equally to formal and informal styles. Traditionally, herbs were grown in small, very trim and formal gardens, the design of which is an art in itself. There are many such examples in horticultural literature that you can study and imitate, and many modern examples to stir the imagination and help you design something unique, intricate, and beautiful. Informal styles, in which the design is less structured, require less time and effort.

Draw the planting beds to fit the site. From the photographs and plans throughout this book and from observations of herb gardens, either adapt a plan or come up with an original. Make the beds a maximum of 5 to 6 feet wide if there is access on two sides, and 3 feet wide or less if there is access on one side. Where wider areas are necessary, add paths or stepping-stones.

Garden paths should be at least 18 inches wide. The most successful paths follow the natural access patterns of the garden, using curves, jogs, or steps only with reason, never just to appear meandering.

## Installing Paths and Edging

Brick or concrete paths are the most permanent and require the least maintenance. Otherwise, paths can be plain turf, or turf inset with sliced timber circles or flagstone. Steps, if necessary, can be constructed of railroad ties, paving stones, or bricks. Paths of mulch can be useful, attractive, and informal. Leaves, grass clippings, pine needles, wood chips, or shredded bark work well. An underlayer of newspaper or weed-blocking fabric, which allows water to pass through but inhibits weed growth, will make a shallow layer of mulch more effective.

RABBIT E. LEE

Edging will be needed to keep the path material from washing into the garden beds. The edging should be compatible with the style and size of the garden. For edges between herb or flower beds and turf, mowing strips installed flush with the ground are most convenient. They should be 4 to 10 inches wide and can be made of concrete, brick, tile, or timber, although timber is easily nicked by the mower blade.

## Installing the Garden

The plants should be arranged with careful consideration for the height, spread, foliage color and texture, flower color, and time of bloom.

The tallest plants should be located at the back. Place space-consuming herbs such as comfrey well away from low-growing and delicate plants. Hot colors, such as orange and strong pinks and reds, should be separated by enough white and blue flowers, and green and gray foliage, so that the hot colors will not clash. Consider single-color gardens, such as one with all white flowers or all blue flowers, or with all gray-green foliage.

Seedlings, cuttings, and young or recovering plants could be located somewhere close to the house and the garden hose but out of the spotlight. This could also be the site of an experiment station for trying new varieties before designating garden space for them.

An herb garden is an excellent place to display garden art, such as a sundial, birdbath, fountain, bee skep (a domed straw structure that provides a home for bees in the garden), or statuary. Any one of these could be a focal point. So could a standard or topiary herb in an attractive pot.

*Garden art seems to belong in herb gardens. Rabbit E. Lee, here at home in Callaway Gardens in Georgia, seems content in an informal patch of rosemary.*

*An herb garden is a lovely spot to locate a bench. This attractive wooden seat is shaded by 'New Dawn' roses.*

A comfortable bench could provide a focal point in the garden as well as a place to relax with a cup of tea. Medieval garden benches were often made of stone or wood; the seat was filled with soil and planted with low-growing chamomile or thyme, both of which make a soft cushion and give off a delightful fragrance when sat upon.

## DESIGNING SPECIAL HERB GARDENS

These suggestions will help you plan herb gardens for specific uses.

Before making a final decision about which herbs to include in your garden, consult the encyclopedia (starting on page 169) and seed and plant catalogs for any special cultural needs. Even the very best

plan will need some minor altering from time to time; hands-on experience will suggest combinations that work better in each particular situation. Most herbs are compact enough to be transplanted if they wind up in the wrong place on the first try. Or cuttings can be taken from such plants and placed in a more suitable location.

Labeling the plants is important. The labels have added interest if they include some information about each plant.

### Kitchen Garden

Because the most well-known herbs are culinary, and even medicinal and cosmetic herbs usually require some preparation in the kitchen, having them handy to the kitchen door can make the difference between using them frequently or forgetting to use them at all.

A kitchen garden plan could include herbs you already use or would like to use. Depending upon space and your inclinations, a beginning plan might include a dozen herbs, among them such favorites as thyme, sage, basil, parsley, chives, and rosemary.

**Italian herb garden** Herbs appropriate to this garden include rosemary, bay, thyme, sage, parsley, oregano, marjoram, arugula, Florence fennel, garlic chives, flatleaf parsley, basil, dill, and summer savory. Depending on your area, some of these (such as rosemary and bay) are best grown in containers that can be brought indoors in winter.

**French herb garden** The French often plant what they call a potager—herbs, vegetables, and fruit all grown together in a space-saving but decorative garden. The plants of choice are often revealed by their common names: French sorrel; French tarragon; French thyme; French lavender; French, or pot, marjoram, with white or pink flowers; and French marigold, which includes many of the common dwarf varieties.

## Informal Garden

Herbs lend themselves graciously to the trend toward natural-looking herb gardens. For busy people it can be a relief to have an unstructured garden. An informal garden can range from the abundance of a cottage garden to more compact designs for regions with little rainfall. The plants should be arranged loosely in sweeping beds with mulch to cover the spaces in between the plants, or in clumps to appear as though they are growing in the wild.

*Informal gardens are easier to design and to care for than formal gardens. This one contains rustic touches in its ornamental bee skep and wattle fence.*

*Shakespearean gardens are composed of plants mentioned by the bard. The one shown here, at Vassar College in Poughkeepsie, New York, features statues of Shakespearean characters. In Shakespeare's day, most people understood the language of the herbs, in which many plants—and especially herbs—were invested with meaning. Mentioning or displaying an herb invoked its associated meaning. Shakespeare utilized the language of the herbs throughout his plays and poems. See page 164 for a "dictionary" of this language.*

## Biblical Garden

In biblical times herbs were more important than they are today. For instance, the Wise Men brought to the infant Jesus gifts of gold, frankincense, and myrrh: gold was a token of kingship, and frankincense of holiness; myrrh was used in embalming and foretold Christ's death.

The "gall" that Christ was given with vinegar as he hung on the cross is believed to have been the juice of the opium poppy. It was given in kindness to dull the pain.

Other herbs mentioned in the Bible that could be included in a biblical garden include aloe, anise, coriander, cumin, garlic, hyssop, mint, mustard, rose, saffron, and wormwood.

## Shakespearean Garden

From *Hamlet* comes the famous line in which Ophelia declares to Laertes, "There's rosemary, that's for remembrance; pray, love, remember." The body of Juliet is borne to the church covered with sprigs of the herb.

A Shakespearean garden would have to have cowslips (*Primula veris*), since the bard mentioned them seven times. This perennial herb has rosettes of soft dark green leaves and fragrant clusters of yellow flowers marked with yellow dots in May and June. The English have long loved them and called them a favorite of the fairies.

Other plants mentioned in Shakespeare's work include lavender, rue, parsley, Madonna lily (*Lilium candidum*), columbine, and English daisy. There's also bay, borage, boxwood, clover, calendula, chamomile, garlic, johnny-jump-up, lemon balm, mustard, sweet myrtle (*Myrtus communis*), pinks (*Dianthus*), strawberry, thyme, winter savory, and yarrow.

## Other Theme Gardens

There is hardly a design idea that cannot be worked into a lovely herb garden. A garden can fit every need, interest, or mood. Cooks can plant dessert, tea, salad, or edible-flower gardens.

A moonlight garden could be planted beside a patio where guests sit and visit after dark. At night blue flowers become white, silver foliage and white flowers reflect the light, and fragrance is at its most intense. White-flowering include white sweet rocket, white honesty, feverfew, white yarrow, yucca, and sweet cicely. Blue-flowering include forget-me-nots and rosemary. Use plenty of silver-leaved thymes, lamb's-ears, wormwood, mugwort, and silver-leaved varieties of santolina. For a focal point include a gray or white statue or birdbath or a fountain with trickling water.

How about a garden of Native American herbs? The North American natives used hundreds of herbs for food, medicine, paint, and other utilitarian and decorative purposes. Such plants included horsetail to polish arrowheads, bearberry leaves to smoke and berries for necklaces and rattles, wild mint to flavor food and mask the human scent in animal traps, and wild rose for fruit and medicine.

Herbal research will inspire more garden themes, perhaps a Chaucer or Charlemagne garden, a Colonial or Shaker garden, or an astrological garden. Nicholas Culpeper, whose *Herbal,* written in 1652, was brought to America by the early settlers, attributed each herb to a ruling heavenly body and urged it for treatment of people with the same zodiacal sign. Reprints of the *Herbal* are still found in libraries.

A horse lover's garden, planted beside the barn door, could include comfrey, arnica, elecampane (also called horseheal, for treating a horse's sore legs), and parsley to add to the feed for stamina. The seed from flax, with its lovely blue flowers, added to horse feed gives a horse a shiny coat. Nicandra (also called shooflyplant) would be helpful in keeping away the flies. One might have to add horsetail and horseradish just for fun.

## Knot and Ribbon Garden

For a delightful formal garden as precise as a piece of embroidery, you could plant one of these intricate and traditional herb gardens

*The herbs in this knot garden have been allowed to grow to lush, full forms that would obscure the design had they not been carefully chosen for color contrast. For examples of more spare, linear knot gardens, see page 29.*

with ribbons of clipped edging plants of contrasting foliage color. The "knots" occur at the intersections of the ribbons. Knot gardens can be fairly simple or extremely complex, an original or a copy of a historical design. The plan should be worked out on graph paper, then the lines should be transferred to the garden with string and stakes or lines of sand, lime, or perlite.

Although it is wise to start small, a knot garden needs to be at least 6 feet square to allow the ribbons to weave. (See Table I on the opposite page for suggestions of suitable plants and their foliage color.) Be-

fore planting, the soil should be prepared deeply and well.

The corner herbs should be planted first, then the spaces filled in with plants. All should be clipped frequently to keep them bushy and neat. To create the illusion of a ribbon crossing over another, the upper ribbon should be clipped in a gentle humpback curve and the lower ribbon in a gentle dip. The last pruning should be made in late summer or early fall so that the plants will have some leaf protection and no tender new growth during the winter.

The space between the ribbons can be planted with other herbs, or the ground can be covered with colored sand or gravel or various mulches. Creeping herbs are good ground covers between the ribbons.

## Dye Garden

Craftspeople, spinners, weavers, potters, and basketmakers prize natural dyes made from plants; the rich, gentle, earthy tones blend beautifully and are not garish or harsh. Extremely bright shades can also be achieved, attested to by Navajo blankets and bright Scottish plaids.

Natural dyeing combines the fascination of botany and chemistry with gardening and visual art. Entire books have been written on the possibilities, problems, and process of dyeing fabrics with herbs and plants. There is a sense of wonder to this idea even for those who might never get so involved as to procure natural wool for the actual dyeing.

More than 500 dye plants can be found in New England alone. See Table II below for plants and the colors they produce.

### TABLE I: HERBS FOR KNOT AND RIBBON GARDENS

The illusion of intertwining ribbons in this type of formal herb garden comes from contrasting foliage colors for each ribbon. An attractive effect is achieved by using two or more of the following low-growing herbs of contrasting foliage color. Herbs are evergreen except the marigolds, which are annuals or tender perennials in the North.

| | |
|---|---|
| Boxwood, dwarf | Light green |
| Germander | Dark green |
| Hyssop | Light green |
| Lavender 'Hidcote' | Green-gray |
| Lavender 'Munstead Dwarf' | Gray-green |
| Marigold, anise-scented | Dark green |
| Marigold, signet | Dark green |
| Rosemary | Dark green |
| Sage | Varies with variety |
| Santolina 'Lemon Queen' | Willow green |
| Santolina 'Nana' | Silver |
| Savory, winter | Dark green |

### TABLE II: HERBS FOR DYEING

Many herbs lend themselves to dyeing. Here are the colors they produce; the addition of a chemical mordant will cause some herbs to produce a different color, such as chrome in the first example.

Agrimony for butter yellow, with chrome for gold

Ajuga for black

Alkanet with acetic acid for soft pink-brown

Bloodroot for orange, with tin for reds, with alum for rust

Broom (dyer's) leaves with alum for green-yellow; flowers with alum for bright yellow, with chrome for deep yellow

Bugleweed for black

Calendula flowers for yellow

Catnip with alum for yellow

Chamomile (dyer's) with alum for bright yellow, with copper for olive

Chicory for orange

Comfrey with iron for brown, with alum for yellow

Coneflower for gray-green

Coreopsis flowers with chrome for orange

Dandelion (whole tops) for magenta, flowers with alum for soft yellow

Feverfew leaves and stems with chrome for greenish yellow

Goldenrod flowers with alum for creamy yellow, with tin for bright yellow, with chrome for gold

Indian-paintbrush flowers with alum for light green

Lady's-bedstraw for purple, with alum for coral pink

Oregano (wild) flowers with alum for violet

Parsley for light green, with alum for cream

Queen-Anne's-lace with alum for pale green

Red clover flowers with chrome for yellow ochre

Rhubarb leaves with tin for yellow and golds

Rue roots with alum for rose

Safflower blooms with alum for yellow

St. John's wort with alum for yellow

Tansy with alum for mustard yellow

# HERBS IN THE GARDEN

*With any type of gardening, one of the inherent satisfactions is handling the plants—planting, tending, and harvesting. The fragrance of many herbs adds to the gardener's pleasure.*

Herbs are as easy to grow as they are rewarding, even for people with "black thumbs." Keeping herbs in bounds may be more of a challenge than getting them to thrive, even with average to minimum care in ordinary conditions. As with all garden endeavors, the secret of successful growing begins with choosing the right plants for the right place.

One of the joys of growing herbs is having conveniently at hand plants that are useful as well as attractive. With vegetables a wise rule is: If your family won't eat it, don't plant it. But this does not necessarily hold true for herbs. A better rule for herbs may be: Plant the herbs that you and your family like best and use most. Some people may always be content with half a dozen of the most useful culinary herbs: parsley, sage, rosemary, thyme, mint, and chives. These alone can make a big difference in cooking, eating, and gardening enjoyment.

## WHAT HERBS TO GROW

Whether your herbs are acquired from neighbors or a nursery, it's wise to ask the grower questions. How tall will the plant get? When does it bloom and what color are the flowers? Will it live over the winter? (See the climate zone map opposite.) Does it need any special care? How is it used?

Advice can make the difference between success and failure. The encyclopedia starting on page 169 will help you determine which plants will grow well in your situation, and where to put them in the garden. The lists on pages 42 to 45 suggest herbs for specific growing conditions, such as dry or damp ground, shade, and seaside gar-

dens, as well as herbs for specific uses, such as foundation plantings, borders and hedges, ground covers, and screening. Here also are lists of herbs that are evergreen except in the North, and herbs given by flower and foliage color.

For gardeners with the time, space, and inclination, the rule for growing herbs may be further amended—from growing what your family likes best and uses most to trying anything once. A single plant of most herbs is enough for a start. If you don't care to continue growing it after a season or two, you can give it away or add it to the compost pile. Most seed catalogs and many nurseries offer perhaps a dozen of the most popular herbs. Specialty catalogs may offer hundreds.

*Left: Although we generally think of herbs as being leafy, many have lovely flowers as well. An entire perennial border can be made of flowering herbs. Right: Leaf colors contribute their own beauty, especially in interesting combinations. These are 'Powys Castle' artemisia and 'Tricolor' sage.*

# CLIMATE ZONE MAP

After finding your location on this USDA map, which is based on minimum winter temperatures, and noting the number of the zone, keep this number in mind when selecting plants from the encyclopedia starting on page 169. To help ensure a thriving garden, 90 percent of your plants should be hardy in your zone.

Most of us can't resist a few challenges that are marginal in our area, but these should be purchased and planted with that in mind. If they don't survive, their loss should be taken with good grace and no guilt. Suggestions for growing in marginal areas are given on page 54. Very favorite plants may be worth trying again and again. Most are not worth the risk, however, especially when one realizes that there are several hundred other more appropriate choices.

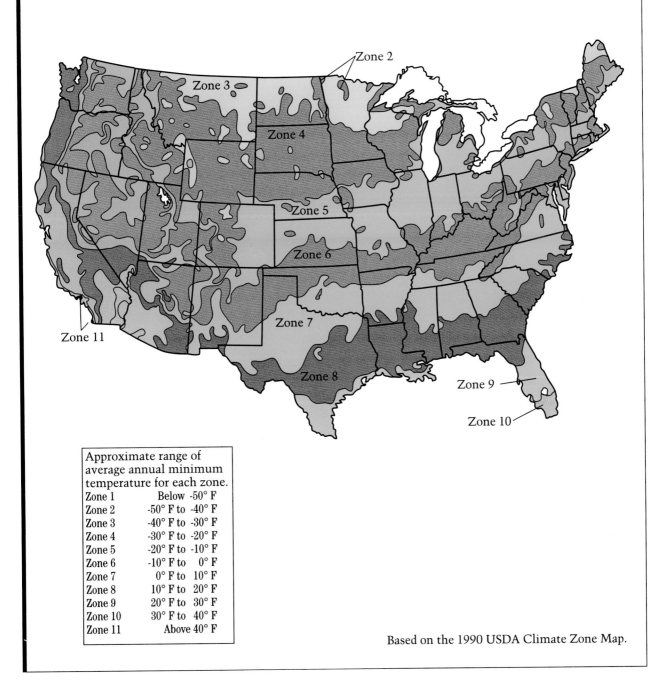

| Approximate range of average annual minimum temperature for each zone. | |
| --- | --- |
| Zone 1 | Below -50° F |
| Zone 2 | -50° F to -40° F |
| Zone 3 | -40° F to -30° F |
| Zone 4 | -30° F to -20° F |
| Zone 5 | -20° F to -10° F |
| Zone 6 | -10° F to   0° F |
| Zone 7 |   0° F to  10° F |
| Zone 8 |  10° F to  20° F |
| Zone 9 |  20° F to  30° F |
| Zone 10 |  30° F to  40° F |
| Zone 11 | Above 40° F |

Based on the 1990 USDA Climate Zone Map.

# HERBS FOR SPECIAL USES

These lists will help you select the most appropriate plant for your situation and needs. Herbs you can expect to find growing in the wild, and those to avoid, are also given. Plants followed by an asterisk are not winter hardy in the North.

## Wild Herbs
Barberry
Bayberry
Betony, wood
Bloodroot
Burdock
Chicory
Couchgrass
Dandelion
Marshmallow
Mint
Mistletoe
Mustard, black
Passionflower
Pennyroyal
Sorrel
Stinging-nettle
Tansy
Valerian
Violet
Yarrow

## Annual Herbs
*In hot climates these herbs will grow from spring to winter or from winter to spring. None are winter hardy in the North.*
Basil
Borage
Calendula
Chervil
Coriander
Cumin
Dill
Fennel
Savory, summer

## Perennial Herbs
Agrimony
Angelica
Artemisia
Bergamot
Bugleweed
Catnip
Chamomile
Chives
Comfrey
Costmary
Feverfew

Germander
Horehound
Hyssop
Lavender
Lemon balm
Lemongrass*
Lemon-verbena*
Lovage
Marjoram
Mint
Mugwort
Oregano
Rosemary*
Rue
Sage
St. John's wort
Savory, winter
Sorrel
Southernwood
Sweet cicely
Sweet woodruff
Tansy
Tarragon
Thyme
Wormwood
Yarrow

## Biennial Herbs
Alexanders
Caraway
Clary sage
Parsley

## Shrubs
Broom
Eucalyptus*
Holly
Juniper
Potentilla

## Trees
Birch
Eucalyptus*
Ginkgo
Holly
Juniper
Linden
Osage-orange
Spruce
Walnut
Walnut, English

## Foundation Plantings
*Herbs suitable for permanent foundation plantings are listed separately from herbs that can be moved once permanent shrubs gain size.*

### With Other Shrubs
Artemisia
Barberry
Bay*
Bayberry
Bergamot
Boxwood*
Juniper
Lavender
Santolina
Scented geranium*
Rose

### Until Other Shrubs Grow
Bergamot
Geranium*
Honesty
Nicandra
Perilla
Santolina
Tansy
Yarrow

## Borders and Hedges
Artemisia
Boxwood*
Catnip
Chives
Germander
Hyssop
Ivy, English
Lavender
Parsley*
Rosemary*
Sage
Santolina
Savory, winter
Society-garlic*
Southernwood
Thyme
Wormwood

## Ground Covers
Bugleweed
Catnip
Chamomile
Germander, dwarf
Lamb's-ears
Lavender
Mint, Corsican*
Rosemary, prostrate*
Santolina
Sweet woodruff
Thyme, woolly
Violet
Yarrow, creeping

## Tall or Screening Herbs
Agrimony
Angelica
Clary sage
Dill*
Elecampane
Fennel*
Lovage
Marshmallow
Mullein
Tansy

## Herbs With Showy Flowers
Alkanet
Aloe*
Bergamot
Calendula*
Chicory
Chives
Gas plant
Hyssop
Monkshood
Orrisroot
Purple coneflower
Saffron crocus
Valerian
Woad
Yarrow

## Herbs for Shade
Agrimony
Angelica
Bergamot
Betony, wood
Bloodroot

Blue-cohosh
Burnet
Cardamom*
Catnip
Chamomile
Chervil*
Comfrey
Coriander*
Costmary
Dill
Fennel*
Feverfew
Flax
Gentian
Germander
Ginger, wild
Goldenseal
Hellebore, black
Hyssop
Lemon balm
Licorice
Lovage
Madagascar-periwinkle
Mint
Monkshood
Parsley
Pennyroyal
Pipsissewa
Rosemary*
St. John's wort
Sweet cicely
Sweet flag
Sweet woodruff
Tansy
Tarragon
Thyme
Valerian
Violet
Wintergreen
Wormwood

### Evergreen Herbs
Aloe*
Bay*
Bugleweed
Chervil*
Feverfew
Houseleek

Hyssop
Rosemary*
Rue
Sage
Santolina
Savory, winter
Southernwood
Thyme
Wormwood

### Herbs for Dry Places
Borage*
Burnet
Chamomile
Chives
Curryplant*
Dittany of Crete*
Fennel*
Geranium, scented*
Germander
Houseleek
Hyssop
Lady's-bedstraw
Lavender
Pennyroyal
Rosemary*
Sage
Santolina
Savory, winter
Soapwort
Southernwood
Thyme
Wormwood
Yarrow

### Herbs for Damp Places
Angelica
Bergamot
Comfrey
Lady's-mantle
Lemon balm
Lovage
Marshmallow
Meadowsweet
Mint (except catnip)
Nasturtium*
Parsley
Pennyroyal
Sweet cicely
Sweet flag

Valerian
Violet
Watercress

### Herbs for Seaside Gardens
Bay*
Evening primrose
Germander
Lemon balm
Rose
Rosemary*
Rue
Sage
Santolina
Sedum

### Herbs for Bees and Butterflies
Agrimony
Anise
Basil*
Bergamot
Borage*
Broom
Catnip
Chamomile
Chives
Comfrey
Dandelion
Evening primrose
Fennel*
Germander
Hyssop
Lavender
Lemon balm
Marjoram
Marshmallow
Meadowsweet
Mint
Parsley
Pinks
Rosemary*
Sage
Savory, winter
Stinging-nettle
Sweet cicely
Thyme
Yarrow

### Herbs for Hummingbirds
Bergamot
Campanula
Catnip
Larkspur
Sage, Mexican*
Sage, pineapple*
Soapwort

### Culinary Herbs
Basil*
Bay*
Borage
Chervil*
Chives
Marjoram
Mint
Oregano
Parsley
Rosemary*
Sage
Savory, summer*
Savory, winter
Tarragon
Thyme

### Herbs for Fragrance
Geranium, scented*
Lavender
Lemon balm
Lemon-verbena*
Mint
Myrtle*
Orange tree*
Sage, pineapple*
Sweet-olive
Thyme

## POSSIBLY POISONOUS HERBS

Herbs that are considered therapeutic but can be toxic in large doses are included here. The botanical names are given to help avoid misidentification. Inedible flowers, some of which are considered toxic, are listed on page 82. Note that aloe is toxic to animals as well as humans.

| Common Name | Botanical Name | Comments |
|---|---|---|
| Aloe | *Aloe vera* | Violent purge taken internally |
| Angelica | *Angelica archangelica* | Contains carcinogens; toxic in large amounts |
| Arnica | *Arnica montana* | Unsafe taken internally |
| Autumn-crocus | *Colchicum autumnale* | High dose can cause nausea, intestinal pain, kidney damage, even death |
| Bayberry | *Myrica cerifera* | Wax can be irritating, may contain carcinogens |
| Bloodroot | *Sanguinaria canadensis* | Unsafe taken internally |
| Blue-cohosh | *Caulophyllum thalictroides* | Toxic taken internally, women should avoid especially if pregnant |
| Broom | *Cystisus scoparius* | Dangerous if smoked, slows heartbeat, can cause paralysis, convulsions, even death |
| Coltsfoot | *Tussilago farfara* | Unsafe taken internally, contains carcinogens |
| Comfrey | *Symphytum officinale* | Carcinogenic to rats when taken internally |
| Cowslip, marsh-marigold | *Caltha palustris* | All parts dangerous if ingested |
| Daffodil | *Narcissus* species | Bulb causes nausea, can be fatal if ingested |
| Deadly nightshade | *Atropa belladonna* | Sap can irritate skin, very toxic if ingested, berries especially dangerous to children |
| Eyebright | *Euphrasia officinalis* | High dose or unsterilized solution can hurt eyes |
| Foxglove | *Digitalis purpurea* | Cumulative effect, can be fatal if ingested |
| Goldenseal | *Hydrastis canadensis* | High dose can cause irritation of external or internal surfaces |
| Hellebore, American | *Veratrum viride* | Very narcotic, skin irritant |
| Hellebore, black- | *Helleborus niger* | Heart stimulant, skin irritant |
| Hemlock | *Conium maculatum* | Lethal, once used to execute criminals |
| Indian-tobacco | *Lobelia inflata* | Causes nausea if ingested, high doses may be fatal |
| Iris | *Iris* species | Ingesting rhizomes can cause severe stomach upset |
| Jimsonweed | *Datura stramonium* | Dangerous, often fatal if ingested |
| Juniper | *Juniperus communis* | High dose or repeated consumption dangerous |
| Larkspur | *Consolida orientalis* | Ingesting seeds or young plants, which can look like dill, can be fatal |
| Licorice | *Glycyrrhiza glabra* | High dose or long repeated use can be toxic; heart or blood pressure patients should avoid entirely |
| Mayapple | *Podophyllum peltatum* | Can be fatal if ingested |
| Mistletoe | *Phoradendron serotinum* | Ingesting berries can cause convulsions, even death |
| Monkshood | *Aconitum napellus* | Poison can be absorbed through skin |
| Moonseed | *Menispermum canadense* | Ingesting berries causes severe stomach upset and pain |
| Pennyroyal, American | *Hadeoma pulegioides* | Unsafe for internal use except in smallest amounts |
| Pennyroyal, European | *Mentha pulegium* | Unsafe for internal use except in smallest amounts |
| Pokeweed | *Phytolacca* species | Berries are dangerous narcotic, can be lethal |
| Rue | *Ruta graveolens* | Can cause rash, unsafe taken internally especially by pregnant women |
| St. John's wort | *Hypericum perforatum* | Toxic taken internally, causes sheep to shed wool, lose appetite, eyesight |
| Sassafras | *Sassafras albidum* | Contains carcinogens, can cause degeneration of heart, liver, or kidneys |
| Sweet flag | *Acorus calamus* | Ingesting rhizomes can cause severe stomach upset |
| Tansy | *Tanacetum vulgare* | Oil very toxic, even lethal, if ingested |
| Violet | *Viola* species | Seeds can be toxic to children |
| Wormwood | *Artemisia absinthium* | Depresses central nervous system if ingested |

# HERBS ACCORDING TO COLOR

Because not all herbs have showy or long-lasting blooms, the color of the foliage is as important as the flower color in creating balance in the herb garden. Plants followed by an asterisk are not winter hardy in the North.

**Silver, Gray, or Variegated Foliage**
Artemisia 'Silver King', 'Silver Queen'
Bugleweed, variegated
Catnip
Comfrey, variegated
Curryplant*
Dittany of Crete*
Eucalyptus*
Germander, silver
Horehound
Lamb's-ears
Lavender
Mint, pineapple
Nettle 'Silver Beacon'
Pinks, clove
Sage
Santolina
Seaholly
Thyme, silver
Wormwood

**Red to Purple Foliage**
Basil, 'Dark Opal'*
Bugleweed, bronze
Cardinal flower
Fennel, bronze*
Orach, red
Perilla, purple
Rose (*Rosa rubrifolia*)
Sage, purple

**Yellow Foliage**
Bay, golden*
Boxwood, golden
Feverfew, golden
Hops, golden
Lemon balm, golden
Meadowsweet, golden
Mint, ginger
Oregano, golden
Rue, variegated
Thyme, 'E. B. Anderson'

**Pink Flowers**
Basil, purple*
Bergamot 'Croftway Pink'
Comfrey, dwarf
Dittany of Crete*

Fenugreek*
Hollyhock
Hyssop
Pinks, clove

**Red Flowers**
Bergamot 'Cambridge Scarlet'
Cardinal flower
Hollyhock
Nasturtium*
Rose
Sage, pineapple*
Scarlet pimpernel

**Orange Flowers**
Butterfly weed
Calendula*
Elecampane
Nasturtium*

**Yellow Flowers**
Calendula*
Curryplant*
Dill*
Germander, silver
Goldenrod
Iris, yellowflag

Lady's-bedstraw
Lady's-mantle
Nasturtium*
Pennyroyal, English
Primrose
Rose, damask
Santolina
St. John's wort
Tansy
Yarrow

**Blue Flowers**
Anise-hyssop*
Bachelor's-button
Borage*
Catnip
Chicory
Comfrey, dwarf
Iris, blueflag
Johnny-jump-up*
Larkspur
Love-in-a-mist
Rosemary*
Sage
Sage, Cleveland
Thyme

**Purple Flowers**
Bergamot, wild
Bugleweed
Catnip
Chives
Johnny-jump-up*
Lavender
Mint, orange, peppermint, spearmint
Saffron crocus
Thyme
Valerian
Violet

**White Flowers**
Angelica
Basil*
Chamomile
Feverfew
Garlic chives
Iris, whiteflag
Mint, pineapple
Orrisroot
Rose
Sweet cicely
Sweet woodruff
Yarrow

*Sage is available in a range of flower colors, many of them vivid. This border sports red pineapple sage* (Salvia elegans), *purple Mexican sage* (S. leucantha), *and pink autumn sage* (S. greggii).

*Wintergreen, like many plants native to regions with cold winters, requires a cold treatment to germinate. Seeds can be planted outdoors where nature applies the cold treatment, or winter can be mimicked with a refrigerator.*

# DIGGING IN

Before bringing home any plants, it's best to select the garden site, draw the plan, and prepare the soil as described on pages 28 to 32.

## Starting With Seeds

All annual herbs and many perennial herbs can be started from seed, which produces the most plants for the least expense. Seeding is a slower and less sure process than starting with plants, but it can be fun and fascinating.

**Indoor planting**  Small or exotic seeds usually do best when started indoors. It is also a good idea to plant tiny seeds of unfamiliar plants indoors so that they can be distinguished from weeds that may germinate at the same time.

The seeds should be started in a warm, dark place; the soil or soil substitute should be kept moist but not saturated. After the seeds have sprouted, the seedlings can be moved to a bright, sheltered indoor spot, such as a windowsill, greenhouse, or cold frame.

Some herbs, such as purple cone-flower, sweet cicely, sweet wood-ruff, and wintergreen, germinate better with cold treatment. (Check the encyclopedia starting on page 169 or seed catalogs for seeds that need this treatment.) Seeds can be cold-treated by sowing them in fall or very early spring directly in the ground or in containers that are then set outdoors to let nature do its work.

Alternatively, the seeds can be soaked overnight or longer in water, then mixed with damp peat moss or vermiculite and placed in a plastic bag in the refrigerator for the required time. If the cold treatment is longer than 30 days, the peat moss should be checked to make sure that it has not dried out. After treatment, the seeds and peat moss should be removed from the refrigerator and spread over soil in a planting tray.

**Outdoor planting** Many herbs do better if sown directly in the garden where they will grow. Some of these are anise, chervil, dill, coriander, cumin, and parsley. Direct seeding prevents transplant shock and crowded roots. It also helps prevent damping-off. Plants started outdoors have the added advantages of abundant light, space for root growth, and better air circulation.

## Starting With Plants

Mail-order plants should be unwrapped as soon as possible after their arrival. Balled roots and potted plants should be watered if the soil is dry. Bare-root plants should be plunged into a bucket of water for at least several hours. If they can't be planted in their permanent location within 24 hours, they should be removed from the water and heeled into the soil, which means positioning the plants at an angle in a shal-

low trench and covering the roots with soil. The plants can stay there for another week or so until they are permanently placed.

## Starting With Cuttings and Divisions

Some herbs, such as true French tarragon and horseradish, do not produce seed. Others have seed that produces offspring with wide variations of flavor or aroma, sometimes even of leaf shape or flower color. In these situations the only way to duplicate the desired plant

## MAKING CUTTINGS

Select stems that are mature, but not woody. The stem should snap when bent sharply.

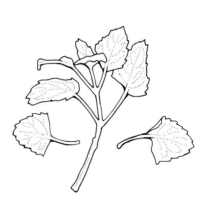

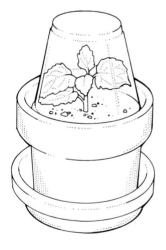

1. Remove any blossoms or bud, and all but about 2 square inches of leaf. Trim the stem to 3 inches long.

2. Place the stem in a mix of 9 parts horticultural vermiculite, perlite or sand, and 1 part peat moss. Cover with a clear plastic drinking glass. Water well and place in a bright spot out of direct sun.

3. Keep the rooting medium moist. After a couple of weeks, tug gently every week to see if roots have begun to grow. When the new roots begin to branch, the cutting is ready to plant.

## LAYERING

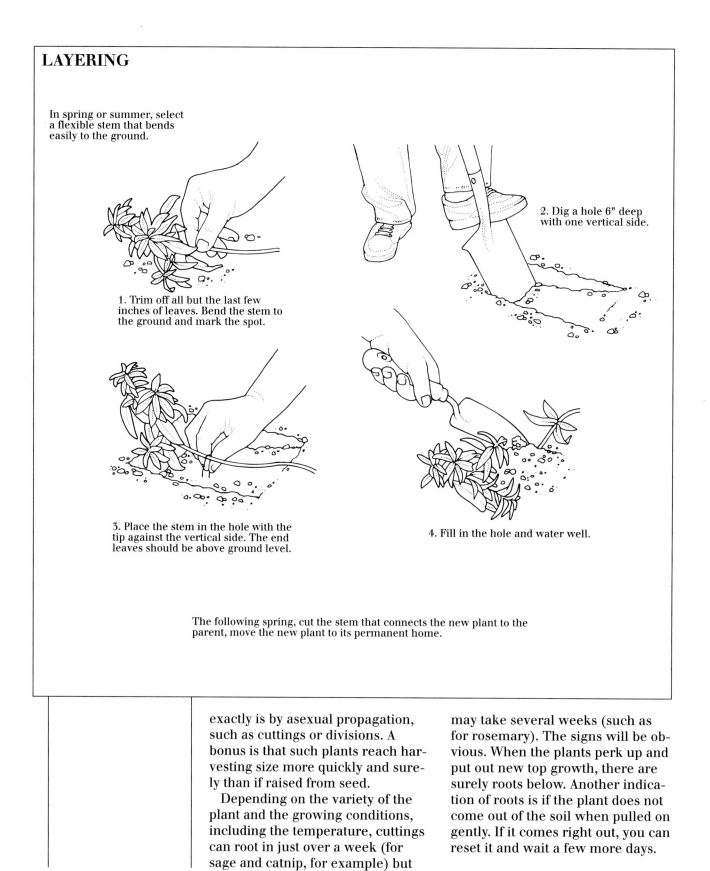

In spring or summer, select a flexible stem that bends easily to the ground.

1. Trim off all but the last few inches of leaves. Bend the stem to the ground and mark the spot.

2. Dig a hole 6" deep with one vertical side.

3. Place the stem in the hole with the tip against the vertical side. The end leaves should be above ground level.

4. Fill in the hole and water well.

The following spring, cut the stem that connects the new plant to the parent, move the new plant to its permanent home.

exactly is by asexual propagation, such as cuttings or divisions. A bonus is that such plants reach harvesting size more quickly and surely than if raised from seed.

Depending on the variety of the plant and the growing conditions, including the temperature, cuttings can root in just over a week (for sage and catnip, for example) but may take several weeks (such as for rosemary). The signs will be obvious. When the plants perk up and put out new top growth, there are surely roots below. Another indication of roots is if the plant does not come out of the soil when pulled on gently. If it comes right out, you can reset it and wait a few more days.

A few herbs, such as horseradish and comfrey, will form new plants from pieces of the root. This works automatically when horseradish and comfrey roots are harvested; pieces that break off and remain in the ground will renew the patch. You can increase stock more quickly by cutting finger-thick pieces of root into pieces 2 to 3 inches long and inserting them vertically into the rooting medium until the tops are ¼ inch below the surface.

Many perennial herbs are easy to propagate by dividing established plants. Clump-forming herbs such as tarragon may need dividing every second year. Others, such as mint and thyme, sprawl and often form roots wherever the stems touch the ground.

Some clump-forming herbs, such as lemongrass, can be propagated by layering. This entails bending down the stems of the side shoots, scratching or cutting partway through the stems where they touch the ground, and covering each cut with soil and a stone to pin it down. A few new plants can often be taken from the side of such a clump without disturbing the main plant.

Other clump-forming plants tend to die out in the middle while producing the healthiest new shoots around the perimeter of the clump. Such plants can be divided by lifting the clump carefully with a spading fork, pulling the pieces apart, selecting those with the best-looking shoots and roots, and replanting them with enough distance in between for natural spreading for the next few years. The less vigorous inner plants of these clumps are best relegated to the compost pile.

## Mound Layering

Some plants defy division. Lavender and santolina, for example, produce a wide, spreading plant from

a single stem and as such cannot be divided. These plants can be coerced into forming a splittable crown, however, by scratching the surface of the underside of the lowest branches to expose the cambium layer, which is just beneath. The soil can then be mounded over all of these points and the crown of the plant.

If this is done in fall, new roots should form by spring. You can check on their growth in spring by digging down in one spot. If the roots look good, you can lift the entire plant and cut it into pieces, each with some roots attached. If not enough roots have formed, the branches should be re-covered and left until fall.

*A member of the mint family, catnip is easy to root from cuttings. Plants that spread by rooting can easily be propagated from cuttings or layering.*

## Transplanting

When seedlings, rooted cuttings, or divisions are moved from the parent plant, everything possible should be done to ease the adjustment. The sudden transition from a warm, humid growing environment to a windy and dry situation, sometimes considerably colder or warmer, can be a shock that sets back a young plant by several weeks. Any such move is bound to cause some damage to the immature root system. The roots cannot keep up with the increased water loss from the leaves, and wilting results.

Hardening off, or gradually acclimating a plant to its new environment, is the single most effective means of reducing the trauma of transplanting. Potted houseplants destined for the outdoors should first be moved to the back porch, a few days later to a protected spot in the garden, then eventually to their permanent outdoor home. A cold frame opened a little more each day also works well as a transition space.

When herbs are transplanted from pots to the garden, the top growth should be cut back to 3 to 4 inches. About ½ inch should be trimmed from the bottom of the rootball. This root pruning will help stimulate new root growth and prevent rot.

## CARE AND MAINTENANCE

The timing of the following tasks—watering, mulching, fertilizing, weeding, and controlling pests and diseases—can make a big difference in how much effort is involved in caring for your herbs. If each job is done promptly as needed, the herbs will respond with vigorous growth. Ignore the care of the herbs and they may eventually recover, but not until after they have sulked and perhaps suffered dieback.

## Watering

Once established in the garden, most herbs require less water than leafy vegetables. In areas with adequate rainfall, that will be enough except in the driest of times. In areas with little rainfall, watering must be part of routine care.

Herbs grown in containers need constant care. Even the most drought-tolerant plants, such as rosemary and sage, should be kept evenly moist. Containers should be checked daily in warm weather; baskets hanging in the sun should be checked twice a day.

In the garden a weekly deep soaking is sufficient in most cases. Watering twice a week may be necessary if the soil is very sandy. Because overwatering is as harmful as underwatering, the soil beneath the surface should be checked to see how often and how much to water. Drip or trickle irrigation is the ideal watering method, but a soaker hose is fine. The apparatus can be hidden under mulch for those who find it distracting.

## Mulching

A layer of mulch keeps the ground at an even temperature—cool in summer, warm in winter—and prevents the alternate freezing and thawing in spring that can thrust roots out of the ground and kill even those plants that have survived the coldest season.

Mulch soaks up water, thus preventing runoff and erosion. It lets the water soak gently and uniformly down around the roots of the plant and then holds it there against drying winds and sun that would otherwise bake, harden, and crack the ground and make it impervious to future rainfall.

# BEST MATERIALS FOR MULCHING

Many materials are effective as mulch in the garden.

**Leaves**   Running the lawn mower over a pile of leaves will shred them so that they will break down quickly. Even when shredded, however, the leaves of silver maple, elm, and birch will mat down and should be mixed with lighter material for use as mulch. Oak leaves are mildly to very acid. Most other leaves are neutral.

**Grass clippings**   A lawn whose clippings are destined for mulch should not have been sprayed with herbicide for the previous 6 weeks. Clippings can be raked up, then placed around plants. Because fresh clippings generate heat as they decompose, they should not actually touch any plant parts until after they've dried out for a week or so. A better use for fresh clippings is to make compost, which can then be used for mulch.

**Newspapers and cardboard**   Both of these come from trees and will break down again. They can be recycled under other mulches, where they will not show. Used this way they permit the top layer of other mulch to be thinner than otherwise necessary.

**Hay, straw, or salt hay**   Although difficult to find, salt hay is the most ideal of these three, since it is the only one without seeds. The seeds contained in regular hay and straw will germinate in the garden, although the seedlings can easily be pulled up.

**Sawdust**   As sawdust decomposes it removes nitrogen from the soil; the amount depends on the type of wood. This can be counteracted by applying nitrogen to the soil. Sawdust mulch should be kept away from the crowns of plants that are subject to crown rot.

**Stones, bark, and wood chips** These mulching materials can be purchased by the bag. Their effectiveness is increased by using newspapers or weed-blocking fabric beneath them; these permit the passage of water but not light.

**Pine needles**   These are airy, fragrant, attractive, weed free, and easy to handle. They are moderately acid.

**Other organic materials**   Mulching materials that may be available locally include ground corncobs, buckwheat hulls, rice hulls, cocoa hulls, walnut or peanut shells, tobacco stems, and hops. You can test a small amount at first and increase use with experience. Some of these materials will not be suitable for certain situations; for example, rice hulls are light and may blow away in a windy area. Some materials may be prohibitively expensive to mulch a large area: cocoa hulls, which attract earthworms, are more expensive on the East Coast than on the West Coast (due to shipping costs). Peat moss, although an excellent soil amendment, is not a good mulching material; if allowed to dry completely, it is very difficult to wet again.

*Straw is an attractive mulch as well as a practical one.*

Mulch that extends to the perimeter of the garden keeps the lawn mower and weed cutter at bay. If the mulch layer is thick enough to keep light from the weed seeds, they will not germinate. The few that do will pull up easily because the soil will be soft and workable. Suggested materials for mulching are listed on page 51.

## Fertilizing

Common sense is the best rule for how often and how much to feed herbs. Do the plants look healthy? Is the soil clay, which holds nutrients until they are used up, or sand, through which nutrients tend to wash? How long is the growing season? How much growth is being harvested? As a general rule, light monthly applications of liquid fertilizer should maintain good foliage color and an acceptable rate of growth.

Slight overfeeding of herbs will not kill them, but it will decrease the concentration of essential oils and therefore the fragrance and flavor. Too much nitrogen can cause rapid, lush growth of foliage but hardly any flowers or seeds.

## Weeding

No plant will thrive if it is crowded by a larger plant that takes all the light, moisture, soil nutrients, and space. So weeding is another matter of common sense.

Some herbs can themselves grow to unwanted proportions; they are noted as invasive in the encyclopedia starting on page 169. One of the best ways to enjoy invasive herbs is to plant them in the center of the lawn, where any runaway shoots can be mowed and their fragrance enjoyed at the same time. Another good idea is to plant them in an area surrounded by sidewalk, driveway, or walls that will act as a natural barrier.

Aggressive herbs can also be planted in a 5-gallon nursery can with the bottom removed. A hole should be dug large enough to accommodate the can with 2 inches of rim exposed above the soil. The can is filled with soil and the herb is planted in it. The can will act as an underground barrier to roots. Some herbs, such as mint, will try to send runners over the edge of the rim, but these can be easily snipped as they attempt their escape.

Some herb seeds are wind-borne and will pop up around the yard in unexpected places. Once the new plants are identified, they can be transplanted back to their allotted space, given away, or removed to the compost pile.

## Controlling Pests and Diseases

Although herbs are among the most resistant of all plants to pests and diseases, they are not completely immune. As a rule, the warmer and more humid the climate, the more frequent and severe the disease and pest problems.

Good soil drainage and aeration and wide enough spacing between plants for air circulation can do much to reduce the incidence of disease. Good cultural practices will keep stress to a minimum and therefore reduce the threat of insects. But a few bugs and spores will find their way into every garden.

Fortunately, common sense can handle most of the problems that arise. Many pests and diseases can be deterred with a strong spray of plain water from the hose nozzle directed at both sides of the leaves. This should be done every day during a warm, rainy period, once or twice a week otherwise. The water will dislodge most of the insects and wash away most of the fungus spores before they can settle in. Not

*The aromatic oils for which we treasure herbs have been developed by the plants as defenses against being eaten, making herbs one of the most insect-resistant groups of plants. But some insects have learned to tolerate those defenses. This caterpillar, the larva of the black swallowtail butterfly, enjoys a parsley plant.*

so much water should be used that it oversoaks the ground; just a brisk, cleansing shower for the leaves is all that's needed.

In the rare case when a plant does not respond to treatment and becomes more a haven for pests than a delight to grow, it should be discarded to a hot compost pile (to kill insects and spores) or in a bag for trash collection.

**Insects**   Herbs sometimes suffer damage from leafhoppers, mealybugs, whiteflies, flea beetles, scale, Japanese beetles, white-fringed beetles, caterpillars, spittlebugs, grasshoppers, or arachnids such as red spider mites. Most can be controlled by careful watching and then treating the first signs of trouble.

New plants should be inspected carefully for insects. A dip in a solution of mild dishwashing detergent is a wise preventive measure. If damage occurs on established plants, a search will usually identify the cause. Sometimes this involves going out at night with a flashlight to catch the nocturnal marauder.

For worms and larvae, either handpicking or treating with Bt (*Bacillus thuringiensis*) is effective, but some larva are worth saving. Among them are the fat green caterpillar with orange dots on black stripes that will change into a black swallowtail butterfly. This caterpillar feeds on celery, carrot tops, and parsley. Another desirable creature is the black caterpillar with white and yellow stripes that becomes the monarch butterfly. These caterpillars are a valued treat when given to a school classroom with plenty of the herb they are already eating; shifting to another plant variety is not recommended.

**Diseases**   Root rot can occur on some herbs, especially in very humid climates or in wet and

## GROWING IN MARGINAL AREAS

It is often possible to grow a plant outside its zone limits by making use of the microclimates in the garden.

▎ The south and west sides of most buildings are sunnier and more protected from the wind than the north and east sides.

▎ If more wind protection is needed, such as from hot, gusty winds in the Midwest, tall species can be planted as windbreaks or fences, or screening panels can be built.

▎ High spots tend to hold less frost than low pockets.

▎ Many herbs that prefer full sun in northern climates will benefit from shade, especially in the afternoon, in southern areas. Tall herbs can shade shorter-growing specimens in the garden; potted plants can be moved between sun and shade.

▎ During the hottest months in hot, dry climates, the sun can be moderated over the herb-growing area by using shade cloth or lath.

▎ Raised beds will help herbs grow in areas of heavy rainfall. Almost all herbs require good to excellent drainage.

▎ Plants can be moved indoors for the winter in areas where it is too cold for them to remain outdoors. These moves should be made gradually, and the plants should be given extra care during their period of adjustment.

▎ Some tender herbs that are too large to be potted up for the winter can be perpetuated by taking cuttings in fall, growing the cuttings on a sunny windowsill until spring, then planting them in the garden after all danger of frost is past.

▎ Winterkill can be reduced by thoroughly watering plants before a hard freeze, then covering them with a loose layer of mulch.

▎ All plants benefit from large and often-renewed amounts of humus in the soil. This is especially true in dry climates, where water can be conserved by working humus into the soil and mulching the surface.

▎ Plants that are marginal for your area should not be pruned in fall. All top growth should be left for maximum winter protection. This is also true after an unexpected frost in the South. The withered leaves will shelter the plant until all danger of frost is past.

▎ Seasons can be extended with cold frames, cloches, or plastic coverings.

▎ Growing plants in rooms with no natural light is possible with fluorescent lighting.

muggy seasons elsewhere. Most susceptible are gray-leaved herbs native to rocky Mediterranean coasts or other arid regions, and low, sprawling herbs, such as some varieties of thyme. Growing practices that will help prevent the problem include raised beds, improved drainage, extra humus for soil aeration, enough space between plants for air circulation, or a gravel or rock mulch.

Damping-off can be prevented in seedlings by watering them with a tea made from 4 cups of boiling water poured over a handful of fresh or 2 tablespoons of dried chamomile flowers. The tea should be steeped for 10 minutes, strained, and allowed to cool before watering the seedlings. Another damping-off preventive is to cover the seeds lightly with peat moss. Because it is very acid, peat moss discourages the germination of damping-off fungus spores.

Teas made from couchgrass rhizomes or horsetail leaves may help control mildew, rust, and other fungus diseases. In many cases the roots aren't affected. The aboveground parts should be removed and burned. As a further precaution, some remaining healthy plants should be moved to a new spot. Or cuttings can be taken from healthy stems when the condition is first detected; these cuttings can be moved to new ground.

## Avoiding Temperature Extremes

To help mature plants survive cold winters outdoors, they can be protected by layering soil, straw, compost, or other mulch around the roots. For other ideas, see Growing in Marginal Areas, at left.

When the growing season ends outdoors, the lives of annual herbs can be extended by some months, and tender perennials can be overwintered indoors. If the plant is not too large, it can be potted up. An easier and more space-efficient way to preserve herbs that are not winter hardy is to take cuttings of the plant and let new plants grow slowly over the winter to renew the beds in spring.

In places where winters are not frigid but summers are long, hot, and humid, herbs are likely to be the victims of summer kill. Susceptible plants can be moved to a shady spot, duplicates can be planted in the shade, or the plants can be grown in containers that can be moved. If your house is air-conditioned, cuttings can be taken and kept indoors during the hottest season.

## GROWING HERB HEDGES

Formal herb hedges can be used to keep the herb garden in bounds and give it a neat, outlined look. Several evergreen herbs are excellent for this purpose: lavender, santolina, germander, curryplant,

*A low hedge, such as this dwarf box-wood, makes a trim edge to a formal garden. The same hedge can be left rounded to make an edging for an informal garden.*

*Opposite: Herbs can be planted in anything that will hold them, from conventional flower pots (bottom) to brightly colored pots (top left) or rusty wagons. Some gardeners enjoy using the most unconventional planters possible, such as used kitchen colanders, old shoes, or fishing creels.*

southernwood, wormwood, and dwarf boxwood. (Also see pages 42 and 43.)

When buying container plants for a formal hedge, it's wise to purchase enough of the same kind at the same time from the same place to be sure of a perfect match. Plants should be selected for the height and shape desired. Most species provide several choices. Most low hedging plants spaced 8 to 14 inches apart will form a solid edging within a year. Cuttings taken in spring may take two years to fill in.

Plants in the herb garden itself should be far enough away from the hedge to leave room for pruning and air circulation. Pruning an herb hedge is best done by laying a piece of plastic, paper, or cloth beside and beneath the hedge to catch the clippings. This not only makes cleanup easier, but the clippings can be used in potpourris, for mulching garden paths, or for adding to the fireplace for fragrance or to the grill for flavor.

Pruning snips will do the job, but shears will do it faster. The hedge should be pruned hard in late spring; most hedge plants can be trimmed to about 9 inches above the ground or to the previous year's growth, as long as green shoots are in evidence below this level. The hedge should be pruned again in mid- to late summer.

Clipping the top of the hedge encourages bushy side growth. The top should be kept narrower than the bottom so that sun and air can reach the lowest branches. This will counteract the natural tendency of hedges to die out at the bottom and spread at the top.

The drawback to hard clipping is that it prevents the growth of most summer flowers. The alternative is to let lovely bloomers, such as

lavender, grow freely through the summer and then cut them well back after harvest in late summer. Germander will usually manage to bloom in spite of frequent clipping.

Informal herb hedges should be trimmed gently at least once a year to prevent a tangle of leggy stems.

Hedges can become excessively woody or die out in the middle after four to five years. If they cannot be renewed by pruning, cuttings can be taken whenever needed to fill in the gaps.

## GROWING HERBS IN CONTAINERS

The variety of foliage colors and textures as well as flowers makes herbs attractive decorations for the patio, balcony, sunroom, or sunny kitchen window. The plants benefit from the microclimate created by grouping them together.

Containers take a bit more care per square foot than in-ground plants, but they offer several advantages.

❚ Because plants in containers are at hand, in view, and easy to watch, they tend to receive more care and stay tidier than in-ground plants.

❚ Containers can be moved indoors for the winter and outdoors for the summer. They can be moved to get enough sun or shade as the seasons change, or to an inconspicuous recovery corner after shearing.

❚ Container plants can be placed at eye or nose level for easy picking, sniffing, watching, and touching.

❚ Because one plant often provides all the fresh herb a cook can use, and several herbs can be grouped in one container, a mini herb garden can be grown in a limited space.

❚ Apartment dwellers with only a balcony, windowsill, or flat roof can grow herbs in containers.

pipe doesn't become clogged with soil. The plants are watered simply by filling the pipe and letting the water trickle through the holes.

Container size is important. Most herbs grow best in 1- to 3-gallon containers. Some herbs, however, such as a mature lemon-verbena or pineapple sage, will eventually need a half barrel. When pots are this large, they are best put on wheels for easy moving. Platforms with casters are available at garden centers and through mail-order catalogs.

Hanging baskets are ideal for herbs. The best types are not the plastic ones often sold at super-markets but sturdy wire baskets at least 12 to 16 inches in diameter. The baskets should be lined well with sphagnum moss or outfitted with ready-made fiber liners.

## GROWING HERBS INDOORS

Many herbs grow well indoors the year around and give constant harvest, interest, and fragrance. You can grow them in any room where nighttime temperatures stay above 55° F.

Herbs grown indoors are relatively pest free. If, however, aphids or white flies become a problem, the plant can be sprayed daily with soapy water until the pests disappear. Plants infested with red spider mites should be discarded.

### Light Requirements

With enough light—five to six hours of sunlight daily in a south- or west-facing window—herbs will do almost as well as outdoors and be much more convenient to use. Most plants do best in the kitchen because of the added humidity. Bathrooms, for the same reason, are good places for fragrant herbs if there is enough space and light.

*Strawberry jars, with their many planting pockets, make excellent herb containers. This one holds a red leaf lettuce and several other salad ingredients.*

Strawberry jars are excellent for holding an assortment of culinary herbs. A space-saving vertical container can be made from a special upright cylinder or wall-like structure made of wood, wire, or pipe with holes cut in the sides and filled with a planting mix.

Deep containers can be made easy to water by positioning one or more pieces of perforated plastic pipe in the container, then adding soil around it. A plastic bag can be used to cover the top of the pipe as the soil is being added and during the planting to be sure that the

*This light garden hides a fluorescent fixture in the top and a waterproof tray in the bottom, so it makes an attractive piece of furniture for a desktop while it provides a ready supply of cut herbs for the kitchen.*

Plants can brighten a room with no natural light by growing them under fluorescent light. Incandescent light will help in combination with natural or fluorescent light, but used alone it produces more heat than the type of light that plants need and can cause burning as well as excessive drying.

Fluorescent fixtures can be combined with counters or shelves in a wide variety of attractive arrangements. The most economical fixtures are at least 3 feet long. They are easy to hang and use little electricity. The same wattage bulb can be used for herbs, flower and vegetable seedlings destined for the garden, and African violets. Special grow lights, some that are colored and some not, are also available.

Fluorescent lights and fixtures should be cleaned once a month. The bulbs should be replaced at least once a year, or when they seem dim.

Mature herbs grow best when their tops are between 5 and 15 inches from the lights. Seedlings should be about 2 inches from the lights to keep them from becoming leggy before they are moved to the outdoors.

Many fixtures can be raised and lowered. If not, or if some of the plants need to be closer, they can be raised on inverted pots or bricks. For very tall herbs, a light positioned lengthwise on the wall will help supplement natural light. The plant can be turned a little every week to keep growth even.

Because plants need a period of darkness every day, it is important that the lights be on for only part of the day—16 to 18 hours for mature plants. A plant under fluorescent light for 14 hours gets the equivalent of 5 to 6 hours of sunlight. An automatic timer that turns the lights on and off is a sound investment and a time-saver.

*This unusual container can be easily moved around the house to follow the sun. The plants it holds, like most herbs, require full sun.*

## Water and Fertilizer Needs

For most herbs the soil should be kept evenly moist. A good test of dryness is to feel the top inch of the soil, or to pick up the pot—it will feel heavy if it has enough moisture. If tapping the pot with a knife produces a sharp ring, the pot is dry; a dull thud means the soil is full of water.

Rosemary and sage are sensitive to overwatering, whereas mint is difficult to overwater. As long as there is good drainage and the pots don't sit in water or dry out too much, watering is more a matter of frequent checking than a difficult science.

Most plants grow best if the thermostat is turned down at night and a little extra humidity is added to the air in the daytime. Setting the plants on a tray of wet pebbles or misting with a spray bottle is always beneficial.

Herbs need little fertilizer in winter because they are not growing very much. The planting mix probably has enough nutrients, unless it contains none and says so on the package, to last the plants through three to five months of winter growing. If it is necessary to use a houseplant food, the recommended amount should be cut by half. Too much fertilizer will reduce the concentration of flavor and fragrance in the plant.

Herbs that grow indoors all year, as opposed to winter only, will benefit from regular, light feedings of a balanced houseplant fertilizer applied in liquid solution. The ideal ratio for herbs is 1 part nitrogen, 2 parts phosphate, and 2 parts potassium, or roughly a 5-10-10 or 10-20-20 analysis. The recommended application rates for houseplants should be halved for all herbs except basil, which is a heavy feeder. The plants should be fertilized as often as every two weeks from late spring to early fall if they are growing vigorously.

An easier way to feed permanently potted herbs as well as outdoor ones is with a spring and summer application of a slow-release fertilizer. The little beads should be worked into the top inch of soil, where they will do their job for three to four months.

## GROWING STANDARDS AND TOPIARY

A standard is a shrub or herb grown with an erect main stem, with its side shoots trimmed off but its top allowed to grow so that it resembles a tree. A topiary is a plant trained and trimmed into an ornamental or fanciful shape. Such plants make excellent focal points for an herb garden. A pair of shaped bay trees, for example, on either side of a formal front door adds an air of elegance. Herbs patiently pruned to

*Rosemary pruned as a standard will probably always require staking; the rosemary trunk will not grow strong enough to safely support the top. The name* standard *refers to a flag or banner, roughly describing the shape of the pruned plant.*

simple or fantastic shapes are no more difficult than a knot garden. They can be grown in containers or directly in the ground.

To grow standards or topiary, preplanning is essential. The branches of an herb seedling are carefully trained to fit the desired shape. Sculpting a mature plant is not satisfactory, because there would be too many bare branches where they weren't wanted and places with no branches where they were needed.

## Standards

The most common herbs for standards are sweet myrtle, rosemary, curryplant, santolina, bay, lemon-verbena, scented geranium, dwarf boxwood, upright germander, and various roses.

The ideal candidate is a strong, healthy cutting or a plant that has a straight single stem. Side branches should be cut off before they become developed, but leafy shoots can stay to give the plant nourishment for faster growth. If necessary, a stake as tall as the desired height can be added and the main stem or trunk tied to it loosely.

The plant should be allowed to grow, mostly straight up, until it is 6 inches taller than you want the finished plant to be. Then the leafy side shoots should be removed on the part of the trunk that you want bare. The top should be left to develop a natural shape; it should be pruned only to keep it in proportion.

## Topiary

You can prune plants to be a simple ball, a series of three graduated globes with a bit of trunk in between, a spiral of foliage around a central trunk, or a fanciful shape.

These topiary shapes are created by pruning as for standards. Then the growing top should be pinched out and the developing shoots pruned down to two or three leaves or sets of leaves. Two buds will develop shoots below each pinch. When these shoots have four to six leaves, they should be pinched back to two or three. This pinching back is repeated until the desired shape is achieved. It may take two to three years of careful pruning to develop full, dense branches.

Once the shape is achieved, only two trimmings a year will be needed to maintain it—once in late spring or early summer after all the new shoots have formed, and again in late summer, so that the next batch of new shoots will clothe the plant for winter.

Another way to shape topiary is to use wires or a frame to guide and train the growth to the desired shape. The wanted growth is retained and all the rest is removed. This method can be used to create a wreath of rosemary or an arch of roses. It can also be used to form a row of espaliered trees (trees grown to a flat plane, perhaps along a wall or fence). Such trees are both striking and useful where a spreading tree would not be appropriate.

## HARVESTING AND STORING HERBS

Herbs can be harvested anytime you have clippers in hand and a use in mind.

When gathering wild herbs, it's best to be sure of their identity. Endangered species should not be harvested (a list can be obtained from the local agricultural extension office). Plants that may have been contaminated by car exhaust or roadside spraying should be avoided. From any plant that is harvested, enough should be left for the plant to regrow.

*In general, herbs can most easily be preserved by drying them. Drying is simple and effective, preserving the fresh taste for months.*

*Herbs preserved in several different ways are on sale here at a farmer's market.*

as arugula should be cut to about 2 inches from the ground, leaving the central growing point intact, or as many leaves as needed can be pulled from the sides of the plant.

Herbs picked for floral bouquets should be cut at midday in dry weather when the flowers are fully open and at their most beautiful. Only the most perfect should be chosen, and they should be kept loose in open containers. They bruise easily and begin to sweat if bunched together.

If you are gathering more than a handful of herbs for immediate use, a basket or box is preferable to a bag, to keep the herbs separate and uncrushed. The herbs should be brought indoors as soon as possible after cutting. Hot sun or a long time spent in a container will wilt them.

## Harvesting for Storage

The time when the leaves, flowers, seeds, or roots of herbs have the maximum oil content and are thus at their peak of fragrance and flavor varies slightly from plant to plant. The encyclopedia starting on page 169 should be consulted for individual species.

The leaves of most culinary herbs reach their peak of flavor when the flower buds just begin to open. After this, the plant directs its energy into reproductive rather than vegetative growth. Then the leaves become fibrous and their flavor is not as strong. Mint is an exception; the leaves taste best when the plant is in full flower.

The leaves should be gathered in midmorning of a dry, sunny day just after the dew has dried and before the sun dissipates the essential oils. You can use a pruning snips, shears, or scissors, or simply pinch brittle stems. Taking the young, tender leaves will encourage the plant to produce new, bushy growth. Not more than a

Growing your own herbs facilitates the harvest. You can pick mint or lemon balm for sun tea in the morning, then set it out to steep in the sun all day. When harvesting vegetables for supper or canning, you can gather the herbs to put with them. In the midst of dinner preparations, you can slip out into the garden to gather a mixed handful of nasturtium flowers and leaves, parsley, arugula, cress, or purslane for the salad. This trip may seem inconvenient, but it provides a minute of escape as well.

Chive leaves should be cut flush with the ground so that new growth will have green tips. Parsley and many of the other leafy herbs such

third of the foliage of perennials should be taken in order not to weaken the plant.

**Short-term storage**   If herbs are placed in a jug of water on the countertop, they will stay at their peak of freshness for only an hour or so. It is better to place them in the refrigerator *unwashed* in a plastic bag with a few holes poked in it for air. Within an hour, heavy condensation will gather in the bag. It should be opened just long enough for the dry air of the refrigerator to absorb the condensation, then the bag should be closed and tied. Or herbs can be stored in the refrigerator in a plastic bag or covered jar with their stems in a bit of water and the leaves dry at the top.

If the herbs have been cut during the heat of the day, it is important to let the heat dissipate before storing them. The herbs can be spread on damp newspapers in a cool place, such as on a concrete basement floor, then covered with more damp newspapers or linen towels. Once the herbs are cool to the touch, they can be placed in plastic bags or rolled in damp newspapers to retain moisture.

**Freezing herbs**   As with vegetables, frozen herbs are second only to fresh for flavor and nutrition. Freezing is appropriate for herbs such as fennel, burnet, chervil, parsley, basil, tarragon, sweet cicely, and chives. Texture preservation varies with the type of herb, although in cooked dishes herb texture is not as important as flavor. When a recipe calls for crumbled herb leaves, as in salad dressings, the leaves should be handled while they are still frozen and brittle.

Some herbs contain enzymes that turn the leaves black when they are frozen. You can check for this by washing and freezing a small test

packet. If the test leaves darken, a new batch of leaves can be spread on a baking sheet and sprayed with nonstick oil spray. If then quickly frozen, they should not darken.

Another option is to place the leaves in a tea strainer, immerse them in boiling water for a few seconds or until the color changes, then cool them for 2 minutes in ice water and shake or pat dry. The leaves can be frozen whole or chopped. Or they can be puréed (1 tablespoon of leaves to 1 tablespoon of water) and frozen in ice-cube trays. After the cubes have frozen solid, they can be transferred to a freezer bag and labeled with the name and date.

*The best time to harvest most herbs is in the morning, after the night's dew has had time to dry.*

*Herbs can be dried in different types of commercial or homemade dryers. This one is a simple frame of wire-mesh racks. Others have heaters and fans built in for faster drying.*

Herbs can be frozen individually or in combinations, such as bouquet garni, fines herbes, herbs for fish, and so forth. All the excess air should be pressed from the plastic bags before sealing. For the ultimate convenience, several meal-sized packets can be stored in a large, rigid, well-labeled container, which will not be crushed or lost in the bottom of the freezer. For the best flavor, frozen herbs should be used within a year.

**Drying herbs**  The most common way of preserving herbs is to dry

them. For the best results drying should start soon after harvest and proceed quickly, although if the moisture evaporates too rapidly, essential oils are lost as well. The herbs should be washed gently and not left in water any longer than necessary. Dead or discolored leaves should be discarded, and the remaining leaves shaken or patted dry. Leaves can remain on stems.

*Oven-drying leaves*  This method preserves color and flavor well but may destroy some therapeutic properties. A gas oven with just the pilot light for heat will usually dry herb leaves spread on baking sheets in about 12 hours. A gas or an electric oven can be used on its lowest setting with the door open a few inches, but the leaves often dry too fast by this method. The herbs should be dried until they are brittle.

To dry herb leaves in a microwave oven, four or five stems of herbs should be spread on a double thickness of paper towels and covered with a single layer of toweling. The oven should be run on full power until the leaves are brittle: in 30- to 60-second intervals for a maximum of about two minutes for small leaves, three minutes for larger ones, turning the leaves halfway through. They can be dried in further 30-second increments if they are not brittle after the recommended time.

When the leaves are brittle and fragile but not so dry that they turn to powder when touched, they are ready for storage.

Strong-flavored herbs, such as lovage, should not be dried in proximity to other herbs or the flavors may mix. Also, fresh material should not be added in the midst of the drying process.

*Air-drying leaves*   Large quantities of herbs are most conveniently dried by this method. The ideal conditions are a dark place with good air circulation, low humidity, and temperatures between 90° and 120° F the first day, 75° to 80° F thereafter. These conditions can be created in a closet, an attic, or a cold frame covered with black plastic, with the addition of a heater or fan if needed.

To air-dry the leaves, the herbs should be cut with long stems, washed only if necessary and dried well, and tied loosely with no more than ten stems to a bundle. If dust or insects will be a problem, the bundle should be covered with a paper bag. Alternatively, small quantities of the herb can be spread on a thin cloth or an open paper bag with many fine holes poked in it. This can be placed on a wire rack so that air can circulate all around it.

The leaves should dry in about four days at optimum temperatures and low humidity, up to two weeks if it is cooler and damper. Then they can be stored as directed on page 69.

*Drying roots*   Roots are best dug in fall when the top growth begins to wither; then they are most full of stored food and concentrated vitamins. For perennials, it's best to wait until the second or third year. The whole plant can be dug, then some can be harvested and the rest replanted; or a hole can be dug beside the plant and part of the root pulled over into it and away from the rest. Some root crops, such as horseradish, can be scrubbed clean; others—valerian, for example—should not be scrubbed, for their desired constituents are in the skin.

All roots should be cleaned before drying, but some very gently. Fibrous parts should be removed. Thick roots should be cut lengthwise and then into small pieces or sliced with a vegetable cutter. The recommended temperature for drying roots is between 120° and 140° F, which can be achieved in a cold frame covered with black plastic, with the addition of a heater if needed. The roots should be turned often until they are fragile enough to break easily. The rhizomes of licorice and the roots of marshmallow should be peeled before drying.

*Drying other plant parts*   Seed heads of anise, caraway, coriander, and dill should be cut when they are almost mature, well turned from green to their final color but before any capsules begin to open. The seed heads can be placed upside down in a paper bag with the name and date written on it; the top of the bag should be closed to keep out insects. When the seeds heads are completely dry, much of the seed will fall out on its own. Shaking or tapping the bag will release the rest. Any large pieces of stem can be removed by hand. The rest

can be winnowed out by tossing handfuls in the air over a sheet on a windy day or in front of a fan, or blowing gently over a tray full of seeds. The lighter chaff will blow away; the heavier seed will fall to the sheet or remain on the tray.

If sunflowers are dried whole, the individual seeds will loosen for easier removal to storage jars after several days.

*There are several ways to dry flowers for display (see pages 156 to 160). Silica gel preserves both the color and the shape of the flowers.*

Many flowers will retain their color if dried correctly; delicate blooms, such as borage, should be arranged so that they will retain their shape. Drying should take one to three weeks, depending on the thickness of the plant parts. They should be laid flat if possible.

Before storing large blooms such as calendula, the petals should be removed. Small flowers such as chamomile and lavender should be kept whole.

The color and shape of flowers not suitable for air-drying can be retained by burying the flowers in clean builders' sand for two weeks or more, or in half borax and half cornmeal, or in silica gel according to package directions.

Fruit such as rose hips can be picked when ripe but not too soft. The hips can become very dry and hard and will then keep indefinitely. Hops should be harvested when they are half dried.

Berries and soft fruit take longer to dry. They can be hung like seeds or dried on a rack with frequent turning.

Before drying bark, it should be washed if necessary, then dried as flat as possible on a rack and turned as needed.

**Salting herbs**   One of the oldest ways to preserve herbs, salting works well for basil, tarragon, parsley, and lovage. Noniodized salt and clean herbs should be alternately layered in a covered crock or jar. The inner layers of salt should just cover the herbs. The bottom and top layers of salt can be a bit thicker. Kosher or canning salt is pure coarse salt and works best.

A modern adaptation of salting is to place a layer of salt on a baking sheet, then add a layer of herb leaves and sprinkle more salt over the top. This is placed in a 300° F oven for 10 minutes, then stirred carefully; any lumps of salt are broken up with a wooden spoon. The baking sheet is then returned to the oven until the leaves are crisp (about another 10 minutes, or a bit longer for parsley and lovage). The leaves are separated from the salt by sifting the mixture through a coarse strainer. The leaves, which remain in the strainer, can be ground and stored as dried herb powder. The salt will contain tiny bits of herbs as well as absorbed flavors and can be used alone or in blends for seasoning.

## Storing Dried Leaves

Herb leaves that have been air- or oven-dried can be stored by removing them whole from their stems, then packing them loosely in dark, airtight glass containers, such as prune juice bottles. Plastic or metal containers may affect the flavor, and paper or cardboard will absorb the oils. Each container should be labeled with the name and date. The herbs should be used within a year; after that, any aromatic ones left over can be used in potpourris or added to an open fire or grill.

The stored leaves should be checked for the first few days. If any condensation forms on the glass, the leaves should be removed and dried further. It's wise to check every so often for moisture, mold, or insects; any affected leaves should be discarded. One or more small pouches of desiccant, such as those found in bottled vitamin tablets, can be added to each jar to absorb moisture.

The leaves of some herbs, such as marshmallow and lady's-mantle, will reabsorb moisture from the air, which can cause chemical deterioration, so their storage should be brief, and the jars should not be left open longer than necessary.

# HERBS IN THE KITCHEN

*From left to right, the herbs in this sunny kitchen are: mint (in the colander), curly-leaf and flatleaf Italian parsley, cilantro, oregano, thyme, and, to the right of the three herbal vinegars, a pot of cut sage and bay leaves.*

Herbs can flavor food subtly, losing their own identity while making familiar dishes taste special, but their absence would certainly be noticed.

Growing herbs is the best way to have a plentiful and self-renewing supply of the freshest foliage, flowers, and seeds for the most intense flavors. You can also grow unusual herbs called for in innovative and ethnic recipes; more and more seed companies now carry exotic herbs. But if you choose to simply use herbs rather than grow them, there are many sources of fresh and dried herbs.

## HAVING HERBS HANDY

Bunches of herbs fresh from the garden and hanging in the kitchen provide a ready supply for cooking and an atmosphere almost as appealing as their flavors.

If your garden doesn't produce all the herbs you need, or if you simply would rather purchase them than grow them, supermarket produce sections carry fresh herbs, either packaged as cut foliage, such as parsley and watercress, or as live plants, such as potted chives.

Natural foods stores often sell dried herbs and spices in bulk, often at much lower prices than the containers found in supermarkets. This practice allows the purchase of only the needed amount. The individual bags should be labeled with the name of the herb and the date purchased.

Many mail-order sources of herb plants also sell packages of dried herbs, usually at lower-than-supermarket prices. Such sources often carry unusual, ethnic, and hard-to-find herbs.

### Herb Centerpieces

In the Middle East a host sometimes passes a bowl of fresh herb sprigs to eat with the meal; in Italy a plant or vase of sweet basil often decorates the table. Placing the stems in water keeps the herbs from darkening or wilting.

You can adapt these customs by gathering from the garden or food store sprigs of several mild herbs that blend with the food being served. These sprigs can be used as a centerpiece, or they can be placed in individual bud vases or vials at each place. Guests can try pinches of various herbs on their food. This is a fine conversation starter as well as a pleasant way to introduce guests to various herb fragrances and flavors without putting too much unaccustomed flavor into favorite foods.

A mixed pot of growing herbs also makes an interesting centerpiece. A pair of scissors can be provided for taste testing, or each guest can be invited to bring a pair of scissors but not told why. The request can add a bit of mystery to a dinner invitation.

*A collection of culinary herbs, planted in a type of basket usually used for trailing flowers, hangs near the kitchen door, ready for the chef.*

*Herbs grow happily in a sunny windowsill. These recycled tins make appropriate containers for small plants.*

## Windowsill and Hanging Gardens

Growing herbs on windowsills or in hanging pots is one of the most serviceable and attractive ways to have herbs handy. Unless you have a greenhouse, it is also the only way to grow fresh herbs during northern winters and, for some herbs, even through southern summers. Seeds can be started or cuttings taken in midsummer, so that the indoor garden will be ready when the first frost arrives.

## Herbal Wreaths

Culinary herbs—both living and dried—can be crafted into wreaths that add scent to the kitchen and flavor to food. Living plants will replenish themselves as they are snipped for cooking. Some of the best plants for living wreaths are thyme, sage, and rosemary.

Herb cuttings should be treated with rooting hormone, then inserted into a moss-filled wire tube, with the stems all going in the same direction. The wreaths should be kept flat under fluorescent lights or hung in a sunny window. They should be misted at least once daily and periodically taken down and soaked in water to which a weak dose of fertilizer has been added. Trimming the growing tips of the plants will keep the wreath compact. Once the plants are rooted and well established, the wreaths are ready to be hung. If you give them as gifts, instructions on watering and misting should be included.

Dried herbs can be crafted into wreaths or swags. The latter is easier—it's simply a cluster of long-stemmed sprigs—and clipping won't upset the shape.

## SOME CULINARY USES

Good cooks and restaurateurs know that it isn't just the flavor of the food but also the way it is served that makes it special. The creative use of herbs can make foods look appealing—pleasing the eye as well as the nose and making one feel wrapped in luxury.

Garnishing with fresh herbs is an elegant touch. Having a small bouquet of mixed herbs in the refrigerator makes it easy. A sprig or two of whatever is being used in the food can be used as a garnish, or appropriate flavors can be combined. Fish dishes can be garnished with dill or fennel. Basil can be minced over a plate of sliced tomatoes. A sprig of mint or lemon balm can be added to hot or iced tea, to the salad plate, or to a slice of chilled melon. Sprigs of parsley can grace the serving platter. Garnishing should not be overdone; simplicity is often the most dramatic touch.

## COOKING WITH HERBS

A few kitchen gadgets and appliances can make using herbs easier and more fun. A mortar and pestle is ideal for grinding and blending dried herbs and seeds. A small electric coffee grinder or spice grinder makes the job go even faster; an extra pepper mill labeled for herbs is a good alternative. A food processor or blender works well for large quantities. Any small amount of flavor lost is well offset by the convenience.

Although kitchen shears or a sharp knife and cutting board do a fine job of mincing fresh herbs, there are several minichoppers available that some cooks find indispensable.

Cheesecloth should be kept on hand to cut into squares; the squares can be tied with fine string for making bouquets garnis. A tea ball of regular or extralarge size will hold herbs for seasoning soups and stews so that the herbs can be removed easily before serving.

Here are a few basics when starting to cook with herbs.

■ Start with small amounts of herb and with only one herb per dish.

■ Remember that the flavor of newly dried herbs will probably be more intense than that of commercial ones. Adjust amounts accordingly; you can always add more. Herbs should enhance, not overwhelm.

■ A general rule of thumb is 1 part dried herb equals 3 parts fresh herb.

■ Don't put herbs in every dish at a meal. One dish is good, two is fine, but three could be too much.

■ Herbs are tender; heat can destroy their flavor or make them taste bitter.

As a rule, add them in the last half hour for long-cooking foods (2 hours or more, such as roasts and stews) and in the last few minutes for quick-cooking foods, such as vegetables, fish, and sauces.

■ Add herbs to cold foods ahead of time and let them stand in the refrigerator for several hours or overnight to absorb the flavor.

■ Crush or bruise fresh herbs with a wooden spoon or between the fingers just before adding to foods to release the flavors.

■ Dominant herbs that don't always mix well with each other are basil, rosemary, oregano, thyme, tarragon, and sage.

■ Herb blends are best with one dominant herb and a few other herbs that complement it.

If you have overseasoned a dish, here are several ways to remedy the situation.

■ Scoop or strain out as much of the herb as possible.

■ Add ½ teaspoon sugar to reduce saltiness.

■ Add more of the bland ingredients to minimize the stronger flavor.

■ Add a peeled raw potato to soak up some of the excess flavor. Remove it just before serving if it isn't appropriate to the dish; otherwise, leave it in.

■ Serve the dish cold, if appropriate, so that the overseasoning will not be as obvious.

■ Make a second, unseasoned batch of the recipe and add it to the first. Then freeze half and turn a mistake into an advantage.

## COMPATIBLE COMBINATIONS

Here are suggestions for herbs and spices to season specific foods. Improvising with your own favorites can expand the list.

*Asparagus*  Chervil, chives, dill, lemon balm, sage, savory, tarragon, thyme

*Avocado*  Dill, marjoram, tarragon

*Beans, dried*  Cumin, garlic, mint, onion, oregano, parsley, sage, savory, sorrel, thyme

*Beans, green or lima*  Basil, caraway seed, dill, marjoram, mint, oregano, rosemary, sage, savory, tarragon, thyme

*Beef and veal*  Basil, bay, caraway seed, chervil, cumin, garlic, ginger, lovage, marjoram, mint, oregano, parsley, rosemary, sage, savory, tarragon, thyme

*Bread*  Anise seed, basil, caraway seed, chives, dill, fennel, garlic, lovage seed, poppy seed, rosemary, sesame seed, sunflower seed, thyme

*Carrots*  Anise seed, basil, chervil, chives, cumin, ginger, mint, parsley

*Cheese*  Caraway seed, chervil, chives, dill, fennel, marjoram, mint, rosemary, sage, savory, thyme

*Cole crops (cabbage, broccoli, cauliflower, brussels sprouts)*  Borage, caraway seed, chives, dill, fennel, marjoram, mint, oregano, parsley, rosemary, sage, savory, sweet cicely, thyme

*Corn*  Chervil, chives, lemon balm, saffron, sage, thyme

*Eggplant*  Basil, cinnamon, dill, garlic, marjoram, mint, oregano, parsley, sage, savory, thyme

*Eggs*  Basil, caraway seed, chervil, chives, dill, fennel, oregano, parsley, rosemary, tarragon

*Fish*  Basil, bay, borage, caraway seed, chervil, chives, dill, fennel, lemon balm, lemon thyme, lovage, marjoram, mint, parsley, thyme

*Fruit*  Anise seed, cinnamon, cloves, ginger, lemon balm, mint, rosemary, pineapple sage

*Ham*  Juniper berries, lovage, marjoram, mint, mustard, oregano, parsley, rosemary, savory

*Lamb*  Basil, bay, chervil, coriander, cumin, dill, lemon balm, lovage, marjoram, mint, parsley, rosemary, sage, savory, tarragon, thyme

*Mushrooms*  Coriander, marjoram, oregano, rosemary, tarragon, thyme

*Onions*  Basil, marjoram, oregano, sage, tarragon, thyme

*Peas*  Basil, chervil, marjoram, mint, parsley, rosemary, sage, savory

*Pork*  Anise seed, caraway seed, chervil, coriander, fennel, garlic, lovage, marjoram, rosemary, saffron, sage, savory, tarragon, thyme

*Potatoes*  Basil, bay, chives, coriander, dill, lovage, marjoram, mint, oregano, parsley, rosemary, sage, savory, tarragon, thyme

*Poultry and game*  Bay, chervil, chives, cumin, dill, fennel seed, fenugreek, garlic, ginger, lemon balm, lovage, mint, marjoram, parsley, sage, savory, tarragon, thyme

*Rice*  Basil, fennel, lovage, saffron, tarragon, thyme

*Soups*  Bay, basil, chervil, garlic, juniper berries, lemon balm, parsley, rosemary, savory, sorrel, tarragon, thyme

*Spinach*  Borage, chervil, marjoram, mint, rosemary, sage, sorrel, tarragon

*Squash*  Basil, dill, garlic, ginger, marjoram, rosemary, sage, savory, tarragon

*Tomatoes*  Basil, bay, chervil, chives, coriander, dill, garlic, lovage, marjoram, mint, oregano, parsley, sage, savory, tarragon

*Turnips*  Dill, marjoram, savory

*Sage is a versatile herb, enhancing most meats and many vegetables.*

## Arugula-Orange Salad

The dressing for this salad is good on any fruit or tossed salad. Left-over dressing can be saved in the refrigerator; it should be stirred before each use.

   2 heads arugula, washed and torn into bite-sized pieces
   1 orange, peeled, sectioned, and cut up
   2 tablespoons chopped almonds, walnuts, or pecans
   Celery Seed Dressing

Mix together the arugula, orange pieces, and nuts. Toss with the Celery Seed Dressing and serve.
*Makes 4 small salads.*

### Celery Seed Dressing

   ¼ cup sugar
   1 teaspoon ground mustard
   1 teaspoon salt
   1 small onion, chopped
   ½ cup distilled white vinegar
   1 cup extravirgin olive oil
   1 teaspoon celery seed

In a blender container combine the sugar, mustard, salt, onion, and vinegar. Add the oil and blend again. Stir in the celery seed.
*Makes about 1½ cups.*

## Summer Salad

   1 cup cantaloupe or honeydew melon balls or pieces
   1 cup chopped tomato
   ½ cup peeled and finely chopped cucumber
   ¼ cup finely chopped fresh mint, basil, or lemon balm
   1 cup plain yogurt
   Salt and pepper, to taste
   4 sprigs fresh mint, for garnish

In a bowl combine the melon, tomato, cucumber, and chopped mint. Add the yogurt and toss to combine. Season to taste with the salt and pepper, and serve garnished with the mint sprigs.
*Makes 4 small salads.*

*Arugula-Orange Salad contrasts the slightly bitter taste of the green with the sweet fruit.*

Using herbs in the kitchen is easier if you have a few gadgets and know a few basics. See page 74 for some suggestions. On the opposite page are more ideas for cooking with herbs. Compatible combinations of herbs and the foods they season are suggested on page 75.

## Herbs in Salads

In the list on page 82, herb flowers from dandelions to violets are suggested salad additions. Recommended salad greens include burnet, chives, dandelion, fennel, hyssop, lovage, nasturtium, purslane, summer savory, sorrel, and sweet cicely. Many are rich in vitamins and minerals as well as having possible therapeutic properties.

# KITCHEN HINTS

Here are a few tips for cooking with herbs and for storing and sharing them.

▮ Add sprigs of mint, lemon balm, or any of the lemon-flavored herbs to a bottle of water kept in the refrigerator for a handy refreshing drink.

▮ After serving sticky foods, offer finger bowls of water with a bit of lemon juice and a floating leaf of scented geranium, or a sprig of lavender, lemon-verbena, or rosemary.

▮ Use dried leaves of stinging-nettle in fall to pack apples and pears and root crops such as carrots and potatoes. Stinging-nettle deters pests and keeps the skins smooth and moist. It can also be used to wrap cheese to preserve it. Wear gloves when handling nettle unless it is well wilted; fresh nettle stings the skin.

▮ When invited to a kitchen shower, consider an herbal gift—containers of dried herbs, live plants, a mortar and pestle, and a favorite recipe.

▮ When cooking vegetables with herbs, to blend the flavors without overcooking the herbs, melt butter in the serving dish. Add the herbs and let stand at least 10 minutes. Then add the vegetables, stir or toss, and serve.

▮ Increase the nutritional value of seeds used in salads, soups, or breads by barely sprouting them first. The fats and starches found in seeds change to vitamins, sugars, and protein during sprouting. Sprouted seeds are more digestible, take less time to cook, and are less fattening than unsprouted seeds. To sprout seeds, place them in a sprouting jar (or any glass jar with a piece of cheesecloth tied to the mouth of the jar), add water to cover, and let stand for several hours or overnight. Pour off the water, rinse the seeds well, drain, and let stand until sprouted, rinsing two or three times a day until the desired growth has been attained. Then refrigerate and use within a few days.

*A small garden near the kitchen door keeps herbs readily available.*

*Pineapple sage can be used to flavor sugar, which will impart an herb-tinged sweetness to cookies, candy, or teas.*

## Wilted Lettuce

1 egg

2 tablespoons *each* sugar, vinegar, and water

½ teaspoon dried herb of your choice

3 cups lettuce, spinach, or any other mild-flavored greens or combination of greens torn into bite-sized pieces

2 slices cooked bacon, crumbled

In a small skillet scramble the egg. Add the sugar, vinegar, water, and herb. Just before serving pour the warm mixture over the greens, sprinkle on the crumbled bacon, and toss.

*Makes 4 small salads.*

## Herb Stuffings

Dried herbs from the garden can be used to make herb stuffings. A delicious blend combines sage, parsley, celery leaves, rosemary, marjoram, oregano, nutmeg, fennel, and thyme. The blend can be used for croutons, scalloped vegetables, and casseroles, to stuff poultry, or as a side dish.

## Herbed Stuffing Mix

30 slices bread, cut into cubes

¼ cup vegetable oil

3 tablespoons instant minced onion

3 tablespoons dried parsley flakes

2 teaspoons garlic salt

1 teaspoon ground sage or thyme, or poultry seasoning

¼ teaspoon ground pepper

Preheat the oven to 300° F. Toast the bread cubes on 2 baking sheets for 45 minutes, stirring occasionally. Remove from the oven when toasted and let cool.

Stir in the oil, onion, parsley, garlic salt, sage, and ground pepper. Toss to coat the cubes. Use immediately or store in an airtight container for up to 4 months in the refrigerator or freezer.

*Makes about 12 cups.*

## Seasoned Flour and Sugar

These seasoned blends will keep indefinitely if stored in the freezer. Small jars labeled with suggestions for use make unique gifts. Seasoned flour can be kept on hand for use in gravies, sauces, biscuits, and pizza or quiche crusts, or to dust over foods before browning or frying. Herbed sugar can be used in tea, as a topping for cookies, cake, or French toast, or to sweeten fruits.

### Seasoned Flour

   3 cups flour
   1 to 2 teaspoons mixed dried
      herbs and spices
   ½ teaspoon salt
   Dash freshly ground pepper

Mix well and store in airtight jars.
   *Makes about 3 cups.*

### Seasoned Sugar

   1 cup granulated or confec-
      tioners' sugar
   2 tablespoons chopped fresh
      herbs, such as rose petals,
      lemon balm, mint, pineapple
      sage, or rose geranium

Mix the sugar and the herbs. Store in an airtight container for 6 weeks for the flavors to blend. The herbs can then be sifted out or left in.
   *Makes about 1 cup.*

## HERBS FOR SPECIAL DIETS

Dishes in which salt, fat, or sugar has been removed or greatly reduced can still be appealing with the addition of herbs, spices, and flavorings.

### Salt-Free Diets

Any or all of the following dried herbs and spices can be used instead of salt to complement the specified dish. Several of these blends can be kept in small jars or salt shakers with large holes. Where savory is suggested, you

can use either winter or summer savory. The dried herbs should be ground as fine as possible with a mortar and pestle or in a spice grinder for use in salt shakers, where mixing them with uncooked rice will help prevent clumping in damp weather. More suggestions for herb combinations are found on page 75.

*For salad* Basil, parsley, lovage, marjoram, dill, tarragon, savory

*For soup* Basil, lovage, parsley, savory, thyme, marjoram, bay

*For beef and veal* Basil, lovage, parsley, thyme, marjoram, savory, sage, rosemary, black pepper, ground cloves, lemon or orange zest, garlic or onion powder

*A classic French bouquet garni (see page 81) is composed of bay, parsley, and thyme tied up in a cheesecloth bundle. But you can use a variety of other herbs for different dishes. You may find a tea infuser is more convenient than the cheesecloth.*

*Five Heavenly Herbs, a staple in Chinese cuisine, is composed of fennel seed, cloves, star anise, Szechuan peppercorns, and cinnamon.*

*For poultry*   Sage, thyme, savory, parsley, lovage, marjoram, basil, ground ginger, orange or lemon zest, garlic powder

*For fish*   Basil, lemon balm, dill, fennel, savory, rosemary, pickling spices, bay, lemon zest

*For yellow vegetables*   Ground cinnamon, ground nutmeg, ground ginger, orange zest, thyme, lovage, celery leaves, bergamot

*For green vegetables*   Savory, chives, onion powder, dill, bay, basil, ground nutmeg, marjoram

*For egg and cheese dishes*   Dill, chives, parsley, paprika, ground nutmeg, ground mustard, black pepper, oregano, thyme, garlic powder

*For beans, rice, and pasta dishes* Ground dried chiles, cumin seed, oregano, garlic powder, parsley, mint, lemon zest, caraway seed

## Low-Calorie Diets

The sugar and fats absent in diets are missed less if the flavor of the food is vibrant rather than bland. Several herbs enhance sweetness without adding calories or chemical substitutes. Herb-infused oils are more flavorful than plain oils, so less oil is used, thereby saving calories (see page 88).

The following herbs, spices, and flavorings can replace some or all sugar for sweetening.

*For salads*   Angelica stems, fennel stalks

*For cakes and cookies*   Ground cardamom

*For pies*   Rose petals, violets

*For tomato sauce*   Ground cinnamon

*For drinks*   Bergamot, cost-mary, mint

*With fruits*   Rosemary, violets, rose petals, costmary, mint

*For sorbets and ices*   Lemon-verbena, lemon balm

*For sauces*   Vanilla extract

## Fines Herbes

This combination of three or four herbs—usually parsley, chervil, thyme, and either basil, chives, or burnet—is most often used in French cooking. Some cooks like to add tarragon, but others find tarragon too distinctive. Fines herbes are delicious finely chopped and added to omelets, tartar sauce, cream soups, sautéed dishes, and cheese dishes at the end of the cooking.

## Five Heavenly Herbs

This combination, also known as Chinese five-spice powder, is a finely ground powder used to add distinctive flavor and fragrance to Asian dishes, especially pork, chicken, and stir-fries, and as a condiment. Although variations are quite acceptable, the usual blend includes 1 tablespoon ground cinnamon; 1 tablespoon fennel seed, ground; ½ teaspoon ground cloves; 6 star anise, ground; and 1 tablespoon Szechuan peppercorns, ground. Szechuan peppercorns have a delayed and intense flavor; black peppercorns can be substituted.

The above amounts make about 4 tablespoons, enough for most recipes. Although five-spice powder is most flavorful if the ingredients are ground as needed, any remaining can be stored in an airtight jar in a cool, dark cupboard or in the freezer.

# CLASSIC HERB COMBINATIONS

Here is a primer of classic herbal combinations.

## Bouquet Garni

The aromatic herbs in this little bundle infuse food with their flavor. The herb bundle simmers in the dish as it cooks and then is removed. The bundle usually consists of parsley, thyme, and bay but can be adjusted to taste, perhaps adding whole peppercorns, ground allspice, ground cloves, chives, celery leaves, rosemary, tarragon, garlic, or marjoram.

Fresh bouquet garni, also known as *bouquet fagot,* is held with a string long enough to tie to the pot handle so that it is easy to remove.

### Louisiana Bouquet Garni

This favorite New Orleans bouquet garni for flavoring crab and shrimp boils is made from dried herbs and spices. They can be placed in a tea ball or infuser, or tied in a small cheesecloth square.

> 1 teaspoon *each* whole allspice, celery seed, black peppercorns, and ground thyme
> ¼ teaspoon *each* whole cloves and cayenne pepper
> 5 bay leaves
> 3 dried hot chiles
> 4 quarts boiling water
> Salt, to taste
> Lemon slices, to taste

Make a bouquet of the herbs, spices, and chiles. Bring the water to a boil and add the bouquet, salt, and lemon slices. Boil for 10 minutes before adding the shellfish.

*Makes about ¼ cup bouquet garni.*

## FLOWERS TO EAT AND NOT TO EAT

Many flowers are edible and indeed are attractive garnishes for food. When using flowers for such a purpose, choose young, blemish-free blossoms of edible flowers (see list below) that have not been sprayed with herbicides or pesticides. Soak them for 10 minutes in cold water with a dash of salt to loosen any insects that might be hiding. Then rinse, drain off the water, wrap gently in a double layer of paper towels, and place in a plastic bag in the refrigerator until mealtime. Here are a few suggestions for using edible blooms.

∎ Use calendula petals and rose petals to add sweetness; use nasturtium blooms to add tang.

∎ Float borage blossoms on cold drinks or freeze them in ice cubes.

∎ Use nasturtiums, pansies, or johnny-jump-ups in a molded salad, to be eaten as is or cut into squares as a garnish. To make the molded salad, pour a thin layer of gelatin into a mold and chill until firm. Arrange the flowers face down on the gelatin, gently pour in enough additional gelatin to cover the flowers, and chill again until firm.

∎ Chop edible flowers into cheese spreads, herb butters, biscuits, or pancake or crêpe batter. Large edible flowers, such as squash blossoms, can be stuffed with cheese spreads.

### Edible Flowers

The blooms of all culinary herbs are edible. This list includes culinary herbs and other edible flowers. Flowers that do not appear in this list should not be eaten. If the edibility of a flower is in doubt, consult your local poison control center.

| Common Name | Common Name |
| --- | --- |
| Anise-hyssop | Impatiens |
| Bachelor's-button | Johnny-jump-up |
| Bergamot | Lavender |
| Borage | Lilac |
| Calendula | Mint |
| Carnation | Nasturtium |
| Chive | Pineapple sage |
| Chrysanthemum | Pinks |
| Citrus | Portulaca |
| Dandelion | Redbud |
| Daylily | Rose |
| English daisy | Savory |
| Fuchsia | Snapdragon |
| Geranium | Squash |
| Hibiscus | Tulip |
| Hollyhock | Violet |
| Hyssop | Yucca |

### Inedible Flowers

Be sure to avoid eating any flower on this list. The botanical name is given to help avoid mistakes in identification. The asterisked herbs are toxic to animals as well as humans.

| Common Name | Botanical Name |
| --- | --- |
| Azalea | *Rhododendron* species |
| Boxwood | *Buxus sempervirens* |
| Buttercup* | *Ranunculus* species |
| Columbine | *Aguilegia* species |
| Cowslip, marsh-marigold* | *Caltha palustris* |
| Daffodil | *Narcissus* species |
| Delphinium | *Delphinium* species |
| Foxglove | *Digitalis purpurea* |
| Fritillaria | *Fritillaria* species |
| Goldenrod | *Solidago* species |
| Heliotrope* | *Heliotropium arborescens* |
| Hydrangea | *Hydrangea* species |
| Iris | *Iris* species |
| Jack-in-the-pulpit | *Arisaema triphyllum* |
| Jimsonweed | *Datura* species |
| Lily, glory | *Lilium humboldtii* var. *ocellatum* |
| Lily-of-the-valley | *Convallaria majalis* |
| Milkweed | *Asclepias* species |
| Mistletoe, American | *Phoradendron serotinum* |
| Monkshood | *Aconitum* species |
| Mountain-laurel | *Kalmia latifolia* |
| Narcissus | *Narcissus* species |
| Nightshade | *Atropa* and *Solanum* species |
| Oleander | *Nerium oleander* |
| Pennyroyal, American | *Hedeoma pulegioides* |
| Pennyroyal, European | *Mentha pulegium* |
| Poinsettia | *Euphorbia pulcherrima* |
| Poppy, oriental | *Papaver orientale* |
| Rhododendron | *Rhododendron* species |
| St. John's wort | *Hypericum perforatum* |
| Scarlet pimpernel* | *Anagallis arvensis* |
| Snowdrop | *Galanthus plicatus* ssp. *byzantinus* |
| Tansy | *Tanacetum vulgare* |
| Wisteria | *Wisteria floribunda* |
| Yellow jessamine | *Gelsemium sempervirens* |
| Zephyr-lily | *Zephyranthes atamasca* |

# HERB PREPARATIONS

These herb preparations can be made ahead and used in a variety of ways, including marinades, stuffings, and sauces.

## Dried Herb Blends

You can combine these herbs and keep them handy in shakers near your food preparation area. Any herbs that are too large to pass through the holes of the shakers can be ground with a mortar and pestle or in a spice grinder before combining them with the other herbs.

*Beef*　1 part *each* basil, chervil, marjoram, parsley, summer savory

*Egg dishes*　1 part *each* basil, chervil, chives, rosemary, summer savory, tarragon

*Fish*　1 part *each* basil, bay leaf, parsley; 2 parts dill, fennel, or tarragon

*Lamb or veal*　1 part *each* chervil, marjoram, parsley, rosemary, summer savory

*Pork*　1 part *each* basil, rosemary, sage, summer savory

*Poultry, stuffing, or chicken soup*　3 parts sage; 2 parts marjoram; 1 part *each* lemon thyme, lovage, parsley

*Salad seasoning*　1 part *each* basil, parsley, tarragon; 1½ parts thyme

*Soups and stews*　1 part *each* lovage, rosemary, savory; 2 parts marjoram

*Tomato sauce*　2 parts *each* basil, oregano; 1 part *each* marjoram, parsley

## Herb Salts

One herb or a blend of several can be used in making herb salts. The flavor imparted by the herbs will help reduce the amount of salt needed. The salt should be noniodized, kosher, or sea salt.

The recommended proportion is about 1 cup of salt to 5 to 8 tablespoons of dried herb. Suitable herbs include basil, chives, garlic, marjoram, oregano, rosemary, savory, tarragon, and thyme. The ingredients can be combined in a blender, then placed in a shaker for immediate use or stored in an airtight glass jar away from heat and light for long-term keeping. Properly stored, herb salts keep indefinitely.

### Herbed Salt

Herbed salt is good on baked potatoes, vegetables, hamburgers, steaks, and any dish that is usually salted. You can substitute, decrease, or increase any of the suggested herbs to taste.

2 cups kosher salt
1 teaspoon garlic powder
2 tablespoons paprika
2 tablespoons ground black pepper
1½ tablespoons poultry seasoning
4 tablespoons *each* dried parsley flakes and dried basil
1 tablespoon ground mustard, celery seed, onion powder, dried dill weed, or dried oregano
2 tablespoons of one of the following ground dried herbs: lovage, mint, rosemary, tarragon, thyme, lemon balm, savory, sage, or marjoram

Combine all the ingredients in the container of a blender or food processor. Process until pulverized. Transfer to a shaker with large holes or store in an airtight jar.

*Makes about 2½ cups.*

## Herbed Rice Blends

For a quick dinner, herbed rice blends can be prepared ahead. Stored in a cool, dry place, they will keep for 6 to 8 months. The following combinations work well. Simply combine the ingredients and transfer to airtight containers. Each

*Opposite: Herb mustards can be made in a variety of flavors. Try marjoram mustard on roast beef sandwiches, or mix basil mustard with sour cream as a vegetable dip.*

blend should be labeled with the ingredients and date.

### Herbed Rice Blend #1
4 cups uncooked rice
4 tablespoons instant chicken bouillon
1 teaspoon salt
2 teaspoons *each* dried tarragon and dried parsley flakes
Dash ground pepper

### Herbed Rice Blend #2
4 cups uncooked rice
5 teaspoons dried grated lemon zest
4 teaspoons dried dill weed
2 teaspoons *each* dried chives and salt

### Herbed Rice Blend #3
4 cups uncooked rice
¼ cup dried green bell pepper flakes
1 teaspoon salt
5 teaspoons dried parsley flakes
1 teaspoon dried basil

## Tangy Mustards
There are black, white, and brown varieties of wild mustard, with such differences as flower size, overall shape, and smoothness of the seed-pods. White mustard is prized as a potherb for salads and as the source of commercially sold mustard seed.

The ground mustard sold in cans is a mixture of black and white seeds (the English ask for "double mustard"), the grinding of which is too complicated for home processing. But it's easy to mix it with other herbs for special sauces and condiments. After trying these basic recipes, you can develop blends according to personal taste.

### Herb Mustard
Combined with an equal amount of mayonnaise and a bit of horse-radish, this mustard is delicious spread on chicken before baking or broiling.

1 cup ground mustard, or to taste
1 cup unbleached or whole wheat flour, or as needed
¼ cup sugar
2 cups distilled white vinegar (or part white wine vinegar)
1 clove garlic, minced
2 tablespoons dried *or* 4 tablespoons chopped fresh herbs such as basil, thyme, parsley, marjoram, or rosemary, or combination of your choice

Blend together the mustard, flour, and sugar. Add the vinegar and stir to a lump-free paste. Add the garlic and dried herbs. Let the mixture stand overnight, then stir again. Add more flour if the mixture is too thin. Transfer to a covered jar. It will keep in the refrigerator for several months.
*Makes about 3 cups.*

### Sweet and Hot Mustard
This mustard perks up green beans or broccoli and is good in dips or on sandwiches or crackers. Mixed with mayonnaise it is delicious for deviled eggs, pasta, or potato salads.

3 tablespoons cornstarch
1 teaspoon salt
½ cup sugar
⅔ cup mint-flavored vinegar
½ cup water
½ cup ground mustard, or to taste
⅛ teaspoon ground turmeric
2 tablespoons butter, melted
1 tablespoon finely minced fresh ginger (or other) mint
1 tablespoon minced fresh basil

Blend the cornstarch, salt, sugar, vinegar, and ¼ cup of the water. In a separate bowl combine the mustard and the remaining ¼ cup water, then blend into the cornstarch mixture. Add the turmeric, butter, mint, and basil; blend thoroughly. Store in an airtight glass jar in the refrigerator. It will keep for several months.
*Makes about 1½ cups.*

## Horseradish

Well known in European and Colonial gardens, horseradish has been used as a condiment by many who use few other herbs. Horseradish sauces will keep for months in the refrigerator, but they taste best if made fresh in small batches. The roots will keep in moist sand all winter. After working with horseradish, it's important not to touch the face or eyes for several hours even after washing your hands; as an extra precaution, you can wear surgeon's latex gloves when handling this pungent herb.

### Creamy Horseradish Sauce

The sauce should be kept cold until right before serving; the contrast in temperature with piping-hot meat accentuates the contrast in flavors.

  1 cup whipping cream
  ½ teaspoon garlic salt *or* ½ teaspoon sea salt and 1 teaspoon paprika
  2 grated horseradish (freshly ground, frozen, or bottled in vinegar)
  1 tablespoon lemon juice (optional)

Whip the cream until very stiff. Add the garlic salt, then mix in the horseradish and lemon juice, if desired. Chill in the refrigerator until serving time.
  *Makes about 2½ cups.*

## Pesto

A famous Italian sauce, pesto is most often made from basil and is delicious served on pasta, rice, baked potatoes, sliced tomatoes, broiled fish or meat, or spaghetti squash. It is also good mixed in deviled eggs, added to vegetable soups, folded into an omelet, or rolled into a loaf of homemade bread. When fresh basil is plentiful in the garden, you can make pesto, then freeze it in meal-sized portions.

Basil is, however, only the beginning. A similar sauce can be made with parsley (or half basil and half parsley) for a different but pleasing flavor. Mint pesto is good with lamb, chicken, rabbit, or squash. Other pestos can be made with oregano or coriander instead of basil, or arugula with ½ cup of basil and the juice of a lemon added to the original ingredients. It's fun to experiment with various herbs for different flavors.

Purists often feel that a food processor or blender affects the flavor of pesto; they prefer grinding the ingredients with a mortar and pestle. You can try both and decide whether convenience is worth the slight loss of flavor intensity.

### Pesto

To store pesto in the refrigerator, add a thin covering of olive oil to keep it from darkening. To freeze pesto, pack it firmly in sterilized jars. Insert the handle of a wooden spoon to eliminate any air bubbles. Cover the pesto with a thin layer of olive oil; if desired, add a teaspoon of herb vinegar to the oil. If the lid is metal, cover the jar top with plastic wrap first. Label, date, and use within 10 months.

  2 cups firmly packed fresh basil leaves, washed and patted dry
  ¼ cup shelled pine nuts, pistachios, or English walnuts
  3 cloves garlic, peeled
  ½ cup freshly grated Parmesan cheese
  ½ cup olive oil

Purée the basil, nuts, and garlic. Blend in the cheese and oil. Serve at once or store in the refrigerator or freezer.
  *Makes about 1 cup.*

# Herb Vinegars

In addition to infusing vinegar with delightful flavors, herbs preserved in vinegar make it possible to save the dill until the cucumbers are ready or preserve other herbs that complement vegetables that ripen at different times. A benefit of using garlic vinegar is the wonderful garlic flavor without odor lingering on the breath.

Vinegars can be made with almost any edible herb; favorites include basil, bay, chervil, chives, dill, fennel, garlic, lemon balm, marjoram, mint, rosemary, sage, savory, tarragon, and thyme. Purple basil imparts an attractive tint to white vinegar.

The following flowers look attractive in vinegar stored in clear glass jars: carnation, chives, clover, lavender, mint, nasturtium, primrose, rose, rosemary, thyme, and violet.

Some good combinations for distilled white vinegar, white wine vinegar, or red wine vinegar include the following.

▮ Basil and chives or burnet
▮ Borage, dill, and shallots
▮ Fennel, bay, and fresh ginger
▮ Fennel, garlic, and parsley
▮ Garlic, cloves, peppercorns, and caraway seed
▮ Lavender flowers and lemon-verbena or rose petals
▮ Mint, honey, and cardamom seed
▮ Nasturtium and garlic
▮ Pinks, rosemary, and rose petals
▮ Rosemary and mint
▮ Rosemary, orange zest, and garlic
▮ Sage, parsley, and chives or shallot
▮ Tarragon, basil, chives, garlic, and lemon thyme or burnet
▮ Tarragon and lemon balm
▮ Tarragon and garlic

With cider vinegar, try dill, nasturtium, and garlic; or hot chile, garlic, and oregano.

The vinegar should be at room temperature. Dried herbs will do, but herbs freshly picked at their prime work best. Wash and dry them well; although water will not affect the flavor, it will cloud the vinegar.

The amount of herb to use is a matter of personal preference. To start use approximately 1 cup of fresh herbs for each quart of vinegar. Remember that some herbs are stronger than others, especially when used in combinations of two or more.

Bruise the herbs with a wooden spoon. If herb seeds are used, bruise them first with a mortar and pestle to release the flavor.

Place the herbs in a clean, dry glass jar, and pour in vinegar to within an inch of the top of the jar.

*Pesto is traditionally made from basil, but other herbs can be used for different effects. When herbs are at their best in midsummer, make and freeze enough pesto for the whole year. You can freeze it in ice-cube trays for convenient single portions.*

Push down and bruise the herbs again, then shake the jar to remove air bubbles. Cover with an acid-proof lid, label the jar, and place on a sunny windowsill. Shake or stir every few days for 2 to 4 weeks. Check that the vinegar still covers the herbs after a few days; add more vinegar if needed.

A quicker method is to bring the vinegar to a boil, add the fresh herbs, and simmer until the vinegar reaches the desired flavor (about 20 minutes).

Taste the herb vinegar to determine when it has reached the desired strength. Should the vinegar become too strong in flavor, add more plain vinegar.

Remove most of the herbs after a month or two or the vinegar may develop an untrue flavor. Strain the vinegar through a fine sieve into dry, sterilized bottles. Add a few sprigs of herbs or flowers for decoration or identification, then cap or cork.

For a special touch, cover the capped bottle with ribbon and sealing wax; the latter is available in stationery stores. Glue a short length of ribbon up the neck, over the top, and down the other side of the bottle. Melt the wax in the top of a double boiler over low heat, dip the capped bottle into the wax until the cap is covered (hold the ribbon so that it doesn't dip into the wax), then let the excess wax drip back into the pan. Take extra care not to let wax drip onto the heating element of the stove, which could cause a fire. The ribbon adds a decorative touch and facilitates lifting the wax to open the bottle. Store the bottled vinegar in a cool, dry place.

The shelf life of vinegars varies, but most will keep up to 18 months. Fruit vinegars sometimes caramelize and become less attractive; these should be used immediately.

### Raspberry Vinegar

This is excellent as a basting sauce with pork chops or chicken. The drippings can be used to make a delicious cream gravy. If necessary, you can substitute frozen raspberries for fresh ones.

> About 1 quart freshly picked clean raspberries
> Distilled white vinegar or white wine vinegar, as needed

Fill a clean 1-quart jar with the raspberries to within 2 inches of the top. Heat the vinegar just until bubbles begin to form around the edge of the pan. Pour it over the raspberries to fill the jar. Cover with a plastic lid or plastic wrap under a metal lid. Let cool. Store in a cool, dark place for 1 to 6 weeks, then strain through a fine sieve into sterilized jars.

*Makes 1 quart.*

## Herb Oils

Ideal for dieters, herb oils are as easy to make as herb vinegars. One tablespoon of robust herb oil contains more flavor than 2 tablespoons of plain oil. You can use herb oils to brown, baste, or marinate meats, to stir-fry vegetables, or in salad dressings. Savory oils are best started with vegetable or olive oil, preferably not strongly flavored. Sweet oils with scented flowers can start with almond oil.

Sweet oils can use clove pinks, lavender, lemon-verbena, or rose petals alone or in any combination. Suggested herbs for savory oils include basil, fennel, garlic, marjoram, mint, rosemary, savory, tarragon, or thyme. Try these delicious combinations for savory oils.

▌Dill weed, garlic, and lemon mint or lemon balm

▌Fennel seed and leaves, mustard seed, and peppercorns

▌Fresh ginger, coriander, and cardamom

*Delicious raspberry vinegar is simple to make and, because of its beauty, it makes a dramatic and unusual gift. Add a label telling what it is and giving some suggestions for use.*

❚ Oregano, garlic, and thyme

❚ Tarragon, chives, and chervil

❚ Tarragon, peppercorns, and thyme

**Caution**    The use of garlic and basil together in oil may encourage the growth of botulism. This combination is best avoided.

A few sprigs of herb, a single clove of garlic, or one chile per cup of oil can change the flavor of the oil appreciably.

For a more robust flavor, fill a 1-quart jar with clean fresh herbs, cover with unheated oil, and seal with a nonmetallic lid. Allow to steep on a sunny windowsill for 2 weeks, stirring daily. When the flavor has reached its desired strength, strain, bottle, and label the oil. If the flavor is still not strong enough, replace the herbs with fresh ones and steep longer.

Another way to make herb oils is to gently heat the oil until it is fragrant (about 5 minutes). Then pour it over the herbs in the jar. Let cool, then cover and store in a dark cupboard for 6 months before using.

## Herb Butters

One of the easiest ways to add herbs to a meal is with herb butters. They can be added to the pan before frying eggs, added to pasta or noodles, melted on broiled meats and fish, and used on breads, baked potatoes, and vegetables. A loaf or two of warm, homemade bread with a choice of three or four different herb butters is a party in itself. The butters can be served in small containers or rolled into balls or logs. Each can be garnished with a leaf or two of the herb for identification as well as decoration.

Fresh herbs work best for butters. The flavor of dried herbs can be enhanced by using a few drops of lemon juice, Worcestershire sauce, or vinegar, added slowly and stirred constantly to prevent curdling.

*The fresh tang of chives combines well with dairy products, such as butters or cheese spreads. Serve chive butter with baked potatoes and garnish the plate with a few stems of chive blossoms.*

For each ¼ pound of butter, use 1 to 2 tablespoons of fresh herbs or 1½ teaspoons of dried herbs or ½ teaspoon of crushed seed. Suitable herbs include basil, chives, parsley, rosemary, tarragon, thyme, or any of the lemon-flavored herbs. Petals of edible flowers can be added for color if desired.

Blend the herbs into the butter by either of two simple methods. Let the butter soften to room temperature, then cream or beat it smooth with a wooden spoon while mixing in the minced seasonings. Or melt the butter in a pan over low heat, then allow to cool. While the butter is still soft, stir in the finely chopped herbs.

Pack the butter into containers. Cover and chill in the refrigerator for at least 3 hours while the flavors blend. Use the butters within a few days. Frozen herb butters will keep for several weeks.

### Chef's Secret Butter

This herb butter can be used when grilling or broiling meats or fish or added to cooked vegetables.

   ½ cup butter, softened
   3 tablespoons minced parsley
   1 tablespoon lemon juice
   ½ teaspoon Worcestershire sauce

Combine all the ingredients, then chill.

   *Makes about ½ cup.*

## Herb Cheeses and Mayonnaise

Cottage cheese or cream cheese mixed with herbs is an easy, low-calorie cracker spread or baked potato topping, or the beginning of a delicious dip. Other cheeses can also be combined with herbs for dips, spreads, and aspics. And herbs can be used to give zest to mayonnaise.

### Herb Cheese Spread

This spread can be made into a dip by adding sour cream, plain yogurt, or mayonnaise as needed for thinning. To make a cheese ball, see the Note below.

   8 ounces cottage cheese *or* 1 package (8 ounces) cream cheese, softened
   2 tablespoons minced fresh herbs *or* 1 to 2 teaspoons dried herbs, such as basil, chives, parsley, arugula, or mint
   Chopped bell pepper or nasturtium flowers and/or leaves, as needed for color

Combine all the ingredients. Refrigerate for several hours or overnight for the flavors to develop.

   *Makes about 1 cup.*

*Note*   Cheese balls make any party table festive and are ideal gifts. Use feta or goat cheese or mild to sharp Cheddar combined with butter, herbs, and spices in about the same amounts as above for cottage cheese or cream cheese. For a festive finishing touch, roll the balls or logs in chopped herbs or nuts. Wrap in foil or plastic wrap and refrigerate for at least a full day for the flavors to blend. Then bring to room temperature to serve.

## Low-Calorie Cottage Cheese Dip
Serve this dip in the center of a tray of crackers or vegetable sticks for a delicious appetizer (see Note).

    1 to 3 tablespoons milk
    1 container (16 ounces) cottage
      cheese
    ½ teaspoon salt
    Dash ground pepper
    3 tablespoons chopped chives
      or 1 teaspoon chopped fresh
      oregano
    ¼ cup grated Parmesan cheese

In a blender container combine the milk, cottage cheese, salt, and pepper. Add the chives and Parmesan, then refrigerate for several hours for the flavors to blend.
    *Makes about 2 cups.*
*Note*   An alternative to the chives and Parmesan is 1 can (6 ounces) tuna and 1 teaspoon *each* fresh dill weed and lemon juice. Or try 1 can (6 ounces) drained minced clams; 1 small onion, chopped; and ¼ teaspoon garlic powder.

## Flowered Cheese Aspic
This aspic makes a memorable hostess gift and can aptly grace the table at weddings or parties.

    2 cups dry white wine or clear
      chicken stock
    1 envelope unflavored gelatin
    8 ounces cream cheese, Cheddar,
      Monterey jack, or Camembert
    Edible flowers and herbs, washed
      and patted dry, for garnish
    Crackers or toasted sliced
      baguette, for accompaniment

In a medium saucepan combine the wine and gelatin, stirring until dissolved and clear. Remove from the

heat and set the pan in ice, stirring gently now and then, until the mixture begins to thicken.

    Place the cheese on a serving plate. Spoon some of the gelatin mixture over the cheese and spread evenly. After about 3 minutes, carefully arrange the flowers and herbs on the top and sides of the cheese. Refrigerate for 15 minutes, then spoon on more gelatin mixture and refrigerate again. Repeat until the flowers are covered. Refrigerate until ready to serve. Serve with crackers or toasted sliced baguette.
    *Makes 1 aspic.*

*Flowered Cheese Aspic makes a striking offering for a special occasion.*

### Cheese-Stuffed Nasturtiums

These attractive cheese balls can be served on nasturtium leaves in a ring around a punch bowl, or served singly as individual salad garnishes.

1 package (8 ounces) cream cheese, softened
2 tablespoons mayonnaise
2 teaspoons finely chopped fresh basil, parsley, or dill weed
*or* 2 tablespoons minced chives, cucumber, or green onion
¼ cup grated carrot
30 nasturtium blossoms and leaves

Combine the cream cheese, mayonnaise, herbs, and carrot (if used). Roll the mixture into about 30 balls, depending on the size of the flowers. Chill until firm, then gently fit the balls into the nasturtium blossoms.
*Makes about 30 pieces.*

### Seasoned Mayonnaise

Stir minced fresh herbs and a little lemon zest into homemade or purchased mayonnaise. Serve as a dip or use as a sandwich spread, salad dressing, or sauce for chilled seafood.

## Herb Honey

If you keep bees and grow herbs, the bees will do their own marvelous blending of flavors. To control the predominant flavors, take off the honey just after certain herbs bloom.

Otherwise, blend herb honey from commercial honey. Herbs enhance the sweetness and add color, fragrance, flavor, and body. Honey, herb or otherwise, will last indefinitely. Should it begin to crystallize, gently heat it to restore its clear liquid state. Avoid overheating or boiling honey. High temperatures will affect the flavor and consistency.

Suitable herbs for adding to honey include anise seed, cardamom seed, stick cinnamon, coriander seed, fennel seed, lavender, lemon balm, lemon-verbena, marjoram, mint, rose, rose geranium, rosemary, sage, thyme, and violet. Use about 1 tablespoon of fresh herb, 1 teaspoon of dried herb, or 1 teaspoon of seed to 1 pint of honey, more or less, depending on taste.

Bruise the seeds, flowers, or chopped leaves and place them in a small saucepan. Pour room-temperature honey into the pan and stir gently over low heat for about 2 minutes. Pour the mixture into sterilized jars and seal. Store at room temperature for about 1 week for the flavors to blend. Then rewarm the honey and strain out the herbs. Reseal or use at once.

## Herb Jellies and Jams

Traditional accompaniments to roast meats, herb jellies and jams are as easy to make as plain fruit ones. You can use commercial apple juice as a base, or you can make your own, as described below.

Pick the herbs after the morning dew has dried. Wash them gently and pat them dry. Almost any culinary herb is suitable; good choices are basil, fennel, mint, rosemary, sage, scented geranium, or thyme.

To make apple juice, cut up tart apples or crab apples; discard only the stem and blossom ends and any bad spots. Add cold water to barely cover and cook over low heat, stirring often, until the apples are soft and tender. If the apples are very sweet, add lemon juice or vinegar to taste.

Strain the juice from the apples through several layers of cheese-cloth in a colander. For clear jelly, do not squeeze the pulp; 4 cups of juice will make about four 8-ounce jars of jelly.

Have the jars clean and sterilized and keep them hot either in a closed dishwasher or on a baking sheet in a 250° F oven.

Follow the recipe below or recipes that come with powdered or liquid pectin from the grocery store. Apples have enough pectin of their own, but the commercial product will make the juice go farther. Use a large pan so that there is plenty of room for a full rolling boil.

## Herb Apple Jelly

Suggested color combinations include dark green for spearmint jelly, light green for thyme jelly, yellow for lemon balm jelly, orange for basil jelly, dark red for opal basil jelly, natural amber for rosemary jelly, and pale pink for rose geranium jelly.

    4 cups apple juice
    1 cup chopped fresh herb leaves
    3 cups sugar
    ½ teaspoon butter or margarine
    Food color (optional)
    Herb leaves or sprigs, for
      decoration

Bring the juice and herb leaves to a full rolling boil and boil hard for 5 minutes (see Note).

Add the sugar and butter; stirring constantly, continue boiling until the mixture reaches 222° F on a candy thermometer or the jelling point of running off the rim of the spoon in drops that merge into a sheet (about 10 minutes).

Remove the jelly from the heat. Skim off the foam. The added butter prevents or greatly decreases the foam, making this step easier. Add the food color, if desired, to the entire batch, or separate the single batch of jelly into 2 or 3 containers of measured amounts so that each will fill 1 or 2 jars completely, then add a few drops of different food color to each.

Into canning jars that have been boiled and kept hot, place 2 or 3 leaves or sprigs of herbs. Pour in

the jelly, leaving ¼ inch headspace for a vacuum and proper seal. Seal with lids that have also been sterilized, then turn the jars upside down for a moment to coat and further sterilize the lid.

Set the jars upright on a thick terry cloth towel; fold part of the towel over the jars to prevent drafts while the jelly sets for 8 hours. The jelly will thicken as it cools.

*Makes about four 8-ounce jars.*

*In this unusual presentation, nasturtium blossoms are filled with cheese balls. Nasturtium blossoms are somewhat peppery; the leaves are more so, with a flavor a little like watercress.*

*Uncooked Rose-Petal Jam has a delightful rose flavor and fragrance as well as vibrant color.*

*Note* To impart a stronger herb flavor to the jelly, instead of bringing the juice and leaves to a full rolling boil, make an infusion of ¼ to 1 cup chopped fresh herbs or 2 to 6 tablespoons dried herbs or crushed seed for every 3 to 4 cups apple juice. The herbs can be bunched, placed in a cheesecloth bag, or left loose. To make the infusion, bring 1 cup of the juice to a full boil in a small pan, pour it over the herbs, and let stand for 20 minutes. Then either strain or remove the bunch of herbs or cheesecloth bag and continue with the recipe.

Different herb jellies can be made with other combinations of herbs and juices. Most of the following will require commercial pectin. Follow the directions that come with the powdered or liquid pectin, and don't interchange among recipes.

▌ Cinnamon with cherry juice
▌ Cloves with tangerine juice
▌ Infusions of basil, chamomile, tarragon, or mint

▮ Lemon balm with grape juice

▮ Lemon thyme with white grape juice

▮ Marjoram with orange juice

▮ Rosemary with orange juice or sherry

▮ Savory with cranberry juice

▮ Sweet woodruff with white wine

▮ Tarragon with grape juice

▮ Thyme with crab apple juice

Here are some suggestions for using herb jellies.

▮ Spoon a dollop of herb jelly in a peach or pear half on each plate beside the meat.

▮ Spread cream cheese on hot biscuits or homemade brown bread, then top with herb jelly.

▮ Use herb jellies in tarts or cookies.

▮ Use herb jelly as a base layer on angel food or pound cake beneath a whipped cream frosting.

▮ Add fresh or dried orange zest to mint jelly for a sauce for Asian foods or to baste chicken.

▮ Use mint jelly with lamb, ham, or pork.

▮ Use lemon balm jelly with fish or poultry.

▮ Use sage jelly with pork, turkey, or chicken.

▮ Use rosemary or thyme jelly with beef.

## Damask Rose Jam

Choose blooms free of pesticides. Damask roses do not have a bitter white end on the petals. If using other rose petals, remove this part. It isn't time consuming; simply take as many petals as can be held between the finger and thumb, pull them from the rose all at once, and cut the white bases from all of them with one clip of the kitchen shears.

5 pounds sugar
1 pound clean damask rose petals
1 quart water
¼ cup lemon juice
1¾ ounces powdered pectin

In a large porcelain pan, layer the sugar and rose petals. Cover and let stand overnight.

Add the water and lemon juice. If desired, chop the mixture a little at a time in a blender, then return it to the pan. Stir in the pectin. Stirring constantly, bring to a full rolling boil and boil for 2 minutes.

Remove from the heat. Continue stirring for 8 to 10 minutes, distributing the petals. Pour into sterilized jars and seal.

*Makes about eight 8-ounce jars.*

## Uncooked Rose-Petal Jam

This jam is quick and easy to prepare and has excellent flavor and fragrance because the roses are uncooked. Make batches of different colors. They will keep for a month in the refrigerator and several months in the freezer. Pick freshly opened roses as soon as the dew is dry in the morning; you can have fresh jam in as little as 15 minutes.

1 cup clean rose petals
1½ cups water
Juice of 1 lemon
2½ cups sugar
1¾ ounces powdered pectin

Place the rose petals, ¾ cup of the water, and lemon juice in a blender; blend until smooth. Gradually add the sugar; continue to blend until dissolved. Let the mixture stand in the blender.

In a small saucepan bring the pectin and the remaining ¾ cup water to a boil. Boil hard for 1 minute, stirring constantly.

With the blender on low speed, add the pectin mixture to the rose mixture. Blend thoroughly. Then pour at once into sterilized jars with lids. Let stand about 6 hours at room temperature, then refrigerate.

*Makes three or four 4-ounce jars.*

*The Holiday Herb Bread Wreath, served with rose-petal butter, is elegantly festive but simple to make because it starts with frozen bread dough.*

## BAKING WITH HERBS

Fresh or dried herbs can enhance the flavor of breads, biscuits, rolls, cakes, cookies, and candy. Herb leaves and flowers can also be made into candied decorations to add a festive note to desserts.

### Baked Goods

Here are several tips and recipes for using herbs in baking.

▮ To any basic bread or biscuit dough, add chives, dill, marjoram, sage, savory, or thyme.

▮ Top breads, rolls, biscuits, and cookies with seeds of caraway, dill, fennel, anise, poppy, or sesame. Brush the dough with egg yolk and sprinkle with seeds before baking.

▮ Add fennel seed to apple or berry pies, cobblers, or tarts. Crushed coriander seed is delicious in hot gingerbread and homemade applesauce. Add the crushed seeds of coriander, anise, dill, sesame, or fennel to any cookie dough before baking. Add toasted sesame seed to a pie crust dough or substitute for pecans in a pecan pie.

## Basic Herbal Quick Bread

6 cups self-rising flour *or* 6 cups all-purpose flour plus 3 tablespoons baking powder and 3 teaspoons salt
  ¼ cup sugar
  3 cups beer, warmed
  1 cup chopped fresh basil, chives, sage, or other herbs

Combine all the ingredients and pour into 2 greased 5- by 9-inch loaf pans. Place in an unheated oven, set the oven to 350° F, and bake 50 minutes.
*Makes 2 loaves.*

## Holiday Herb Bread Wreath

Serve this with herb butter made festive for the holidays by mixing softened butter with pimientos or red rose petals for Christmas dinner, with pastel flowers for Easter.

  1 pound frozen white bread dough, defrosted 15 minutes
  Vegetable oil, for brushing
  Melted butter, as needed
  2 tablespoons grated Parmesan cheese
  2 tablespoons chopped parsley

With a sharp knife carefully cut the dough crosswise into 10 or more slices. Arrange the slices in a circle, sides just touching, on a greased baking sheet. Brush with the oil, and let rise until completely defrosted and doubled in bulk.

Preheat the oven to 400° F. Bake the bread until lightly browned (about 12 minutes). Remove from the oven; brush with melted butter and top with grated cheese. Return to the oven and bake until the cheese is lightly browned (2 to 4 minutes). Sprinkle with the parsley; let bread cool before serving with herb butter.
*Makes about 10 servings.*

## Herbed Quiche Pastry

The dry ingredients for this simple herbed pastry can be prepared in advance and in quantity and stored in an airtight jar. Fill the pastry with the filling of your choice, and continue baking according to the directions in your filling recipe.

  1½ cups flour
  1 tablespoon dried parsley flakes
  2 teaspoons dried dill weed
  1½ teaspoons ground mustard
  ¼ teaspoon salt
  ½ cup butter or margarine, softened
  4 tablespoons cold water, or as needed
  1 egg, beaten

Preheat the oven to 450° F. In a large bowl combine the flour, parsley, dill, mustard, and salt. Add the butter; combine until the mixture resembles cornmeal. Stir in the water a little at a time until the dough pulls away from the sides of the bowl.

Roll out the dough on a lightly floured surface, then use it to line a 9-inch pie pan. Prick the dough with a fork in several places, then brush with the beaten egg. Bake for 10 minutes.
*Makes one 9-inch pastry.*

## Anise Seed Cookies

  1 cup butter, softened
  1½ cups sugar
  2 eggs
  2 teaspoons vanilla extract
  3 cups flour
  2 teaspoons baking powder
  1 teaspoon salt
  1 teaspoon grated lemon zest
  1 tablespoon crushed anise seed (see Note)

In a medium bowl cream the butter and sugar. Add the eggs one at a time and beat after each addition. Mix in the vanilla.

In another medium bowl sift together the flour, baking powder,

*Herb Candy can be made with many herbs for a wide range of flavors. Experiment to find your favorite.*

## Herb Candy

For herb leaves, stems, and flowers, use mint, horehound, wintergreen, or lemon-flavored herbs. (The optional cocoa is good with mint.) For seeds, use fennel, anise, caraway, or coriander.

2 cups boiling water
1 cup herb leaves, stems, and flowers *or* 1½ cups seeds (see Note)
¾ cup firmly packed brown sugar
¾ cup granulated sugar
½ teaspoon butter
1 tablespoon cocoa (optional)

Pour the water over the herbs and steep 20 minutes for a strong infusion. Strain. Add the sugars and butter; cook over medium heat to the hard-crack stage (300° F) on a candy thermometer (a few drops of the mixture dropped into a cup of cold water should form a hard ball).

Pour the mixture into a buttered 8-inch-square pan or 5- by 9-inch loaf pan. Score into pieces before it sets; as soon as it hardens, invert the pan, and tap to remove the candy. Cut or break into pieces. Wrap each piece in plastic wrap and store in an airtight container.

*Makes about 50 pieces.*

*Note* About 1½ teaspoons dried mint leaves or anise seed can be added to horehound to vary the flavor.

## Candied Herb Decorations

Sugar-coated herb leaves, petals, or flowers make exquisite garnishes for fruit salads, cakes, custards, parfaits, or other desserts, and are also good to eat by themselves as candy.

Appropriate candidates for crystallized leaves are borage, sage, mint, catnip, or other sweet foliage. Pick perfect leaves of moderate size.

When crystallizing flowers, select freshly opened blooms, and leave

and salt. Add it gradually to the egg mixture. Add the zest and anise seed and blend well. Chill for several hours or overnight.

Preheat the oven to 350° F. Roll the dough into a thin rope; cut into disks. Arrange on a greased baking sheet and bake for 10 minutes.

*Makes 4 to 5 dozen cookies.*

*Note* One tablespoon fennel seed or cumin seed or 2 tablespoons dill seed or coriander seed can be substituted for anise seed.

enough stem to hold onto while candying. Cut away the bitter white base of rose petals before separating the individual flower petals. (See the recipe for Damask Rose Jam on page 95 for how to do this easily.) For whole flowers, such as violets, borage, geraniums, johnny-jump-ups, or other edible blooms, wash and gently pat them dry with a paper towel.

Assemble bowls of superfine granulated white sugar. Make colored sugars by adding 2 drops of food color to ½ cup of sugar and shaking in a jar until the color is evenly mixed. Colored sugars will deepen, not change, the natural flower color.

Beat an egg white until it is slightly frothy. (Adding the juice of 1 lemon to each egg white will improve the flavor of catnip leaves.) Hold the flower or leaf in one hand and paint egg white over all surfaces with a small, soft camel's hair brush. Use a toothpick to separate the petals if the brush will not do the job.

Hold the flower or leaf over a bowl of sugar to catch the spills. Coat all surfaces with the sugar. Place the coated herb on waxed paper and allow to dry for 2 days in a warm place. The candied herbs can be stored in the refrigerator for 4 to 6 months in an airtight container with waxed paper between the layers.

To candy angelica stems for garnish or for a fruitcake ingredient, harvest the mature stems. Clean them, peel off the outer skin, and cut them into pieces. Soak for 12 hours in a solution of cold water and 1 tablespoon *each* salt and distilled white vinegar. Drain the stems, cover with fresh water, and boil until almost transparent and quite green.

Then make a syrup of 2 cups of sugar and 1 cup of water. Add a few drops of green food color if desired. Add the angelica stems and simmer until translucent and glazed. Remove with a slotted spoon to a tray covered with waxed paper. Dry and store as for flowers. Or place in a sterilized jar, cover with syrup to exclude air, and seal.

*Candied flowers and leaves make beautiful garnishes. Shown here are borage flowers (the blue stars), sage flowers, and mint leaves.*

*A calendula-petal glaze graces a ham. You can add the petals to any clear ham glaze (see below).*

## MAIN DISHES

Here are a few main dish ideas and recipes in which herbs add intriguing flavors.

▌ Add chives, borage, oregano, sage, or savory to rice casseroles.

▌ After sautéeing liver, sauté fresh sage leaves and grapefruit or orange sections in the same pan. Use to garnish the liver.

▌ Add ½ to 1 cup calendula petals to a brown sugar ham glaze.

▌ Marinate pork chops in 2 tablespoons olive oil, 2 crushed cloves garlic, salt and pepper to taste, and 6 crushed juniper berries (enough marinade for 4 thick pork chops). Another good marinade combination is lemongrass, olive oil, onion, garlic, pepper, and Chinese five-spice powder (see page 81).

▌ Make a fish sauce by heating ¼ cup *each* butter, lemon juice, and water. Stir in 1 teaspoon chicken bouillon and salt, pepper, dill weed or thyme, and paprika to taste. Pour over cooked fish.

▌ For a delicious crust for baked fish, brush uncooked fish with olive oil. Sprinkle with finely chopped fresh herbs, such as parsley, chives, dill weed, fennel, and lemon thyme; press them into the oil. Drizzle with a bit more oil; sprinkle with dried bread crumbs and press into the oil. Bake at 350° F until the fish flakes at the touch of a fork.

▌ Chop fresh herbs or crumble dry ones into the flour, cornmeal, or batter for frying fish.

### Delicious Fish

2 cups orange or lemon juice
2 tablespoons pickling spices
Salt, to taste (optional)
Enough fish fillets for 4 servings
1 tablespoon cornstarch

In a heavy skillet combine the juice, pickling spices, and salt (if used); simmer over low heat. Add the fish fillets; cover and simmer until the fish flakes at the touch of a fork (about 10 minutes). Remove the fish to a serving platter and remove the pickling spices with a slotted spoon. Add the cornstarch to the skillet and heat until the sauce has thickened. Serve over or with the fish.

*Makes 4 servings.*

### Broiled Fish With Herb Butter

To make herb butter, soften butter and blend in minced onion, dill weed, thyme, savory, basil, or any of the lemon-flavored herbs.

Enough fish fillets for 4 servings
Herb butter, as needed
Grated Parmesan cheese, for sprinkling
Paprika, for sprinkling

Place the fish fillets on a greased baking sheet and brush both sides with the herb butter. Bake at 350° F until almost done, then sprinkle with the cheese and paprika and broil until the cheese is melted. Serve hot.

*Makes 4 servings.*

# VEGETABLE DISHES

Cooked vegetables almost always benefit from seasoning with herbs. Here are a few suggestions.

### Stinging-nettles

Cooked nettles are stingless and delicious. Fresh nettles, however, cause a painful sting, so wear gloves when handling them.

4 slices bacon
½ teaspoon salt
3 tablespoons sugar
3 quarts stinging-nettles, well washed (see Note)
Water, as needed
3 tablespoons butter or margarine
Cider vinegar, for sprinkling
Salt and pepper, to taste

In a large skillet fry the bacon until crisp; then crumble and set aside. Add the salt, sugar, and nettles to the skillet with just enough water to boil the greens without burning. Cook until tender. Drain, then add the butter, a few sprinkles of cider vinegar, and the salt and pepper to taste. Add the reserved crumbled bacon; toss and serve.

*Makes 4 servings.*

*Note* Mustard greens and young dandelion greens can be used instead of stinging-nettles, in which case omit the sugar.

*Stinging-nettles give a nasty burn when fresh, but lose their "bite" as soon as they wilt. Wear gloves and long sleeves to gather nettles, then spread them in the sun for an hour to wilt. Then they can be handled like any greens.*

### Stir-Fried Vegetable Strips

Although any summer squash can be used in this recipe, the flesh of the chayote is firmer and crisper than that of summer squash, so it holds its texture better.

3 carrots, peeled
2 tablespoons butter
1½ pounds summer squash or chayote, peeled only if skin is tough, and cut into thin strips
2 cloves garlic, peeled and minced
2 tablespoons chopped fresh oregano
Salt and pepper, to taste

Cook the carrots briefly in boiling water, then drain and cut into thin strips.

In a large skillet over medium heat, melt the butter. Add the carrot strips, squash, garlic, and oregano; cook until tender (10 to 15 minutes), stirring frequently. Add the salt and pepper to taste; serve hot.
*Makes 6 to 8 servings.*

### Dandelion Greens With Cheese Sauce

Collect young dandelion greens early in spring before the plants bloom and dress with this delicious Cheddar cheese sauce.

2 teaspoons salt
3 quarts dandelion greens, well washed
Water, as needed
¼ cup butter or margarine
¼ cup flour
¼ teaspoon ground pepper
½ teaspoon ground mustard
2 cups milk
2 cups grated medium-sharp Cheddar cheese
1 can (4 ounces) mushrooms, drained

In a large skillet combine 1 teaspoon of the salt, the greens, and just enough water to boil the greens without burning. Cook until tender. Drain and set aside.

In a small saucepan over low heat, melt the butter. Add the flour, the remaining 1 teaspoon salt, the pepper, and mustard; stir until smooth. Add the milk gradually, stirring constantly. Bring almost to a boil; reduce the heat and simmer until thickened (about 1 minute). Add the cheese and stir until melted. Add the mushrooms and reserved cooked greens. Stir and cook until heated through. Serve at once.
*Makes 6 servings.*

### Gertrude's French Sorrel Soup

2 shallots, peeled and chopped
4 tablespoons butter
2 handfuls sorrel leaves (8 to 10 large leaves), washed and patted dry
2 cups chicken stock
3 tablespoons flour
2 tablespoons chopped fresh lovage or celery leaves
Salt and pepper, to taste
4 tablespoons chopped fresh chervil
2 egg yolks, slightly beaten
1 cup whipping cream
Croutons, for garnish (optional)
Sour cream and chives, for garnish (optional)

In a large saucepan brown the shallots in the butter.

Remove the midribs from the sorrel leaves by folding the leaves along the rib, then tearing down the center starting at the top of the leaf. Chop the leaves, then add to the pan. Sauté, stirring constantly, until the leaves soften almost to a purée.

Add the stock, flour, lovage, salt, pepper, and chervil; bring to a boil. Add some of the liquid to the beaten egg yolks, stirring constantly to prevent curdling. Then return this mixture to the pan and continue to stir carefully to prevent lumps from forming.

Add the cream; cook over low heat only until thickened. Serve hot with croutons, if desired, or serve cold topped with a spoonful of sour cream and chives, if desired.

*Makes 4 servings.*

## HERBAL TEAS AND DRINKS

Herbal teas can be made by steeping dried or fresh herbs in just-boiled water until the liquid reaches the desired strength. Stronger infusions are steeped for 20 minutes or so. The recommended proportion per cup of water is 1 to 2 teaspoons of crushed dried leaves or 2 to 3 teaspoons of chopped fresh or thawed frozen ones.

You can use a tea ball or a refillable tea bag (available in natural foods stores), or pour the water directly over the herbs and strain them out when pouring the tea. A nonmetallic teapot gives the truest flavor and keeps the tea hot the longest.

Decoctions are made with the seeds or tough plant parts, such as the roots, which should be ground or bruised with a mortar and pestle. They are simmered in boiling water for 15 to 20 minutes. A heaping teaspoon of seeds or ground roots is used for each cup of water.

Sun tea is made by placing loose herbs and/or regular or herbal tea bags in a jar of water (which should be clear glass to absorb the most rays) and setting the jar in the sun for several hours to all day.

Any edible herb or herb part can be used to make tea. Popular herbs include chamomile, lemongrass, and mint. Therapeutic but bland-tasting herbs or those that make a bitter brew can be blended with others to improve the flavor of the tea. Herb teas can be sweetened as regular tea is sweetened, but some may not need sweeteners at all. Lemon can be added, if desired. Any tea that is left over can be frozen as ice cubes for flavoring other drinks.

Here are some good blends for herbal teas.

▮ Mint and lemon balm
▮ Borage and any lemon-flavored herb
▮ Lemongrass and rose geranium
▮ Rose petals, rose hips, and raspberry leaves
▮ Rose hips and bay
▮ Pennyroyal, peppermint, and fresh ginger

*Gertrude's French Sorrel Soup, a variation on a classic French dish, tempers the sour bite of the sorrel with a creamy base.*

## Lemon Balm Tea Mix

Use 2 teaspoons of this mix per cup of boiling water. The tea can be sweetened with honey.

 1 cup crushed dried lemon balm leaves, stems removed
 ½ cup dried rosebuds or rose petals
 ½ cup dried orange blossoms

Combine all the ingredients and store in an airtight container.
*Makes 2 cups mix.*

## Lemon Balm Cooler

This lemon mixture can be combined with ginger ale or orange or other fruit juice, using equal parts of each, or it can be served with light rum.

 1 cup packed fresh lemon balm leaves
 3 sprigs fresh lemon-verbena or lemongrass (optional)
 4 cups boiling water

Steep the lemon balm and verbena (if used) in the water for 20 minutes. (If using lemongrass, simmer the mixture for 5 to 10 minutes.) Let cool and strain.
*Makes 4 cups mix.*

## Pineapple-Rosemary Cooler

 1 teaspoon chopped fresh rosemary leaves
 ½ cup chopped fresh mint leaves
 1 large can (46 oz) pineapple juice
 ¼ teaspoon salt
 2 cups water
 ½ cup sugar
 ¾ cup lemon juice
 1 can (6 oz) frozen limeade, defrosted

Simmer the rosemary and mint in 1 cup of the pineapple juice. Strain, then to the liquid add the salt, water, sugar, lemon juice, limeade, and remaining pineapple juice. Chill before serving.
*Makes about twenty-four 4-ounce servings.*

*On a hot afternoon, set out Citrus Mint Bubblies in the shade of a tree. Kids love them.*

## Citrus Mint Bubbly

 2 cups fairly strong mint tea
 1½ cups lemonade
 2 cups orange juice
 2 cups crushed ice, plus more for serving
 2 cans (12 oz each) ginger ale
 10 slices orange, for garnish
 10 sprigs mint, for garnish

Combine the tea, lemonade, orange juice, the 2 cups crushed ice, and ginger ale. Pour into glasses over additional ice. Garnish each glass with an orange slice and a mint sprig. Serve at once.
*Makes ten 8-ounce servings.*

## Ginger Tea

2 tablespoons grated fresh ginger
Half a lemon
4 cups water
Honey, to taste
1 stick cinnamon *or* 6 cardamom seeds *or* 6 whole cloves (optional)

Add the ginger and lemon to the water. Bring to a boil, then simmer, uncovered, 15 to 20 minutes. Strain into cups and add honey to taste. The cinnamon, cardamom, and cloves can be used to add variety.

*Makes 4 cups.*

## Mulled Cider

4 gallons apple cider or apple juice
3 oranges studded with whole cloves
Cinnamon stick (optional)

Heat but do not boil the cider. Transfer to a punch bowl. To serve, float the oranges in the bowl. Add a stick of cinnamon if desired.

*Makes sixty-four 8-ounce servings.*
*Note* An alternate method is less decorative but more flavorful and quicker to fix. Make a cheesecloth packet of 4 teaspoons *each* whole cloves and whole allspice, 2 tablespoons slivered dried orange zest, and 2 cardamom seeds. Float in the warmed cider to flavor it, but remove before serving.

## Modern Switchel

Traditionally, switchel is made of molasses and rum, flavored with ginger and vinegar. This updated nonalcoholic version, sweetened with honey, is a low-calorie drink that gives quick energy. It is high in potassium and can also act as a diuretic.

2 cups boiling water
1 to 2 tablespoons honey
2 tablespoons herb vinegar

Combine all the ingredients. Serve hot or iced.

*Makes 2 cups.*

## Breakfast Fruit Shake

This makes a delicious instant breakfast. Any fruits can be substituted. The apple juice provides natural sweetening, the orange juice gives a pleasant tartness, and the mint sets it all off with a zesty flavor.

1 cup apple juice
½ cup orange juice
1 banana, peeled, halved, and frozen
½ cup strawberries, frozen
3 leaves mint or lemon balm
Water, if needed

In a blender container combine the juices, fruits, and mint. Blend until smooth, adding water if the mixture is too thick to swirl.

*Makes 2 servings.*

*Mint Julep is a Southern tradition. If you can't go to the Derby, sip it slowly over quiet conversation. The recipe is on the next page.*

*Dandelion wine was more popular in a time when people had the leisure to gather gallons of petals. If you make it, be sure the dandelions have not been treated with herbicides.*

### Mint Julep

The imbibing of juleps has always been a ceremony. They are meant to be sipped for an entire afternoon, not downed quickly as a thirst quencher. To make a julep to be drunk quickly, half or more of the whiskey can be replaced with club soda.

    4 sprigs mint, about 4 inches each
    4 teaspoons confectioners' sugar
    2 ounces rye whiskey
    Crushed ice, as needed

Place 3 mint sprigs and 3 teaspoons of the confectioners' sugar in the bottom of a tall glass. With a pestle or the handle of a wooden spoon, bruise the mint until syrupy. Add 1 ounce of the whiskey and enough crushed ice to fill the glass halfway. Stir well. Add the remaining 1 ounce whiskey, additional crushed ice, and the remaining teaspoon confectioners' sugar. Stir, then fill the glass with more crushed ice. Stir again, then let stand until the glass is frosted (10 to 15 minutes). Garnish with the remaining mint.
    *Makes 1 julep.*

### Dandelion Wine

    2 gallons dandelion blossoms,
       stems and green parts
       removed
    16 cups sugar
    2 gallons boiling water
    3 lemons, sliced
    3 oranges, sliced
    1 box (16 oz) golden raisins
    1 package active dry yeast

Rinse the blossoms in cool water, then place in a large crock. Add the sugar, then the water. Stir and let cool.

Add the lemons, oranges, raisins, and yeast. Stir well, then cover with cheesecloth. Let stand for 48 hours. Strain, then let the liquid stand for 5 days covered with cheesecloth. Strain again and let ferment in a warm spot until all bubbling stops. Decant into bottles and store in a cool, dry place for 6 months.
    *Makes about 3 gallons.*

## GRILLING WITH HERBS

Here are a few suggestions for using herbs when grilling meat, vegetables, even fruits.

▮ When grilling steak gather a few sprigs of parsley, sage, rosemary, and thyme and make a basting brush by tying them together in a bundle or to a wood handle. Dip this in butter or sauce and spread it on the meat as it cooks.

▮ Add herb prunings to the grill just as the chicken begins to brown.

▮ Marinate fish for an hour or more in a mixture of olive oil, lemon juice, minced garlic, and your choice of bay leaves, dill weed, parsley, or fennel. Grill the fish only until it begins to flake at the touch of a fork, brushing frequently with the marinade.

▮ Slice potatoes and onions—more than needed, for leftovers—onto a sheet of aluminum foil; fold into a packet with parsley or thyme and butter or any herb butter. Grill until tender (20 to 30 minutes).

▮ Marinate eggplant and bell pepper strips in herb vinegar, or sprinkle the strips with tarragon, basil, or oregano. Grill them in aluminum foil packets until tender (10 to 15 minutes).

▮ Pull back the husks of corn on the cob, remove the silk, spread each ear with butter, sprinkle with chopped fresh marjoram or mint, and replace the husks. Grill for 10 to 15 minutes, turning frequently.

▮ Cook peeled sweet potatoes in salted water until barely tender. Then slice lengthwise, place around the cooler edges of a grill, and brush with a mixture of butter, lemon juice, garlic, thyme, and rosemary. Grill 10 to 15 minutes.

▮ Cut apples, pineapples, or papayas into rings and thread onto skewers alternating with fig halves. Brush with butter and chopped fresh mint. Cook on a lightly greased grill for 4 to 6 minutes, turning frequently.

*Vegetables grilled with herbs are delicious fresh off the fire—and the leftovers are terrific in casseroles and other dishes.*

# HERBS IN THE CUPBOARD AND CLOSET

*Lavender wands are an easy way to bring herbal scent into the closet or bureau. If they are hanging in the open, as in a closet, they can be decorated with ribbons and bows. See page 120 for directions on making them.*

The fresh scent imparted by herbs was historically more essential than enjoyable. In this day of daily baths, automatic washing machines, and deodorant soap, it is difficult to imagine pioneer life, when a farm animal might have been kept in the family cabin for winter warmth. Yet interest in herbs for fragrance transcends time and culture. Today every garden, field, and roadside offers treasures for potpourri and other fragrances. And like the growers and gatherers down through the ages, we use herbs today for fragrance in the closet and cupboard.

Fragrances are frequent in the gardens of our minds. The fragrance of white roses may bring back the magic of the night of the senior prom, or the heavy scent of stephanotis the wonder of a wedding day. Scents also take us back on everyday trips—to last summer's garden in the cold of winter, to sunshine on a dreary day, to the blossoming of roses when we are confined to the office, to a spring meadow from our childhood. Rudyard Kipling wrote, "Scents are surer than sound or sight to make your heart strings crack."

*Opposite: Dry Potpourri is easy to make. The materials can be accumulated over a long period, then quickly assembled.*

# POTPOURRIS

The housewife of old prepared her fragrances with loving care. It was both a duty and a delight to finish cleaning the parlor and then open the potpourri jar, stir the contents, and let the fragrance fill the room. Although fragrant commercial aerosol sprays are currently available, potpourri has recently regained its former popularity.

The art of making potpourri is almost as old as the cultivation of flowers. The ancient Greeks and Egyptians placed potpourri in the tombs of their dead to assuage their grief; the scent wafted out when the tombs were opened in the early twentieth century, 5,000 years later.

Around the sixteenth century the Europeans and English began making potpourri for household uses. The practice came to the colonies with the first cherished roses and lavender.

The first potpourris were moist, actually pickled, flowers and leaves; the name came from the French words for "rotten pot." The herbs were salted and mixed with spices, oils, a fixative, and a bit of brandy or good perfume and were stored in dark-glass jars. The fragrance of such a mixture is very long-lasting. Instructions for making moist potpourri are given on page 116.

Today, most people make dry potpourri for the ease of preparation. Material can be gathered over several weeks or an entire growing season. The needed additions can be purchased, and a large amount of mix can be prepared in as little as half an hour.

You can grow herbs for potpourri or gather them in the wild. Or you can purchase all needed potpourri supplies from craft shops or herb growers. Many plant catalogs also offer dried flowers, leaves, fixatives, and essential oils. Having at least one fixative on hand can be motivating when the dried herbs accumulate.

Examining commercial mixes can provide ideas for improving the visual appeal of homemade potpourri. Commercial potpourri often contains bits of bark, tiny pine or hemlock cones, berries, cloves and other whole spices, rosebuds, globe amaranth, pieces of statice or baby's breath, pearly everlasting, lemongrass, or citrus zest.

Although some commercial mixes are largely wood chips treated with artificial color and fragrance and very few if any actual herbs, some wood is desirable in potpourri. Cedar, sandalwood, and the twigs of lavender, rosemary, southernwood, and thyme all have scent. In addition, they absorb and then slowly release the scents of essential oils or of the herbs used with them.

Flowers for potpourris should be gathered as they open; leaves can be gathered whenever the plants need pruning. Both can dry gradually on paper towels spread in a warm place, such as the top of the refrigerator, so that by autumn there will be a good supply of fragrant material.

## Dry Potpourri

Herbs for potpourri are listed on pages 112 and 113 according to fragrance, color, and texture. You can use these suggestions to create potpourris based on varying themes, such as a soothing mix or a spice blend. A soothing potpourri might include rose petals, calendula flowers, and lemon-verbena leaves. Spice potpourri could include rose petals, lavender flowers, anise seed, cloves, nutmeg, cinnamon, crushed benzoin for a fixative, and oil of jasmine, rose geranium, or rosemary. There are as many recipes for potpourri as there are people who make it. See page 114

# HERBS FOR POTPOURRI

## Herbs for Fragrance

| Common Name | Botanical Name | Part Used |
|---|---|---|
| Acacia | *Acacia* species | Flowers |
| Ambrosia | *Chenopodium botrys* | Leaves |
| Anise-hyssop | *Agastache foeniculum* | Leaves, flowers |
| Artemisia | *Artemisia* species | Leaves, flowers |
| Balsam, garden | *Impatiens balsamina* | Flowers |
| Basil | *Ocimum* species | Leaves, flowers |
| Bay | *Laurus nobilis* | Leaves |
| Bergamot | *Monarda* species | Leaves, flowers |
| Broom | *Cytisus* species | Flowers |
| Cardamom | *Elettaria cardamomum* | Leaves, root |
| Carnation | *Dianthus* species | Flowers |
| Chamomile | *Chamaemelum nobile* | Leaves, flowers |
| Chamomile, German | *Matricaria recutita* | Leaves, flowers |
| Clary sage | *Salvia sclarea* | Leaves, flowers |
| Costmary | *Tanacetum balsamita* | Leaves, flowers |
| Eucalyptus | *Eucalyptus* species | Leaves |
| Fennel | *Foeniculum vulgare* | Leaves, flowers |
| Feverfew | *Tanacetum parthenium* | Leaves, flowers |
| Freesia | *Freesia* species and hybrids | Flowers |
| Gardenia | *Gardenia augusta* | Flowers |
| Geranium, scented | *Pelargonium* species | Leaves, flowers |
| Honeysuckle | *Lonicera* species | Flowers |
| Hyacinth | *Hyacinthus orientalis* | Flowers |
| Jasmine | *Jasminum* and *Trachelospermum* species | Flowers |
| Lavender | *Lavandula angustifolia* | Leaves, flowers |
| Lemon balm | *Melissa officinalis* | Leaves, flowers |
| Lemongrass | *Cymbopogon citratus* | Leaves |
| Lemon-verbena | *Aloysia triphylla* | Leaves |

| Common Name | Botanical Name | Part Used |
|---|---|---|
| Lilac | *Syringa vulgaris* | Flowers |
| Lily-of-the-valley | *Convallaria majalis* | Flowers |
| Linden | *Tilia* species | Flowers |
| Marjoram | *Origanum majorana* | Leaves, flowers |
| Mignonette | *Reseda odorata* | Flowers |
| Mint | *Mentha* species | Leaves, flowers |
| Mock orange | *Philadelphus* species | Flowers |
| Narcissus | *Narcissus* species | Flowers |
| Nicotiana | *Nicotiana alata* | Flowers |
| Orange | *Citrus* species | Flowers |
| Oregano | *Origanum* species | Leaves, flowers |
| Orrisroot | *Iris germanica* var. *florentina* | Root |
| Patchouli | *Pogostemon cablin* | Leaves |
| Peony | *Paeonia* hybrids | Flowers |
| Pinks, clove | *Dianthus caryophyllus* | Flowers |
| Rose | *Rosa* species | Petals |
| Rosemary | *Rosmarinus officinalis* | Leaves, flowers |
| Sage | *Salvia* species | Leaves, flowers |
| Sage, Cleveland | *Salvia clevelandii* | Leaves, flowers |
| Santolina | *Santolina chamaecyparissus* | Leaves, flowers |
| Stock | *Matthiola incana* 'Annua' | Flowers |
| Sweet flag | *Acorus calamus* | Leaves |
| Sweet rocket | *Hesperis matronalis* | Flowers |
| Sweet woodruff | *Asperula odorata* | Leaves, flowers |
| Tansy | *Tanacetum vulgare* | Leaves, flowers |
| Tarragon | *Artemisia dracunculus* | Leaves, flowers |
| Thyme, lemon | *Thymus × citriodorus* | Leaves, flowers |
| Violet, purple | *Viola odorata* | Flowers |
| Yarrow | *Achillea* species and hybrids | Leaves, flowers |

## Herbs for Color

### White

| Common Name | Botanical Name |
|---|---|
| Baby's breath | *Gypsophila* species |
| Bergamot | *Monarda didyma* 'Alba' |
| Feverfew | *Tanacetum parthenium* |
| Mint | *Mentha* species |
| Statice | *Limonium* species |
| Strawflower | *Helichrysum bracteatum monstrosum* |
| Yarrow | *Achillea millefolium* 'White Beauty' |

### Blue

| Common Name | Botanical Name |
|---|---|
| Borage | *Borago officinalis* |
| Chicory | *Cichorium intybus* |
| Cornflower | *Centaurea cyanus* |
| Delphinium | *Delphinium* species |
| Forget-me-not | *Myosotis* species |
| Hyssop | *Hyssopus officinalis* |
| Larkspur | *Delphinium* species |
| Mint | *Mentha* species |
| Salvia | *Salvia* species |

### Pink to Lavender

| Common Name | Botanical Name |
|---|---|
| Allium | *Allium* species |
| Baby's breath | *Gypsophila* species |
| Bergamot | *Monarda didyma* 'Croftway Pink' |
| Geranium | *Pelargonium* species |
| Globe amaranth | *Gomphrena globosa* |
| Heath | *Erica carnea* |
| Heather | *Calluna vulgaris* |
| Lavender | *Lavandula angustifolia* |
| Pinks, clove | *Dianthus caryophyllus* |
| Rose | *Rosa* species |
| Strawflower | *Helichrysum bracteatum monstrosum* |
| Yarrow | *Alchillea millefolium* 'Purpurea' |

### Red to Purple

| Common Name | Botanical Name |
|---|---|
| Bergamot | *Mondarda didyma* 'Burgundy' |
| Globe amaranth | *Gomphrena globosa* |
| Poppy | *Papaver* species |
| Rose | *Rosa* species |
| Salvia | *Salvia* species |
| Tulip | *Tulipa* species |
| Zinnia | *Zinnia elegans* |

### Yellow to Orange

| Common Name | Botanical Name |
|---|---|
| Calendula | *Calendula officinalis* |
| Fennel | *Foeniculum vulgare* |
| Goldenrod | *Solidago* species |
| Marigold | *Tagetes* species |
| Nasturtium | *Tropaeolum* species |
| Pansy | *Viola cornuta* |
| Santolina | *Santolina chamaecyparissus* |
| Strawflower | *Helichrysum bracteatum monstrosum* |
| Tansy | *Tanacetum vulgare* |
| Yarrow | *Achillea millefolium* |

## Herbs for Texture*

| Common Name | Botanical Name | Part Used |
|---|---|---|
| Artemisia | *Artemisia* species | Flowers |
| Baby's breath | *Gypsophila* species | Flowers |
| Grasses | | Blades and seed heads |
| Hemlock | *Tsuga canadensis* | Cones |
| Myrtle, sweet | *Myrtus communis* | Leaves |
| Palm | | Fronds |
| Pine | *Pinus* species | Needles and cones |
| Rose | *Rosa* species | Buds and petals |
| Statice | *Limonium* species | Flowers |

*Pods of various species can also be used for texture.

# DRY POTPOURRI MIXES

Here are some potpourri mixes for various uses. If not indicated otherwise, the ingredients in each mix should be combined according to the Basic Recipe.

## Basic Recipe

A few drops essential oil
1 to 3 tablespoons fixative
4 cups dried flowers and leaves
Up to 3 tablespoons spices

In a covered container, blend the essential oil with the fixative. Let stand for 2 days, to give the oil a chance to be absorbed.

Place the dried flowers and leaves in a large bowl. Add the fixative-oil mixture, then add the spices, a little at a time, until the combination of fragrances is just right. Blend and store for 4 to 6 weeks in a dark, closed container or large plastic bag to cure, stirring or shaking occasionally.

*Makes about 4 cups.*

## Special-Occasion Potpourri

Save the flowers from special occasions—roses from prom corsages, lilacs from the bouquet at a graduation party, the most fragrant flowers from your wedding bouquet, the flowers from anniversaries. Dry the petals of each, then store them in an attractive covered container. Add fixative when the first few cups accumulate, then revive the mixture with drops of essential oil as needed.

## Woodsy Mix

4 cups dried leaves of bayberry, chamomile, clary sage, eucalyptus, lady's-bedstraw, marjoram, rosemary, santolina, thyme, wormwood, yarrow, or pine needles
1 cup sandalwood or cedar shavings or chips
1 to 3 tablespoons oakmoss or vetiver
A few drops oil of any of the above dried plants

## Mix for Men

4 cups dried lemon balm, thyme, rosemary, santolina, or yarrow
Up to 3 tablespoons ground spices, such as nutmeg, cinnamon, or allspice
2 tablespoons orrisroot

## Christmas Mix

1 cup *each* dried red rose petals, balsam tips, hemlock cones, red and white strawflowers or white statice, and bay leaves
Up to 1 cup whole cloves, broken cinnamon pieces, and/or whole allspice
1 to 3 tablespoons orrisroot or oakmoss
A few drops oil of balsam or pine

## Citrus Mix

4 cups dried leaves of bergamot, lemon balm, lemon basil, lemongrass, lemon thyme, lemon-verbena, or marigold flowers
1 cup *each* slivered citrus zest, cedar shavings, and whole cloves
1 to 3 tablespoons sweet flag or angelica root pieces
A few drops oil of sweet orange, lemon, or citronella

## Flower Garden in the Moonlight Mix

4 cups dried petals of rose, carnation, cornflower, delphinium, gardenia, hyacinth, jasmine, lavender, lilac, lily-of-the-valley, orange blossom, peony, scented geranium, sweet pea, or violet, for scent
4 cups dried statice or everlasting, for color
Up to 1 cup juniper berries, sweet cicely seeds, slivered citrus zest, or coriander seed
1 to 3 tablespoons orrisroot, oakmoss, or other fixative
A few drops oil of any flower (optional)

## Spicy Mix for the Kitchen

4 cups dried leaves of anise, basil, bay, caraway, eucalyptus, hyssop, lemon balm, lemon-verbena, mint, pennyroyal, sage, scented geranium, or thyme
Up to 1 cup broken cinnamon pieces or vanilla bean pieces, whole cloves, or whole nutmeg
2 tablespoons vetiver or other fixative
A few drops oil of basil or scented geranium

*A potpourri garden*

for more ideas on making theme potpourris. You can use the recipes as is, or change them to fit the materials you have on hand.

Rose petals and rosebuds often make up the bulk of potpourri; preferred roses include damask, cabbage, Kansanlik, gallica, and the modern 'Dainty Bess'. When making large quantities of potpourri, the petals of all roses can be used.

Citrus zest is another good addition to potpourri. You can save and dry zest (the colored portion of the rind) throughout the year. The zest is best removed from the fruit in thin strips with a vegetable peeler or sharp paring knife. The pith (the white portion of the rind) should not be used in potpourri.

The supermarket or natural foods store is a convenient source of seeds of allspice, anise, and coriander, cinnamon by the stick, and whole nutmeg, cloves, and vanilla beans. The nutmeg can be grated by hand; the cloves and vanilla beans can be ground in a blender or with a mortar and pestle just before using.

Dried roots are available from herb-craft suppliers, or you can dig and dry your own. Likely candidates include angelica, cowslip, elecampane, sweet flag (*Acorus calamus*), and valerian. Pet stores are a good source of wood chips that absorb other scents, such as cedar, sandalwood, and cassia.

All spices, zests, roots, and wood chips have a strong scent and should be used sparingly, about 1 tablespoon to 4 cups of dried herbs.

**Fixatives**  Available through herb-craft catalogs, fixatives absorb and hold the essential oils of other herbs and make all the fragrances last longer. They also add a bit of their own scent. The recommended proportion is 1 tablespoon of fixative per cup of dried herbs.

Orrisroot is the most popular fixative, although it can cause allergies in some people. Citrus zest is somewhat of a fixative. So is oakmoss, the root of sweet flag, violet root, frankincense, and myrrh. Some fixatives, such as benzoin, storax, and ambergris, can be purchased from a drugstore.

## GROWING YOUR OWN FIXATIVES

Here are five fixatives you can grow yourself.

■ Clary sage (*Salvia sclarea*) is a tall, lanky, easy-to-grow biennial with spires of white or blue flowers in purple bracts the second summer. Seed can also be sown in late winter and the plant grown as an annual. It self-sows readily. Clary sage is used to make muscatel oil, which is used for a musky fragrance in perfume. The leaves and stems have a tangy lemon fragrance. The leaves are used as a fixative with citrus or floral blends, jasmine, rose geranium, or lavender.

■ Clevelandii sage (*Salvia clevelandii*) is a tender perennial that grows into a woody, semievergreen shrub up to 3 feet tall and 2 feet wide if fed regularly. Northern gardeners will do best to buy new plants each spring or grow plants in containers and overwinter them indoors.

■ Patchouli (*Pogostemon cablin* or *P. patchouli*) is a tender perennial that prefers humusy soil and ample warmth. It will grow 4 feet tall and wide in southern gardens. If grown in a container, it needs a large one. The leaves and oil have a heavy, exotic yet earthy aroma that is good with lavender, rose, rose geranium, sandalwood, cloves, cinnamon, and exotic or musk blends. Patchouli is a good insect repellent.

■ Sweet flag (*Acorus calamus*) is a perennial bog plant; it does well in deep, rich, wet, humusy soil in full sun or part shade. The rhizome has a mellow, violet scent and is good with rose, vanilla, and fruity scents and blends.

■ Orrisroot, or Florentine iris (*Iris germanica* var. *florentina*), is a perennial iris with lovely white flowers. It needs fertile soil with plenty of bonemeal and water. The plant must be 3 years old before the rhizome is large enough to harvest. The tuber eyes can be replanted to replenish the stock. The dried rhizome has little scent at first but when stored for about 2 years develops a mild violet fragrance that is good with lavender, cloves, vanilla, and woodsy or exotic mixes.

Fixatives are available powdered or in pieces. Both forms work well, but powder can cloud a glass container or seep through the fabric of a sachet. See page 115 for fixatives you can grow in the garden.

**Essential oils**  These substances are highly concentrated extracts from plant parts—some say the vital force of the plant. They are available from herb-craft suppliers and often gift shops and natural foods stores.

Because essential oils are so concentrated, they should be added to dry potpourris with an eyedropper. Only one or two types of oil should be used in each potpourri mixture. Potpourri that has lost its fragrance can be revived by adding a drop or two of oil.

Some of the best essential oils for potpourri are attar of roses and oil of violet, carnation, jasmine, lemon-verbena, lavender, sandalwood, heliotrope, and orange blossom (neroli oil).

Essential oils should never be taken internally, so it is important to keep them out of the reach of children. Stored in the small dark vials they come in, they should remain viable for about two years. They should not be purchased if they have been displayed in a sunny window. And they should not be refrigerated; the ideal storage temperature is 65° F.

The best oils are the result of steam distillation. (It takes 250 pounds of rose petals to make 1 ounce of oil by this method.) Sometimes peel pressure is used to extract oils from citrus fruits. Solvents are used to extract some oils, such as jasmine, tuberose (*Polianthes tuberosa*), and carnation.

Many oils are made entirely by chemical means; a good supplier will indicate which oils are natural and which are synthetic. Although no chemical can replace all the qualities of a plant, synthetic oils are less expensive than natural oils and can be quite true to scent or flavor and useful for potpourris. Natural oils are preferred for therapeutic purposes.

It's wise to ask about purity: If a product is sold as an "herbal essence," it probably contains pure oils mixed with alcohol. Tinctures contain 1 part essential oil to 10 parts fine-grade alcohol. "Fragrance" oils are also diluted to various degrees.

Pure essential oils vary greatly in price. Pure jasmine, rose, and neroli oil are much more expensive or come in much smaller containers than sweet orange or eucalyptus oil. Most pure oils cost two to four times as much as eucalyptus or orange oil.

## MAKING MOIST POTPOURRI

Rose petals can be fermented with salt to make moist potpourri. Use 1 cup of noniodized salt (sea salt is ideal) to 3 cups of packed petals. Rosemary or bay leaves can be pulverized and mixed with the salt. This potpourri will stay fragrant for years with the addition of a bit of brandy every few years or whenever the mixture dries out a bit.

Dry the rose petals until leathery and limp and only half to one third of their original bulk (about 2 days).

In a bowl place a layer of petals ¼ inch thick. Sprinkle with salt. Repeat until all the petals are used. Cover the layers with a plate, and weight it with a heavy rock. Let stand in a dark, dry, warm place with good air circulation for 10 days as the petals and salt cake together.

Continue to add more petals and salt every 2 to 7 days all summer. Also add grated lemon or orange zest whenever they're available. If a sweet-smelling liquid gathers, pour it off and save it to add to bathwater. If the petal mixture froths, stir it daily with a wooden spoon for another 10 days.

When the petals become a dry, layered, sweet-smelling cake—from pink to dull brown in color, depending on the additions—break up the caked petals into small pieces. Add more dried flower petals as well as dried leaves, spices, roots, or citrus zest. Fixatives or essential oils are not necessary, because the fermentation process produces such a strong, lasting scent.

Seal the potpourri in an airtight container or a plastic bag for 6 more weeks, opening it daily to stir. Then transfer to smaller opaque containers and keep covered when not in use.

**Preparing dry potpourri** Let the flowers and leaves dry until they are crisp, then strip the flowers and leaves from the stems and discard the stems. Accumulate the flowers and leaves in a covered container. When you have about 4 cups of dried material, use it in the recipe on page 114 to make your own dry potpourri.

With their many bits of memorable color, dry potpourris are lovely displayed in clear glass jars or open containers. To preserve the scent longer, keep the lid on except when the room is occupied. Covered baskets or porous fabrics will let just a slight scent escape constantly. (Moist potpourri, which is less attractive than the dry form, is usually kept in opaque jars with lids or in covered boxes. Directions for making moist potpourri are given on page 116.)

The scent from dry potpourri is most noticeable in warm, light, and airy rooms. A constantly humid atmosphere can alter the scent or keep it from pervading the room. Dry potpourri should be kept out of direct sunlight, which will fade its colors and dissipate the fragrance too quickly.

Although some scents will last for years, others begin to diminish after as little as three months. Dry potpourris can be revived as needed with fresh crushed spices, dried petals and herbs, or essential oils. The original recipe or theme should be followed as closely as possible.

When the potpourri loses its scent or balance beyond reviving, it can be set by the fireplace to be added in small bits for a fragrant fire.

## Simmering Potpourri

Potpourri mixtures can be simmered in water to release their fragrance. The scented moisture of the simmering herbs will add humidity and decrease static electricity in a heated house while bringing back the fragrance of summer. A pleasing mixture is bay, rosemary, lemon balm, eucalyptus, rose petals, lavender, and whole cloves or cinnamon sticks. To 3 cups of water add ¼ to ½ cup of crushed dried herbs or twice as much chopped fresh herbs. Or you can steep the herbs in water, then strain out the herbs and use the water in a vaporizer.

Potpourri burners may seem like a new idea, but herbal mixtures were once burned directly in metal containers called perfume pans. Herbs were also smoldered over the fires in wayside inns to make the rooms smell fresh and ready for guests. Rosemary was sometimes called *incensier* and was

*In a simmering potpourri burner, a potpourri mixture is combined with water and then heated to diffuse the fragrance. Because the scent is short-lived, use inexpensive mixtures in these burners.*

*Damask roses have a strong and delightful scent. They are the source of the rose oil used in perfumes and other rose scents; the petals can be used in potpourris and sachets.*

used in churches instead of more costly incense.

Any herbal mixture can be burned like or with incense in a potpourri or incense burner. The incense will keep the herb smoldering longer. Consider using a mixture of inexpensive ingredients, since it will have a short life. Avoid powders, because they will float to the top. You can reheat the blend several times—at least three—until all the scent is gone.

Decorated ceramic incense burners are increasingly popular in gift shops. Some depend for heat on a votive type of candle at the base. Others need to be plugged in and are warmed electrically.

No burner? Place a few spoonfuls of dry potpourri or a drop or two of essential oil in a metal pan of water on the back of a woodstove or on top of a radiator, or in a crockpot or in a saucepan over the lowest heat on the stove.

## Potpourri Ball

A fragrant potpourri ball can be made with potpourri mix and a Styrofoam ball. The ball is held by a toothpick or yarn needle, then it is painted with or dipped in white glue, then rolled in potpourri mix until the surface is covered with colorful bits of fragrance. Ribbons and other decoration can be added as desired.

# SACHETS

Colonial housewives tucked sachets among the clean sheets fresh off the washline and the winter woolens packed away in spring. These packets of aromatic herbs can be as simple as a few dried lavender leaves or rose petals tied in a clean handkerchief. Or you can place the herbs in tea bag papers, sold in natural foods stores. Or you can spoon the herbs into plain or fancy sachet holders (see right). Sachets can also be small bags containing perfumed powders or potpourri.

You can make sachets simply by filling small cloth bags with any combination of rosemary, thyme, rose petals, lavender, or sweet woodruff, and make their fragrance last with a bit of ground cloves from the spice shelf or purchased fixatives such as gum benzoin or calamus root powder.

The sachets can be tucked in empty suitcases, the pockets of winter coats when they're stored during warm weather, and in purses, shoes, and boots. They can be placed in drawers with lingerie, gloves, linens, and especially sweaters; herbs smell much better than mothballs. With added loops the sachets can be hung on hangers with dresses and suits.

Thin sachets can also be tucked behind books on bookshelves to scent the book pages and also help protect the books from insects. Herbs appropriate for this use are lavender, southernwood, santolina, or wormwood; any of these should be fixed with cinnamon or cloves.

## OTHER FRAGRANT CUPBOARD HERBS

Lavender wands, scented drawer liners, and pomanders make lovely gifts of long-lasting fragrance. Here are easy directions for making them.

## QUICK AND EASY SACHETS

Sachets can be plain or lacy and fancy. By following these directions you can make many plain but useful ones in only a few minutes.

One piece of fabric 20 by 16 inches, folded double lengthwise, will make 40 sachets if you make each sachet 2 inches wide and 4 inches long.

Fold the fabric in half to make a rectangle 20 inches by 8 inches. With chalk or a light pencil mark, indicate on the fabric the size you want to make your sachets. Machine stitch ⅛ to ¼ inch on each side of all long chalk lines and along the long edges. Then make similar lines of stitching just *above* the short lines and above the bottom short edge.

With pinking shears, cut the sachets apart along the short chalk lines. (Or finish the edges with a zigzag machine stitch in thread of a contrasting color.) Fill the sachets with a mixture of your choice, then stitch them closed along the top. Cut apart the filled sachets on the long chalk lines between the two rows of machine stitching.

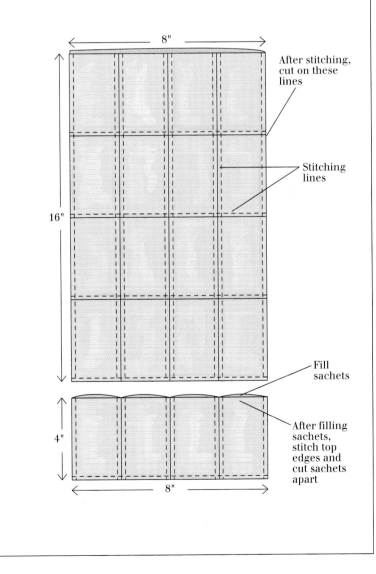

After stitching, cut on these lines

Stitching lines

16"

8"

Fill sachets

After filling sachets, stitch top edges and cut sachets apart

4"

8"

## MAKING A LAVENDER WAND

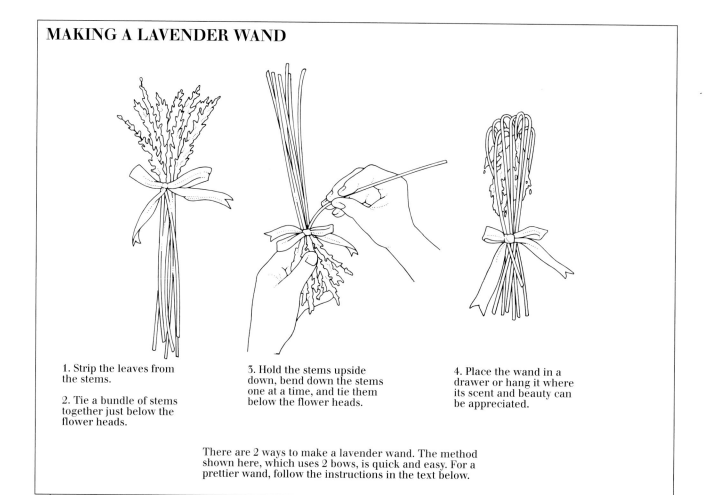

1. Strip the leaves from the stems.

2. Tie a bundle of stems together just below the flower heads.

3. Hold the stems upside down, bend down the stems one at a time, and tie them below the flower heads.

4. Place the wand in a drawer or hang it where its scent and beauty can be appreciated.

There are 2 ways to make a lavender wand. The method shown here, which uses 2 bows, is quick and easy. For a prettier wand, follow the instructions in the text below.

## Lavender Wand

A favorite herb for drawers and wardrobes, lavender has a lovely, long-lasting fragrance and also deters moths and fleas.

One of the most charming ways to preserve these summer blooms is to make lavender wands, sometimes called lavender bottles. Pick 13 to 19 (an uneven number) of the longest stems just after the dew has dried. Select stems on which the lower blooms are fully open and the ones at the top of the spire are just beginning to open.

Bring the stems indoors, then strip off all the leaves and set them aside to dry for another use. Make the wand at once while the stems are supple.

Select 3 to 5 yards of ribbon; you will weave it in and out of the stems. Gather the stems so that the base of the flower heads is even. Place one end of the ribbon under your left thumb and hold it at the base of the blossoms. Then weave it in and out among the stems for a few rows. Holding the flowers gently in your left hand, very carefully bend each stem over the flower heads; the result will look like a cage with the flowers inside. As you bend more stems, tighten the ribbon with a toothpick or crochet hook, but be sure not to get it so tight that the stems stain the ribbon.

When the weaving has gone beyond the flowers, wrap the ribbon around the outside of the stems and secure it with a pin. Let the lavender dry for 2 weeks; the stems will shrink a bit. Again tighten the ribbon to take up the slack, then wrap it around the outside of the stems and secure it with a bow and a loop for hanging. Trim the stem ends evenly or at a slant.

Lavender wands can adorn a gift box. They are also attractive when set on a dressing table or hung from a bedpost. To scent and protect clothing, they can be hung in a closet or cupboard or placed in drawers.

## Scented Drawer and Shelf Liners

Potpourri or sachet mixtures can be used to make scented drawer liners and closet shelf liners for the bedroom and bath. If you have wallpaper remnants, the liners can match the room. Inexpensive wallpapers absorb fragrances best.

Cut sheets of wallpaper to fit the drawers and shelves. Assemble a favorite potpourri or sachet mixture and a matching essential oil. Lavender, lemon-verbena, mint, and rose petals all work well. Put a few drops of the oil on a cotton ball and rub this over the underside of the first sheet of paper.

Then sprinkle the mixture generously over the patterned side of the paper. Place another piece of paper on top of this and again sprinkle with the mixture. Rub the oiled cotton ball over the back of every third or fourth sheet. When all the sheets are treated, roll them up together and seal them in a plastic bag for 6 weeks to absorb the fragrance.

When you unroll the papers to line drawers and shelves, gather up the herbal mixture and save it for another use.

## Pomanders

Perforated containers have been used as pomanders since medieval times. Now these containers are made of porcelain with a perforated

*Lavender has been a favorite scent for centuries. Bring its scent into your home with sachets (page 119), lavender wands, or pillows (page 152).*

moths in closets, repel flies from the kitchen, and freshen a sickroom.

**Fruit pomander**   You can make fruit pomanders with citrus fruits or green or red apples. You can expect all fruit to darken to a brownish color as it dries. Purchase whole cloves (the least expensive way is to buy them in bulk from a natural foods store), then select those with large heads and strong stems. It takes about 1 ounce of cloves to entirely cover an average-sized piece of fruit. Simple lines or designs rather than a solid covering will take fewer cloves.

Before inserting the cloves into citrus fruits, squeeze the fruit gently to soften the skin. If necessary, use a darning needle to start the holes for the cloves. Leave one clove space between each to allow for shrinkage as the fruit dries. Be sure to leave a strip of fruit free of cloves so that a ribbon can be added later if desired.

After inserting as many cloves as desired, roll the fruit in a mixture of orrisroot powder and ground cinnamon, nutmeg, coriander, or allspice. Each fruit will require about 2 ounces of orrisroot mixed with 2 ounces of spice. A large batch of this mixture can be made ahead; kept sealed in a plastic bag, it will last up to 3 months.

Place the finished pomanders in a paper bag together with any leftover spices. Check them every few days until they are dry and sound hollow when tapped. This can take from 1 to 3 months. Or let the pomanders dry by hanging them in a closet or setting them in a bowl as a centerpiece.

If the pomanders are to be used in drawers or anyplace where the powdered spices would be undesirable, place the finished pomander in a bag of see-through fabric and tie the top with a ribbon.

*Citrus zest pomanders make lovely Christmas presents. Tucked into pretty fabric bags, they will release their fragrance for years to scent closets or drawers.*

surface and a ribbon at the top. These can be filled with moist potpourri or a perfume-soaked sponge or cotton. Fruit pomanders—lemons, limes, oranges, or apples studded with whole cloves—have been popular since the sixteenth century and are still made today. Small ones were once worn around the neck or waist and used like nosegays to ward off germs or cover unpleasant odors.

Pomanders can be hung, used as centerpieces, or placed in drawers. They look attractive as they deter

Use ribbons to suspend pomanders in cupboards or closets. Or turn them into decorations as well as room fresheners by trimming them with ribbon, a few sprigs of dried herb flowers, rosebuds, baby's breath, tiny pinecones, or a bay leaf.

The scent of the pomander will last for a year or more. Renew the fragrance by rolling the pomander in a mixture of orrisroot and 2 drops of essential oil, then sealing it in a plastic bag for 2 weeks.

**Citrus zest pomander**   Spices, essential oils or fixatives, and citrus zest can be combined to make these pomanders. Save citrus zest in a plastic bag in the freezer. When 4 cups of zest have accumulated, assemble ground spices—cinnamon, cloves, nutmeg, ginger, or allspice—and essential oils or fixative powders, such as orrisroot, calamus, or sandalwood. Each 4 cups of zest will make about 50 pomanders.

Grind the zest in a blender, then add about 6 tablespoons of spices, 1 tablespoon of fixative, and a few drops of oil. The mixture should be doughy. If necessary, add a few drops of glycerin to help bind it together. Remove the mixture to a work surface and roll it into walnut-sized balls. Allow them to air-dry, turning occasionally, or wrap them at once in organdy or other breathable fabric. Drying will take a week or two.

Wrapped in red fabric and decorated with a sprig of evergreen or holly, these pomanders make lovely Christmas gifts. Later they can be used in drawers or closets to release their delightful scents over the years. A few drops of essential oil can be used to revive them when necessary.

# STREWING HERBS

Good housekeepers in olden days combated household odors with strewing herbs. Spring cleaning meant taking all the rugs outdoors, beating the dirt out of them, then tacking them back down over a padding of straw and sprigs of herbs, which released their fragrance when trodden upon. Although modern sanitation has made this use for herbs all but forgotten, the principle is still sound and worthy of revival both indoors and out.

## Freshening the Air

Sprigs of fresh or dried herbs, dry potpourri mixtures, or the prunings from herb bouquets can be placed under a doormat. Herb sprigs or sachets can be folded in a sofa bed or chair or placed under the cushions of upholstered furniture. This can be especially refreshing in winter, when stale household odors linger.

## Repelling Insects and Rodents

Plants with repellent qualities have been used for centuries to keep away insect pests and rodents.

**Roaches and waterbugs**   Where Osage-orange (*Maclura pomifera*) grows wild or remains from former hedges, from Texas across the Midwest to Pennsylvania, one of the rites of fall is bringing home a few fruits for insect control. Six of these grapefruit-sized, crinkly lime green fruits will keep a large house free of roaches and waterbugs for up to two years. The fruits do not kill the insects; rather they seem to prevent insects from entering the premises. Some people claim that the fruits also discourage mice, spiders, and crickets.

Pick the fruits off the tree (be careful of the thorny branches) or

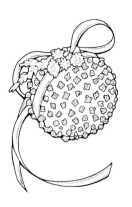

*Simple sachets filled with insect-repelling herbs can be placed among woolens.*

ondary scents can come from citrus zest, lemon-verbena, tansy, bay leaves, fennel, cedar shavings, tobacco leaves, or black peppercorns.

A combination of at least two to four herbs works best. Select herbs whose scent you enjoy, because the scent will cling somewhat to clothing.

Pick the leaves and flowers in the morning after the dew has dried, preferably on a sunny day when the last rain was three days past. Dry the plant matter until it is crisp, then strip the leaves from the stems and discard the stems; roll the leaves with a rolling pin or blend in a blender to reduce them almost to a powder.

Mix in 1 tablespoon of ground cloves for every 4 tablespoons of herbs. Fixative is not necessary, although it will prolong the mixture's effectiveness against moths. The best fixative for this purpose is chipped orrisroot and half again as much essential oil as for a plain potpourri. The best essential oils to use are those that are insect repelling: cedar, lemon, lavender, pennyroyal, peppermint, or bayberry.

Pack the mixture into cloth bags, using at least ¼ cup per bag. Place a bag in every bureau drawer, the knitting basket, the dog's bed, and every closet. The herbs will lose their fragrance, so they should be replaced once a year.

Cedar chests also lose their fragrance over the years as the oils near the surface of the wood evaporate. To restore the insect-repelling quality of cedar, sand the wood periodically or rub it with fresh cedar oil.

gather them from the ground, and tuck them in closets, the cupboard under the sink, behind the stove, and in the basement. There is no noticeable odor even as the fruits shrivel and dry out over the winter.

**Moths**   Since the days of ancient Greece and Rome, certain herbs have been used to keep moths from clothes and linens. These include lavender, southernwood, tansy, camphor, basil, eucalyptus, pyrethrum (only the dried yellow disk flowers in the center of the daisy), wormwood, rue, santolina, costmary, rosemary, thyme, pennyroyal, and most mints. The mints, peppermint especially, may also deter mice from nibbling in closets. Sec-

**Ants**   Colonial women planted tansy around the foundation of the house because ants are supposed to avoid the herb. Some people claim that catnip sprinkled along an ant path will cause the ants to turn around and go the other way. A time-honored remedy for ant infestations is to squeeze lemon juice into the places where the ants could enter, then scatter bits of the zest in likely spots. Ants are supposedly repelled by the scent of lemon. Other ant deterrents are catnip, cayenne (dried or an infusion), and walnut leaves.

**Fleas**   You can deter fleas by hanging fresh or dried sprigs of pennyroyal or tansy, using cocoa hulls in pet bedding, and using solutions of wormwood or cloves in the pet's bath. Or you can use the same herbs for strewing about the house. Another flea remedy for the house is to burn sprigs of fleabane (*Pulicaria dysenterica*), ploughman's spikenard (*Inula conyzae*), wormwood, or mugwort and let the fumes fill the room. The room should be well aired before anyone enters it.

**Flies**   The easiest and most effective herbal fly deterrent is shooflyplant (*Nicandra physaloides*, see page 245). Other known fly deterrents are mint, pennyroyal, lavender, mugwort, rosemary, rue, southernwood, thyme, and tansy. They can be used in potpourris or as strewing herbs (see page 123). The sticky roots of elecampane were once used as a natural flypaper.

**Mosquitoes**   To keep mosquitoes at bay while working in the garden, rub fresh lavender leaves on any exposed skin. This will help for about 20 minutes. Keep a sprig in your hair, pocket, or belt loop to renew the rub as needed. Other mosquito-repelling herbs are chamomile, mosquitobush (*Agastache cana*), and mosquito-shoo geranium (*Pelargonium citrosum vanieenii*).

**Rodents**   Mice and rats can be deterred with mint, stinking cham-

omile (*Anthemis cotula*), tansy leaves, and spurge (*Euphorbia lathyris*). Catnip of course works, not to mention the helpers it attracts.

# THE HOUSEKEEPING CLOSET

Herbal home-care products can be effective, fun to make, and easy and enjoyable to use.

## Soap
Any cake of soap can be transformed into a fine lathering and effective herb soap by using the following recipe.

### Herb Soap
Select pleasing molds to determine the final shape of your soaps. The oils listed first have the strongest antiseptic properties.

¼ pound (about 1 cup) soap shavings, scented or unscented
4 tablespoons honey
2 tablespoons corn oil
1 teaspoon oil of lemon, thyme, orange, bergamot, juniper, cloves, lavender, neroli, peppermint, rosemary, sandalwood, or eucalyptus
Vegetable oil, for coating molds

In the top of a double boiler, combine the soap shavings with the honey and corn oil. Simmer for 20 minutes, stirring occasionally with a wooden spoon. Add the herbal oil, place the top pan directly over low heat, and stir constantly until the mixture has the texture of soft modeling clay.

Coat the molds with the vegetable oil. Scoop the mixture into the molds; let cool. Remove from the molds and coat the soap with vegetable oil. Store the soaps unwrapped in a warm, dry place until hard.
*Makes 1 large or 4 small bars.*

*Herbs strewn under an ironing board cover will impart their fragrance to the clothes as the hot iron passes over them.*

## Furniture Polish

The oils contained in herbs can make your furniture shine.

▌ Rub the leaves of lemon balm on wood furniture and it will clean, shine, and leave a fragrance that has been known to keep away cats.

▌ Grind the seeds of sweet cicely with a mortar and pestle; wrap in a soft cloth and use to polish wood.

### Herbal Furniture Polish

Use this mixture on a dust cloth and it won't be necessary to buff the furniture.

2 ounces linseed oil
2 ounces malt vinegar
3 drops peppermint oil
20 crushed sweet cicely seeds *or* ½ teaspoon *each* lemon and lime oil *or* ¾ teaspoon lavender oil

Pour all the ingredients in a jar and shake well.
*Makes about 4 ounces.*

## Metal Polish

▌ Scrub copper pans with a handful of bruised leaves of yellow wood sorrel (*Oxalis stricta*). The oxalic acid in the leaves makes an effective metal polish.

▌ Use a cluster of stems of horsetail like a scouring pad to polish metal. Be sure to wash the pans before using them again for cooking to remove all the abrasive bits of silica contained in the plant.

▌ Use a strong infusion of horsetail to polish metal. Add 1 ounce of dried or 3 handfuls of fresh horsetail to 2 cups of water and let steep for 2 hours or more, then simmer in the same water for 15 minutes. Strain. To polish, soak the article in the liquid for 5 minutes, then allow to dry slowly before polishing with a dry cloth. For large pieces or mixed metals, use a cloth to coat the desired part with the liquid, let dry, then polish with another cloth.

## Laundry Freshener

Herbs can be used to scent the laundry during washing and ironing.

▌ Scent laundry with a strong infusion of one or more herbs, such as the flowers of pinks, lavender, roses, or violets, leaves of costmary, angelica, bay, bergamot, marjoram, mint, lemon-verbena, rosemary, or sweet myrtle, or the powdered root of rose. Strain the infusion and add it to the rinse water at the end of hand washing or to the final rinse cycle of the washing machine. Or add it to the mister or into the steam iron when ironing.

▌ Place crushed herbs or a sachet mixture under the ironing board cover. Or add a sachet to the clothes in the dryer; this will sweeten even the laundry that was left wet in the washer overnight.

*Herb vinegars are simple to make (see page 134). To freshen the air in a house, use them in water to clean windows.*

## Other Housekeeping Products

Herbs can be used to make housekeeping products from glue to bleach. Here are a few suggestions.

▮ Boil the leaves, stems, and especially the bruised roots of soapwort (*Saponaria officinalis*) for 30 minutes with just enough water to cover. Strain, then use the solution to wash and give softness and sheen to any natural fabric.

▮ Dab the juice from the leaves of yellow wood sorrel on stained fabric and leave for 30 minutes. Rinse and repeat if needed. The juice contains enough oxalic acid to be a natural bleach that will even remove rust spots from white cotton and fade ink to a shadow.

▮ Use herb vinegar in hot water to clean and shine windows; it leaves the house smelling pleasantly fresh and fragrant.

▮ To make an herbal disinfectant, boil the leaves of thyme, juniper, eucalyptus, pine, sage, rosemary, or lavender, or the roots of angelica, in water for 30 minutes. The more herb in the water, the stronger the germ-killing action. Strain and use alone or with soap for kitchen and bathroom cleaning.

▮ Use the bulbs of wild hyacinth (*Hyacinthoides nonscripta*) for glue. Simply scrape the side of the bulb with a knife and use the viscous juice right away. Keep the rest in the refrigerator. The glue can be used on paper; historically it has been used by bookbinders and for affixing feathers to arrows.

# HERBS IN THE BEDROOM AND BATH

*Herbal bath preparations are (from left to right): Floral Water (page 130), Moisturizing Bath Foam (page 133), Sage Toner (page 145), Cucumber Cleanser (page 144), and Oily Bath Oil (page 132).*

The pleasures of garden fragrances and the good feelings they can evoke need not stop at the garden gate. Herbs can be a part of cleansing, relaxing, and beauty care as well. Many of the herbal preparations in this chapter are simple to make; some take a bit more time. All allow you to know and control the ingredients so that the preparations are natural and much less expensive than commercial products.

There are many easy ways to utilize herbs in the bedroom and bath that are practical and aesthetically pleasing. A sprig of sage or mint kept in a glass of water by the bed can be rubbed over the teeth first thing in the morning to sweeten the breath. Aloe juice used as a facial moisturizer tightens and soothes the skin. A bowl of pomander balls or a cluster of eucalyptus in the bathroom will release scent with the steam from every shower. Herbal tea bags can be used in the bathwater—up to four at a time for strong fragrance. And potted lavender or rosemary plants will thrive in the extra humidity of the bathroom. If the room is dark or otherwise less than ideal, the plant can be left there for a few days, then returned to a bright windowsill. Rotating the selection adds to the interest.

# HERBAL BATH PREPARATIONS

Many herbal preparations help you pamper yourself in the bath or shower. Floral waters, soaking herbs for a scented bath, herbal bath oils, bath bags and mitts, bubble bath, scented vinegars, after-shower splashes, and herbal soaps are all easy and delightful.

## Floral Water

Also called toilet water, floral water is refreshing in an herbal bath or as an after-shower splash. Floral waters distilled for the commercial

*Fruit pomanders (see page 122) can scent the bathroom as well as the closet. The heat and steam from a bath will release the fragrance.*

market will keep indefinitely. Homemade waters will keep for only 2 weeks in the refrigerator. When making them it's best to use nonmetallic containers and distilled water.

### Basic Recipe for Floral Water

You can prepare floral water for specific effects. Herbs to ease aches and those that are invigorating, relaxing, antiseptic, astringent, or decongestant are listed on page 131.

> 6 tablespoons chopped fresh herbs *or* 3 tablespoons crushed dried herbs (see Note)
> 2 cups water
> 1 ounce fresh flower petals *or* ½ ounce dried flower petals

Place the ingredients in an enamel pan. Bring to a boil, then cover, reduce the heat, and simmer 30 minutes. Let cool, then strain, bottle, and refrigerate.

*Makes about 2 cups.*

Note  Floral water intended mostly for bathing should be made stronger by using up to 1 pound fresh material and increasing the dried material and water proportionally. Add 3 ounces vodka after straining. Use ½ cup floral water per bath.

### Rose Water

Add 1 cup of this floral water to a tub full of hot water. Or splash it on the body after a shower.

> 2 cups distilled water
> ¼ cup vodka
> ½ cup unsprayed freshly gathered rose petals *or* ¼ cup dried (red ones look best)
> Up to 15 drops rose oil, depending on strength of rose petal fragrance

Combine all the ingredients in a jar and place in the sun for 1 day. Strain and refrigerate in a covered bottle. Use within 2 weeks.

*Makes about 2 cups.*

## Soaking Herbs for a Scented Bath

Although a shower may be faster than a bath, there are times when the multiple benefits of a slow, soaking bath make it a good use of time. Hydrotherapy has been used for centuries to relieve stress of body and mind. It still works. And it works better with the addition of herbs for their fragrance and therapeutic properties.

Herbs can aid relaxation; refresh the skin, body, and soul; and help heal sore muscles. Herbs for specific uses are listed below. You can hang herbs from the faucet or showerhead while the water is running; use them to make herbal tea bags, which are then added to the bathwater (page 132); or use floral waters in the bathwater as described on page 130.

Water temperature that is close to body temperature is the most relaxing. Just a trace of a chill can be stimulating and can renew the body's energy. Very hot water can make you sleepy. Anything over 104° F can dehydrate the skin and exhaust the body. Perspiring skin cannot absorb therapeutic herbal properties or scents. Ex-

---

### BATH AND SOAKING HERBS AND THEIR EFFECTS

These herbs can be used in the Basic Recipe for Floral Water (opposite page). The plant leaves are used unless otherwise noted.

**Relaxing Herbs**
Catnip
Chamomile flowers
Comfrey
Evening primrose
  blooms
Hops
Hyssop
Jasmine flowers
Juniper berries
Lemon balm
Linden flowers
Marshmallow root
Mullein
Passionflower blooms
Rose petals
Tansy flowers
Valerian root
Vervain
Violet

**Muscle-Soothing Herbs**
Agrimony
Bay
Juniper berries
Mugwort
Oregano
Sage
Strawberry leaves

**Invigorating Herbs**
Basil
Bay
Blackberry leaves
Borage
Calendula blooms
Citronella
Eucalyptus
Fennel
Horseradish root
Ivy
Lavender flowers
Lemon balm
Lemon-verbena
Lovage root
Marjoram
Mint
Orange zest
Parsley
Pennyroyal
Pine needles
Rosemary
Sage
Savory
Stinging-nettle
Tansy
Thyme
Vetiver root

**Decongestant Herbs**
Eucalyptus
Feverfew flowers

**Antiseptic Herbs**
Eucalyptus
Sandalwood
Sorrel

**Astringent Herbs**
Agrimony
Alum root
Bay
Bayberry bark
Clary sage
Comfrey
Lady's-mantle
Lemongrass
Lemon-scented herbs
Mullein
Nasturtium flowers
Raspberry leaves
Rosemary
Rose petals
Sage
Sorrel
Stinging-nettle
Strawberry leaves
Vinca
Wintergreen
Yarrow flowers

*Filled with herbs, bath mitts take the place of washcloths. Parsley acts as a natural deodorant.*

Essential oil should be added to the bath drop by drop after the tub is filled. If it is added as the water is running, much of it will evaporate. See the lists on page 138 for essential oils for specific uses. And see the advice on page 139 about using essential oils.

> 3 parts vegetable or nut oil or red turkey oil (see Note)
> 1 part essential oil of your choice

Place the vegetable oil in a bottle. Add the essential oil and shake well. Let stand for 2 weeks for the scent to blend into the oil. Use 1 to 3 teaspoons per bath.

*Note* The lubricating oil that will disperse best in bathwater is red turkey oil, a treated castor oil that is available in drugstores and some herb outlets. Most other oils lie on the surface of the water and coat the body only when you are getting in or out of the bath or when the water is agitated. Mixing lubricating oils with 1 tablespoon milk will help disperse them through the bathwater.

## Bath Bag and Mitt

An easy way to use herbs in the bath is with a bath bag or mitt. They are easy to make and luxurious to use.

A bath bag can be as simple as a pouch made of cheesecloth or any thin cotton material; herbs are added to the center of a square of the fabric and the corners are tied together. Ribbon or yarn can be used to hold the pouch closed; the ribbon is looped over the hot water faucet so the running water passes through the pouch. The ribbon should be long enough so that the loop can be released and the bag left to steep in the water for a while after the tub is filled. A bath bag can also be hung from a shower-head or used in place of a wash-cloth in the shower.

treme heat can even lower blood pressure and lead to fainting.

## Herbal Bath Oil

The ideal use of herbal bath oils is to add them after washing and then have a lovely soak. Otherwise the lubricating oils can keep moisture from penetrating the skin instead of later keeping the moisture in. It's best not to stay in the bathwater more than 20 minutes altogether or the bath will begin to dry rather than moisturize the skin.

## Oily Bath Oil

Oily oils can help moisturize the skin, which aids in carrying scent.

A bath mitt is made in the shape of a mitten with three thicknesses of cloth—the outer one of terry, the two inner ones of lightweight cotton. The herbs are placed between the inside cotton layer and the terry; the hand goes between the cotton layers. Different colors of terry can be used for each member of the family.

The bags or mitts can be filled with a handful of one type of herb or a combination. Lovage, parsley, or sage can be used for a natural deodorant; equal parts oatmeal or coarse cornmeal can be added to soften the water and the skin. A cache of bath bags or mitts can be kept on hand in airtight containers to use instead of washcloths.

The bags and mitts should be dried thoroughly after each use. They can be reused until the scent is gone—usually at least three uses. Then they can be opened, emptied, washed, and refilled.

## Bubble Bath

There are several ways to add bubbles to an herbal bath. Because bubble baths can be drying to the skin, they should be used only once a week. Or for a bath that won't be drying at all, you can use a bath foam (see below) with an essential oil.

### Homemade Bubble Bath

Use up to 3 tablespoons under fast running water for each frothy bath.

    2 cups springwater
    4 tablespoons dried herbs
    2 cups mild liquid soap or baby
       shampoo

Place the water and herbs in a large saucepan and bring to a boil, then reduce the heat, cover, and simmer until the liquid has reduced to 1 cup (about 30 minutes). Strain and let cool, then add the liquid soap. Mix well and store in stoppered bottles.
    *Makes about 4 cups.*

### Moisturizing Bath Foam

The glycerin and sugar are not necessary, but they will make the bubbles last longer. Use 2 to 3 tablespoons of foam per bath.

    1 cup mild dishwashing liquid
    ¼ cup glycerin (optional)
    1 teaspoon sugar (optional)
    5 to 10 drops essential oil of your
       choice

Combine all the ingredients and store in stoppered bottles.
    *Makes about 1¼ cups.*

*Sage is not only a kitchen herb. It can be used in bath mitts or to make soaps, lotions, and skin toners.*

## Scented Vinegar

Vinegar has long been used as an astringent cleanser and a hair rinse, and to soften the skin, soothe itchiness, and ease aching muscles. Adding herbs increases the benefits and makes the vinegar more pleasant smelling.

Herb vinegars for beauty care are made in the same way as those for cooking. It is best to use a pure, light-colored, lightly scented cider vinegar or a white wine vinegar for a base. Add 1 cup of chopped fresh herbs or 3 to 6 tablespoons of crushed dried herbs per pint of

vinegar, and let steep on a sunny windowsill in a tightly stoppered bottle for 2 to 3 weeks, shaking it daily. When the scents are well blended, strain and rebottle, adding a single sprig of herb for decoration and identification. Dilute with distilled water if desired.

Or make an infusion by adding the herbs to the vinegar, bringing just to a boil, and letting the mixture stand overnight before straining and bottling.

Experiment with combinations of herbs and also with uses. Add 1 cup of scented vinegar to a tub full of

*Herbal vinegars have many uses in the bath. Their astringency makes them a refreshing aftershave splash.*

bathwater to refresh the skin. Open a bottle of scented vinegar and inhale the scent to help clear a stuffy head. Use the vinegar to close pores and remove excess oil from the face after cleansing with a creamy cleanser, or use scented vinegar between washings to refresh and tone the skin. Men often find scented vinegars excellent for aftershave lotions.

## After-Shower Splash
Floral waters and scented vinegars, both discussed above, are stimulating and refreshing to splash on the body or the face after a shower. Similar preparations can be made in the same way using rubbing alcohol or witch hazel for a base.

Mint and yarrow make a masculine scent. Lavender is a good addition to any mixture, and eucalyptus will add a mentholated fragrance.

## Garden-Fresh Soap
Making your own herb soap allows you to select the fragrances and soothing properties you desire. Lavender is antiseptic and relaxing. Any of the lemon-scented herbs are refreshing. Chamomile relaxes and

*Herbal soaps can be shaped by hand into balls or formed in molds. Begin with chips of a mild soap and scent it with herbs from your garden.*

softens the skin. Herbs that are said to help heal acne include agrimony, burdock, clover, horsetail, iris, lavender, lemon balm, Solomon's-seal, southernwood, and tansy.

### Herbal Soap

Save soap chips until you have the equivalent of 2 large bars. Or grate bars of a mild castile soap (see Note). Use soaps with a pleasant feel and minimal scent.

> About 10 ounces castile soap
> ⅓ cup boiling water
> 2 tablespoons chopped fresh herbs *or* 1 tablespoon crushed dried herbs
> Essential oil (optional)

Grate the soap. A blender will make it almost powder-fine for the smoothest, quickest soap; a hand grater will give interesting textures.

*Adding clover to soap may help heal acne.*

Make a tea of the boiling water and herbs; let steep for 15 minutes. Strain, then add essential oil drop by drop.

Add the mixture to the grated soap. Knead it into balls or other shapes or pack it into molds coated with vegetable or nut oil (candy molds or paper cup molds are fine). As soon as the soap is firm, pop it out of the molds. Then let it dry in an airy place, turning as needed, for 2 to 5 days.

*Makes 1½ to 2 cups.*

*Note*   An alternate method is to grate or blend soap scraps or pieces of new bars into a saucepan with a little water or herbal tea. Add herbs or essential oil to suit. Place the soap mixture over low heat until the soap is dissolved, then pour the hot liquid into molds to harden.

An even easier way to make herb soap is to sprinkle 6 drops of essential oil on a piece of soft, absorbent cotton, such as flannel, and wrap this around a bar of minimally scented soap. Place the wrapped soap in a plastic bag, seal, and leave for at least 8 weeks. You can reuse the fabric to wrap another bar.

To make liquid soap, which can be used in a pump dispenser, mix soap chips in a blender. It is best to keep deodorant and facial soaps separate. Add enough herbal infusion to make a thick liquid; add a few drops of essential oil if desired.

Many herbs contain saponins, which produce a soapy lather and are fun to try as substitutes for regular soaps. Such herbs include soapweed (*Yucca glauca*), Spanish bayonet (*Yucca aloifolia*), soapwort (*Saponaria officinalis*), saltbush (*Atriplex hortensis*), papaya (leaves), and wild gourd. The herbs are added to warm water and rubbed to produce a lather. You may want to grow these herbs or look for them in mail-order catalogs (see page 287).

# BODY CARE PREPARATIONS AND COSMETICS

You can make your own body care preparations, such as massage oil, facial masks, aftershave lotion, and shampoo, as well as your own herbal cosmetics, such as lipstick, eye shadow, moisturizer, and perfume. When making herbal cosmetics, it is perfectly all right to substitute ingredients; few people have all the exact ingredients on hand, and the preparations should be unique. It's important to keep a record of what you put in each preparation. Some will be such successes that you will want to repeat them exactly.

Herbal body care products and herbal cosmetics are just some of the easy ways you can enjoy herbs daily. Below is a list of sources for ingredients.

## Massage Oil

Essential oils and lubricating oils are combined to make massage oil, which can relieve stress and tension, improve blood circulation, and accelerate the elimination of wastes, thus cleansing and nourishing the blood.

Essential oils enhance the benefits of the lubricating oils because of the effect of their fragrance on the olfactory nerves. The olfactory nerves are linked directly to the part of the brain in which emotions

### SHOPPING LIST

Many of the ingredients you need to make the herbal products in this chapter can be found in a grocery store, drugstore, or natural foods store. Fixatives, essential oils, and the herbs themselves that can't be found elsewhere are available from the mail-order sources listed on page 287.

**From the Natural Foods Store**
▌ Dried herbs, for all herbal preparations; available in bulk

**From the Grocery Store**
▌ Almonds, for facial masks
▌ Borax, for skin toners and moisturizing creams; a white laundry powder that acts in creams as an emulsifier
▌ Buttermilk or plain yogurt, for facial masks and cleansers; soothing and astringent and good for oily skin
▌ Distilled or mineral water, for floral waters
▌ Honey, for facial masks; soothes, moisturizes, and binds other ingredients
▌ Oatmeal, for facial masks, soaps, and bath bags and mitts

▌ Almond oil, for perfumes, skin cleaners, muscle massage, and aftershaves; has little scent, is slow to turn rancid, is rich in protein, and is nourishing to the skin
▌ Avocado oil, for muscle massage; penetrates deeply but becomes sticky when used in large amounts
▌ Calendula, carrot, evening primrose, jojoba, sesame, and wheat germ oils, for muscle massage
▌ Olive oil, for massage and itch relief; has a distinctive odor
▌ Safflower, soy, and sunflower oils, for cosmetics and muscle massage. Soy is the least sticky and has the most pleasant texture; sunflower oil has the shortest shelf life but is rich in vitamin E.
▌ Whole milk or sour cream, for moisturizing creams

**From the Drugstore**
▌ Beeswax, for cleansing and moisturizing creams; a good emulsifier for the oil and water in creams. Usually sold by the block, it should be melted slowly over low heat. Cool in 1-tablespoon amounts, or the amounts you will most often

need, in foil-lined muffin pans or egg cartons. When these portions cool and resolidify, they can be wrapped and labeled for a ready supply.
▌ Cocoa butter, for cleansing and moisturizing creams; a rich emollient that is actually a thick fat from the cocoa bean. It is inexpensive and has long been used to reduce scarring.
▌ Fuller's earth, for facial masks
▌ Glycerin, for softening the skin in cosmetics; a clear, thick syrup that is a by-product of the soap-making industry
▌ Witch hazel, for muscle massage, itch relief, and cleansing; an alcohol-like liquid
▌ Rose water and other floral waters, for perfumes, skin toners, skin cleansers, and astringents; will keep indefinitely
▌ Red turkey oil, for oily bath oil; a treated castor oil
▌ Tincture of myrrh, for skin cleansers; antiseptic and healing, good for treating skin irritation and inflammations
▌ Tincture of benzoin, for fixative and antiseptic astringent

*Eucalyptus oil has a warming and penetrating quality, making it good for massage oils.*

and memories are stored. In addition, essential oils permeate the skin and enter the bloodstream more quickly and thoroughly than lubricating oils, and their benefits are more long-lasting.

Lubricating oils can improve dry or oily skin and increase elasticity. Lubricating oils used in massage oil include almond, jojoba, olive, sesame, corn, soy, sunflower, calendula, carrot, evening primrose, and wheat germ oil.

**Choosing essential oils** The fragrance of essential oils is so concentrated that it is sometimes only slightly similar to the herb itself. It is best to sniff before you buy. See the lists below of essential oils for specific uses.

**Preparing massage oil** Pour 2 ounces of lubricating oil in a bottle and add from 15 to 30 drops of essential oil (either purchased or your own—see below). Start with an average amount or less and see what works best. Adding 1 teaspoon of wheat germ oil will preserve freshness; 1 teaspoon of avocado oil

---

## ESSENTIAL OILS AND THEIR EFFECTS

A single essential oil can be selected for the quality most desired, or two to four essential oils can be blended to combine the qualities of each.

**Relaxing Oils**
Chamomile
Cypress
Frankincense
Geranium
Jasmine
Marjoram
Neroli
Patchouli
Rose
Sandalwood
Ylang-ylang

**Mood-Lifting Oils**
Basil
Lemon balm
Patchouli
Rose

**Muscle-Soothing Oils**
Eucalyptus
Juniper
Lavender
Marjoram
Rosemary
Thyme

**Invigorating Oils**
Basil
Camphor
Eucalyptus
Ginger
Juniper
Lemon
Peppermint
Rosemary

**Antiseptic Oils**
Bergamot
Juniper
Lavender
Lemon

**Astringent Oils**
Cypress
Geranium
Rose

**Insect-Repellent Oils**
Eucalyptus
Geranium
Lavender

will enhance absorption. A full body massage takes 2 to 4 teaspoons of mixed oils. Label and date each mix, store them in a cool, dry place, and use them within 2 to 3 months.

The easiest way to make a massage oil from garden herbs is to combine 4 ounces of mixed herbs with 1 quart of mixed vegetable oils or pure olive oil in a nonmetal container. Let steep in a warm place for 2 weeks. Then strain, add some essential oil if desired, label, and use immediately or store in the refrigerator.

For a stronger extraction, start as above but strain after as little as 24 hours. Then add more herbs to the same oil and repeat the process from 6 to 10 times. This makes a lovely fragrant oil for massage, baths, moisturizing the face or hands, lotions, soaps, and candles. It will last for several months in a tightly sealed, dark bottle, longer if a perfume fixative is added. Fixatives such as musk civet, ambergris, or castoreum are available from pharmacies and mail-order suppliers.

The following advice should be heeded when using essential oils.

▌Before using any herbal massage oil, test for an allergic reaction by placing a small portion on the gauze of a bandage and wearing it on the inner arm for 24 hours. If there is any adverse reaction, eliminate ingredients until the offender is obvious.

▌Use only pure essential oils for massage. These are very concentrated and powerful, so use common-sense care.

▌Keep essential oils out of the reach of children.

▌Never use the essential oils of anise seed, bitter almond, cedar, cinnamon bark, cloves, hyssop, pennyroyal, sage, or wintergreen.

▌When pregnant avoid the essential oils of basil, clary sage, fennel, juniper, marjoram, myrrh, peppermint, rose, and rosemary.

▌People with high blood pressure should avoid rosemary oil.

▌If you are sunbathing or working outdoors, avoid bergamot and citrus oils; they can cause intensive burning by the sun. (Oil of bergamot comes from bergamot orange [*Citrus bergamia*], a citrus tree grown in Italy, not from the garden perennial *Monarda*, which is often called by the common name bergamot also.)

▌Avoid using massage oil for an hour after a very hot bath, a steam bath, or a sauna. During that time the skin will be eliminating heat, toxins, and moisture and won't be

*The essential oil of lavender is pleasantly soothing in a massage oil. One of the most commonly used herbs in commercial perfumes, lavender has been a favorite scent for hundreds of years. This is Spanish lavender.*

*Less intense than perfume, cologne is simple to make at home. Rose-Petal Cologne is made by steeping the petals in alcohol.*

## Perfume and Cologne

Essential oils can be used by themselves as perfume. You can select a main scent and complementing secondary scents or simply a single scent. Some herbalists advise striking a high, a medium, and a low note. The first gives the initial impression. In commercial perfume making, if the scent is not detectable after 24 hours, it is considered a high note. The second note is the body of the perfume, which takes 5 to 20 minutes after exposure to the air to be detectable, and lasts from 24 to 60 hours. The low note is the lingering fragrance, still detectable after 60 hours; it is the fixative in the blend.

For people who do not use perfume often, essential oils are ideal because they keep much longer than dilutions. And most essential oils are considerably less expensive than commercial perfumes.

Most perfumes contain a base of undenatured 60 to 90 proof ethyl alcohol (vodka is often used) and essential oils. Although perfume can be made with lubricating oils as well, alcohol-based perfumes have a stronger scent.

The best way to wear perfume is in the hair, because the protein in the hair causes the scent to last much longer than it does on the skin.

Making your own perfume allows you to create a purely personal scent—one that you can carry through other cosmetics you make. It's best to prepare perfume in small quantities, store it in a stoppered bottle, opaque if possible, and use it up within three months. The bottle should be shaken every day for the first two weeks to blend the scents. And the bottle should be labeled with the ingredients, so that the perfume can be duplicated if desired. Here are several suggested

ready to absorb anything, so the benefits would be largely wasted.

▌Do not use massage oil on the abdomen right after eating.

▌Do not use massage oil on anyone with heart trouble or severe back pain.

▌Do not massage any area if it causes discomfort.

▌Do not use massage oil on anyone with a fever, virus infection, or suspected cancer, or who has lately undergone major surgery.

▌Avoid areas of fractures, sprains, bruises, swelling, rashes, and torn muscles.

mixes using either alcohol or lubricating oils as a base.

▌Add 20 drops of essential oil to ¼ ounce of jojoba oil. Unlike other lubricating oils, jojoba oil does not turn rancid if kept for a long time. It is a good emollient for dry or oily skin and is an excellent hair conditioner.

▌To 2 ounces of almond oil add a few drops of one or more essential oils. Almond oil has little scent of its own, is rich in protein, is a nourishing skin oil, and keeps well. Use this mixture as both a perfume and a skin conditioner.

## Homemade Cologne

Originally manufactured in Cologne, Germany, cologne contained, for every 2 ounces of alcohol, approximately 44 drops of bergamot oil, 15 drops of lemon or orange oil, 4 drops of neroli oil, and 1 drop each of rosemary and lavender oil. The exact ingredients varied from source to source. Also called eau de cologne, this scented liquid is weaker, less long-lasting, and less expensive than perfume. This version is easy to make at home.

   1 cup fresh lavender flowers, rose petals, orange blossoms, or jasmine blossoms
   2 ounces ethyl alcohol

Steep the flowers in the alcohol in a stoppered jar at room temperature, shaking well every day for 6 days. Strain and store in a dark glass bottle with a tight lid and almost no air space.

## Steam Facial

The beauty aid that improves the skin most rapidly is a steam facial. It's best to choose a time when you can relax and won't be going out soon. Herbs suitable for steam facials are listed on page 142.

   Fill a teakettle with 4 to 6 cups of water and put it on to boil. Then take a large bowl and a pruning

snips and head into the garden. Gather the equivalent of 2 handfuls of fresh herbs. In winter as little as 3 tablespoons of dried herbs will do. Gatherings may include a branch of sage and some lemon balm, mint, and basil flowers or leaves. Basil and mint can help clear the head and make you feel more alert. If you have a cold or a headache, add eucalyptus to open the breathing passages.

   Cleanse your face in the usual way. Then pour the boiling water over the herbs in the bowl and stir them gently to immerse them all

*An herbal steam facial refreshes and cleanses the skin. Gather a combination of fresh herbs from your garden.*

## HERBS FOR STEAM FACIALS

### Base for All Facials
Comfrey
Fennel
Houseleek

### Normal to Dry Skin
Borage
Burnet
Clover
Comfrey
Cornflower
Fennel
Houseleek
Lady's-mantle
Licorice root
Marshmallow root or leaves
Parsley
Sorrel
Violet flowers or leaves

### Oily to Normal Skin
Comfrey
Fennel
Lavender
Lemongrass
Lemon zest
Rose petals
Sage

### For an Astringent
Herbal vinegars
Witch hazel
Yarrow

### For Calming and Cleansing
Applemint
Chamomile
Chervil
Lady's-mantle
Lavender
Lemon balm
Linden
Rose petals
Spearmint
Thyme

### For Increasing Circulation and Stimulation
Pansy leaves
Peach leaves
Rosemary
Stinging-nettle

### For Tightening and Stimulating Mature Skin
Anise seed
Comfrey
Dandelion
Lavender
Lemon-verbena
Peppermint
Red clover leaves or flowers
Tansy leaves or flowers

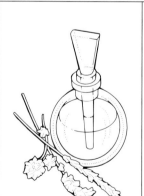

and begin the infusion. Take a towel and the bowl of steeping herbs to a comfortable place, preferably with a table or counter in front of you. Or sit on the sofa, put a pillow on your lap, and settle the bowl gently on it.

Close your eyes and carefully lower your face into the steam as much as is comfortable, keeping 12 to 18 inches from the water. Make a tent of the towel to hold in the steam; open an end whenever you need more air. Try to stay that way for 10 to 15 minutes while your face perspires and the herbal steam softens the skin and draws the impurities from your pores.

An alternate method is a compress facial. Make the same herbal infusion. Arrange a towel over your shoulders to catch drips. Then soak a soft cloth in the hot infusion, lift it out with tongs, and press it to remove excess water. Let the cloth cool until it will not burn, then apply it carefully to the face. Repeat the dipping until the infusion cools. This also feels wonderful on the back of the neck.

End a facial with a tepid and then a cool rinse. Then use an astringent to close and tighten the pores. Or proceed to a facial mask (see below). Try to avoid temperature changes for an hour or more.

Facials are recommended once a week for normal skin, two to three times a week for oily skin, and only every two to three weeks for dry skin. Avoid them if you have thread veins, serious skin problems, or breathing or heart problems.

## Facial Mask
The ideal time—although not the only time—for a facial mask is while the pores are open right after a steam facial. Make this a project for a stay-at-home celebration, for the face sometimes remains flushed for several hours.

Preparing a facial mask is as simple as whirling the strained herbs from the facial steam in a blender, then applying this green mix to the face.

Any facial mask can be thickened to the desired consistency with ground almonds, oatmeal, or fuller's earth (available at drugstores). These three ingredients, used alone or in combination, make a good base.

Other ingredients for a facial mask might include 1 tablespoon of milk or sour cream for softening and toning dry skin, or 1 tablespoon of buttermilk or yogurt to dry oily skin; 1 teaspoon of honey for

healing and moisturizing; a few drops of lemon juice or cider vinegar to restore the pH balance of the skin; egg yolk for dry skin or beaten egg white to tighten oily skin; brewer's yeast to nourish the skin and extract impurities; wheat germ oil for dry skin; or a few drops of essential oil for fragrance.

Spread the paste over the face except for the eye and mouth area. Lie down and relax for 10 to 30 minutes, with cucumber slices or cotton balls soaked in an herbal infusion over the eyes. Your skin should feel tight and stiff. Then wash off the mask with warm water. Apply a pore-closing infusion of yarrow or rose, and a moisturizer, or just end with a cold cloth compress.

Do not attempt to store leftover facial masks. They may spoil.

## Skin Cleanser

A traditional skin cleanser can be made with equal parts rose water (see page 130) and glycerin, which is available in drugstores. These are mixed together, heated just to boiling, allowed to cool, and stored in closed containers.

Cream cleansers are made with melted beeswax, oils (lanolin, almond oil, or glycerin), and herbal or scented waters (rose water, lavender water, or orange blossom water). More wax can be added for a thicker cream or more oil for a softer one. A little more herbal water may make the preparation fluffier, but you risk separation of the ingredients. Herbs such as houseleek and marshmallow, which contain mucilage, make a cream spongier.

*Yarrow has an astringent effect in herbal facials. Add it to close the pores and tighten the skin.*

The ingredients must be at the same temperature or they may curdle; while the wax is melting in one enamel pan, the oils can be warming in another or in the microwave. Slowly pour the oils into the wax while beating constantly. Add the herbal infusion and/or essential oils. When the mixture is cool, spoon it carefully into wide-topped jars or bottles, then label them with the ingredients and date.

The creams will last for a few weeks in the refrigerator. They should be dipped into only with clean hands or a spatula so as not to introduce bacteria.

*Use violets in milk to cleanse dry skin. This one is the freckles violet (Viola obliqua)—but don't expect it to either increase or diminish your freckles!*

### Easy Milk Cleanser
3 to 4 ounces unsweetened plain yogurt
1 tablespoon safflower oil
½ teaspoon lemon juice
2 drops essential oil of rose, lavender, or geranium

Mix all the ingredients and use within 2 days.
*Makes about ½ cup.*

### Cleanser for Dry Skin
2 tablespoons fresh or dried chamomile flowers, violets, or linden flowers
½ cup whole milk

In the top of a double boiler, combine the flowers and milk. Heat for 30 minutes at a temperature low enough so that the milk does not form a skin.

Remove the pan from the heat and let stand for 2 hours, then strain and use. The cleanser will keep 1 week in the refrigerator.
*Makes ⅓ to ½ cup.*

### Fennel Seed Cleansing Milk
This simple cleanser is good for oily skin.

½ cup buttermilk
2 tablespoons crushed fennel seed

Heat the buttermilk and fennel seed in the top of a double boiler for 30 minutes. Let cool for 2 hours, then strain and bottle. It will keep 1 week in the refrigerator.
*Makes ⅓ to ½ cup.*

### Cucumber Cleanser for Oily Skin
1 teaspoon beeswax
4 tablespoons soy oil
¼ cucumber, peeled and diced
6 teaspoons yarrow infusion
5 drops tincture of myrrh

Melt the wax in a double boiler over low heat. Warm the oil and add to the wax, beating constantly. Purée the cucumber in a blender to extract 2 tablespoons juice.

Warm this and the yarrow infusion; add to the oil-wax mixture, again beating constantly. Remove from the heat and let cool, then stir in the myrrh. Spoon into labeled jars. Store in the refrigerator.

*Makes ⅓ to ½ cup.*

## Astringent

An astringent is usually the second step in a facial; it removes all traces of the cleanser, closes the pores, and removes excess oil. Also called a toner or refresher, an astringent is good to use for quick cleansing and refreshing between more thorough cleansing routines.

Any of the floral waters or vinegars or after-shower splashes mentioned earlier in this chapter make fine astringents, especially if made with some of the astringent herbs listed on page 131. Traditional refreshers good for all skin types include rose water, lavender water, and orange flower water.

### Basic Skin Toner

⅓ cup herb extract (see Note)
½ cup witch hazel
2 teaspoons glycerin
½ teaspoon boric acid
½ teaspoon tincture of benzoin

Mix well and keep in a closed bottle. Shake well before using.

*Makes about 1 cup.*

*Note* To make an herb extract, steep the chosen herb or herbs in an equal amount of ethyl alcohol or vodka. After a week, strain and add more herbs. After one more week, strain again.

### Skin Toner for Dry Skin

10 tablespoons rose water
    (see page 130)
2 tablespoons orange flower
    water
2 tablespoons witch hazel

Mix all the ingredients and store in a stoppered bottle.

*Makes about ¾ cup.*

### Sage Toner for Oily Skin

¼ cup crumbled dried sage
¼ cup ethyl alcohol or vodka
¼ teaspoon borax (optional)
3 tablespoons witch hazel
10 drops glycerin

Blend or grind the sage with the alcohol. Let stand 2 weeks, then strain and add the borax dissolved in the witch hazel. Add the glycerin and mix well. Keep in a stoppered bottle and shake before using.

*Makes about ⅓ cup.*

## Moisturizer

The third and final step in facial care is a moisturizer to protect the skin from dryness and dirt. The ingredients are assembled using the same method as for skin cleansers (page 143). The moisturizer is massaged into clean skin to add moisture to the outer layers and speed the renewal of skin cells. Both almond and sunflower oil soften as they moisturize.

### Comfrey and Cocoa Moisturizer

This moisturizer is nourishing for all types of skin, especially winter-dried hands and faces.

1 teaspoon beeswax
1 tablespoon lanolin, warmed
1 tablespoon cocoa butter,
    warmed
1 teaspoon glycerin, warmed
½ teaspoon borax
2 tablespoons comfrey
    infusion (tea)
A few drops essential oil (optional)

Melt the beeswax and add the lanolin and cocoa butter. Stir together. Add the glycerin. Dissolve the borax in the comfrey infusion and add to the wax mixture with the essential oil (if used). Stir as the cream cools and thickens. Spoon into labeled jars.

*Makes about ¼ cup.*

*An herbal after-shave is refreshing as well as functional. This one is pine-lemon, made with essential oils and vinegar; for a milder preparation, make it with witch hazel.*

## Aftershave Lotion

A cool application of an herbal aftershave will refresh and heal the face. You can add your choice of fragrance. Herbal aftershaves tend to be more subtle, freshly natural, and less overpowering than commercial products, and considerably less expensive.

Any of the herbal waters, astringents, or after-shower splashes already described in this chapter are suitable. Substituting witch hazel for the alcohol makes any recipe more soothing.

Here are some essential oils that are good for aftershave lotions.

■ Basil is said to clear the head for mental sharpness.

■ Bergamot is supposed to relieve anxiety and depression and may be a good way to begin a difficult day.

■ Black pepper has a light, stimulating odor and aids circulation.

■ Coriander has a sweet, uplifting fragrance.

■ Frankincense is a warming, relaxing tonic said to be rejuvenating.

■ Lemon is invigorating, antiseptic, and insect repelling.

■ Patchouli relieves anxiety and is calming and antiseptic.

■ Pine has a woodsy scent that is refreshing and antiseptic.

Aftershave lotions can be made with fresh herbs instead of essential oils.

### Herbal Aftershave

The fresh herbs can be used alone or in any combination. The glycerin can be added for dry skin.

> 1 part chopped fresh basil, dill, eucalyptus, lavender, marjoram, mint, sage, rosemary, thyme, or yarrow
> 1 part cider vinegar or cider vinegar and witch hazel
> 1 teaspoon glycerin or almond oil (optional)

Combine the herbs and vinegar in a covered jar; the container should be no more than half full. Leave it in a warm place, shaking once a day, for 2 weeks. Strain, then add glycerin if desired. Store in an airtight bottle.

## Suntan Lotion

There are no herbal substitutes for commercial sunscreen with a high sun protection factor (SPF). Common sense and moderation, especially for fair-skinned people and children, is very important. Wearing a hat is wise when working outdoors for long periods of time. A lavish application of aloe vera gel can relieve sunburn.

## Moisturizing Suntan Lotion

This moisturizing lotion contains a small enough portion of bergamot oil to be safe (see page 139); it will help a skin that tans easily to tan more deeply and quickly.

    1 tablespoon lanolin
    4 tablespoons sesame oil,
      warmed
    6 tablespoons floral water,
      warmed
    1 teaspoon cider vinegar, warmed
    2 drops bergamot oil

In a double boiler over medium heat, melt the lanolin, then add the sesame oil and beat well. Add the floral water, vinegar, and bergamot oil and beat until smooth and thick. Let cool; bottle and label.
    *Makes about ¼ cup.*

## Sunburn Relief

This soothing mixture should be gently applied to reddened skin.

    6 tablespoons olive oil
    3 tablespoons vinegar
    ½ teaspoon iodine
    Up to 10 drops essential oil of
      lavender

Blend all the ingredients together. Bottle and label.
    *Makes about ½ cup.*

# Lipstick and Eye Shadow

Beeswax is used in many herbal cosmetics.

## Herbal Lipstick

To redden the lips or cheeks, the ancients used alkanet root.

    2 tablespoons ground alkanet
      root
    ½ cup sesame oil
    4 tablespoons melted beeswax

Combine the alkanet and oil and let stand for 1 week. Strain, warm, and add to the beeswax. Beat the mixture until it is at room temperature. Store in small jars.
    *Makes about ⅓ cup.*

## Herbal Eye Shadow

For lavender shadow use black mallow flowers and alkanet. For green eye shadow use parsley. Use calendula petals for yellow. To darken the eyebrows, use a strong decoction of sage boiled in a black cast-iron pot.

    1 part fresh herbs
    4 parts oil
    1 part beeswax

Soak the herbs in the oil until the oil is well colored. Melt the beeswax. Warm the oil, then add the beeswax, and beat until cold. Pack in small containers.

*The juice of the aloe vera plant is soothing and healing. To use it, break off a leaf and squeeze the mucilaginous juice on a burn or minor irritation. The plant is easy to grow in a sunny window.*

*This fragrant Herbal Body Powder, made in moments, combines lavender, rosemary, and rose petals.*

## Dusting Powder

Here's a fragrant, soothing body powder that makes a lovely gift.

### Herbal Body Powder
  2 cups dried herb leaves or flowers: lavender buds, rose petals, or leaves of patchouli, rosemary, lavender, or yarrow
  A few drops essential oil of your choice
  1 pound arrowroot

Whirl the herbs in a blender; transfer to a large bowl. Combine the oil with the arrowroot; add to the herbs and stir to mix. Store in jars or powder boxes, or put in decorative containers for gifts.
  *Makes about 2 cups.*

## Hand Care

An occasional soak in warm herbal tea is beneficial to your hands. A recommended combination is tea made with the essential oils of benzoin, patchouli, or rose and any of the following herbs: calendula petals, chamomile flowers, or leaves of comfrey, fennel, marshmallow, or yarrow.

## Foot Care

Soothing foot soaks and foot powder can ease tired feet. An effective soak is warm herbal tea made from a handful of fresh or 3 tablespoons of dried leaves of bay, lavender, lemon balm, lovage, marjoram, mint, rosemary, sage, or thyme. Sage and lovage help deodorize the feet. You can add ¼ cup of apple cider to relieve itchiness, 1 teaspoon of cayenne pepper to warm cold feet, or 1 teaspoon of crushed dried comfrey leaves to soothe athlete's foot.

## Deodorant Foot Powder

4 ounces cornstarch
8 ounces unscented talcum
  powder
2 ounces baking soda
2 teaspoons powdered orrisroot
5 drops essential oil of your
  choice (optional)

Combine all the ingredients and mix well. Store in a dusting powder box with a puff or in a can with a perforated lid.

*Makes about 1 cup.*

## Mouth Care

Herbal products for mouth care can be just as effective as, and perhaps safer than, the abrasives, detergents, and sweetening ingredients used in commercial toothpastes or the powerful agents in mouthwashes. Here are a few ways to use herbal products for a healthy mouth.

▮ If you forget your toothbrush on a camping trip, cleanse your gums and teeth by chewing the end of a twig of flowering dogwood.

▮ To freshen the breath, chew parsley, watercress, or peppermint leaves; all are high in chlorophyll, which is a green plant pigment as well as a breath freshener. Or chew juniper berries. Any of these will help eliminate the odor from onion, garlic, or alcohol.

▮ To help remove tea and smoking stains, whiten the teeth, and remove plaque, rub the inside of a lemon rind over the teeth.

▮ To help heal mouth ulcers, rinse your mouth with about 10 drops of goldenseal tincture in a glass of warm water.

▮ For a simple, refreshing mouthwash, rinse or gargle with a tea of peppermint, rosemary, sage, marjoram, black currant leaves, thyme, and/or anise seed. Peppermint and thyme add antiseptic qualities. Or use rose water (page 130) or lavender water.

▮ For a spicy mouthwash, add just a few drops of the following preparation to a glass of water. Grind cloves, caraway seed, cinnamon, and nutmeg with a mortar and pestle, then add to a blender with an equal amount of sherry. Add a few drops of tincture of myrrh, peppermint, or lavender and let the mixture stand for 1 week to blend.

### Herbal Toothpaste

1 tablespoon arrowroot
1 teaspoon sea salt
½ teaspoon baking soda *or* 1 teaspoon ground cinnamon
Up to 15 drops oil of peppermint

Mix all the ingredients, then grind to a dry paste with a mortar and pestle. Store in an airtight container.

*Makes about 4 teaspoons.*

### Herbal Tooth Powder

2 parts chopped fresh sage
  leaves, including growing tips
1 part sea salt

Combine the sage and sea salt. Bake in a 300° F oven for 20 minutes. Remove and grind the dried sage to a fine powder. Return to the oven for another 15 minutes. Let cool, then store it in an airtight container.

### Lip Balm

1 ounce beeswax
½ cup almond oil
1 tablespoon honey
½ teaspoon essential oil of lemon,
  orange, or vanilla

In a double boiler over medium heat, melt the beeswax in the almond oil. Add the honey and essential oil. Let cool, then store in a small covered container.

*Makes about ¾ cup.*

## Eye Care

Herbs can help soothe tired, red, or strained eyes. Eyebright (*Euphrasia officinalis*) is the most famous eye-care herb and indeed is called

## Herbal Eye Compresses

These compresses should be used only when fresh. Any remaining decoction can be frozen in an ice cube tray, then stored in labeled plastic bags in the freezer. The cubes can be melted as needed.

2 tablespoons chopped fresh *or* 1 teaspoon crushed dried herbs
2 cups water

Simmer the herbs in the water for 20 minutes. Let cool, then strain up to 3 times through a fine sieve to remove all flecks of leaf or blossom.

Prepare the compresses by dipping sterile cotton or gauze into the cool decoction. Rest the compresses on the eyelids for 10 to 15 minutes.

## Hair Care

Many herbs and their oils make excellent shampoos, conditioners, or hair-coloring agents; some can serve as all three.

An ideal base is castile soap or any avocado, coconut, baby, or soapwort shampoo. Essential oils or a strong infusion of the chosen herbs are then added to the base. Some suggestions for herbs are given on the opposite page.

### Soapwort Shampoo

This shampoo produces little lather but excellent, gentle cleansing. It won't sting the eyes, so it is good for small children. The dried leaves, stems, or roots of soapwort are available from natural foods stores.

4 cups boiling water
¼ cup ground dried soapwort root *or* 2 handfuls fresh leaves and stems
2 handfuls fresh *or* ⅓ cup dried herbs for specific hair types (see opposite page)

Pour the boiling water over all the herbs. Steep for 30 minutes, then strain. Use ½ to 1 cup per shampoo, more for longer hair.

*Makes about 4 cups.*

*Scented Lip Balm (see page 149) will provide pleasant relief to dry or chapped lips.*

*casse-lunette,* meaning "discard your spectacles" in French. Eyebright can also help watery eyes caused by a cold or allergies.

Calendula soothes, chamomile reduces the appearance of weariness, cornflower relieves puffiness, fennel seed or agrimony add sparkle to the eyes, horsetail helps reduce redness and swelling, mallow softens the surrounding skin, and mint reduces the dark bags under the eyes. Other herbs used for eye care include borage, lady's-mantle, marigold, rose, and wormwood.

Also good for a quick pickup are cooled tea bags of regular or herbal tea held over the closed eyes for 10 minutes.

## Dry Shampoo

This is good for the ill or infirm or anyone who doesn't have time for a full shampoo. To apply, part the hair in sections and shake the powder onto the scalp. Massage in, leave on 10 minutes to absorb grease and impurities, then brush out until the hair is shiny.

> 3 tablespoons powdered arrowroot
> 3 tablespoons powdered orrisroot

Stir the ingredients together.
*Makes about ⅓ cup.*

## Hair Oil Treatment

Use any of the herbs or essential oils for specific hair types (at right). Just before shampooing, add ½ cup of chopped fresh herbs or 2 to 4 tablespoons of crushed dried herbs to 2 tablespoons of almond or sunflower oil. Alternatively you could use 6 drops of essential oil instead of the herbs. Warm the mixture in the sun or microwave oven. Strain out the herbs, then apply to the hands and massage into the scalp and along the hair strands to the ends. Repeat as needed for complete coverage.

Cover the hair with a plastic shower cap, then wrap the head in a hot towel. Redip the towel as it cools and leave it on for 20 to 30 minutes. Then shampoo as usual.

## Hair Rinse and Conditioner

Make an herbal tea of any of the herbs for specific hair types (at right). Strain and let cool. Add a few drops of essential oil if desired. For dark hair add 1 tablespoon of cider vinegar; for light hair add 1 tablespoon of lemon juice. Pour over the hair. Catch the runoff; repeat several times, massaging the liquid into the scalp. Leave the final rinse to dry on the hair. This hair rinse will remove all traces of soap, aid circulation, and leave the hair soft and shiny.

## HERBS FOR HAIR CARE

The following herbs can be used for specific hair colors, types, and conditions.

❚ For light hair use calendula, chamomile, linden flowers, mullein, orange blossoms, orrisroot, stinging-nettle, tumeric, or yarrow. Rhubarb root is one of the best lighteners.

❚ For dark hair use cloves, henna, lavender, marjoram, mint, rosemary, sage, thyme, or yarrow. To highlight natural colors, use crushed walnut shells, sandalwood, or redwood bark.

❚ Make red hair shine with calendula, marigold, or hibiscus flowers, or cloves.

❚ For gray hair use a decoction of blue-purple hollyhock flowers to remove yellow tones, or wood betony (*Stachys officinalis*) to highlight yellow tones. To darken gray hair and add sparkle, use a decoction of bay, marjoram, sage, or wood betony.

❚ For oily hair use calendula, horsetail, lavender, lemon balm, lemongrass, lemon juice, mint, orrisroot, rosemary, southernwood, or yarrow.

❚ For dry hair use burdock root, citrus zest, comfrey, marshmallow, parsley, red clover, sage, or stinging-nettle.

❚ For added body and luster, use calendula, cleavers (*Galium aparine*), fennel leaves, goose-grass (*Potentilla anserina*), horsetail, linden flowers, nasturtium, parsley, rosemary, sage, southernwood, stinging-nettle, or watercress.

❚ Encourage hair growth with catnip, fenugreek seed, horsetail, or southernwood.

❚ To prevent dandruff use burdock root, chamomile, cleavers, garlic or onion bulbs, goose-grass, parsley, rosemary, southernwood, stinging-nettle, or thyme.

❚ To prevent static electricity, loosen a too-curly permanent, or simply add fragrance to the hair, sprinkle a few drops of rosemary oil on the hairbrush before using.

## Natural Hair Coloring

Any of the herbs listed for specific hair types (above) will gradually lighten, darken, or add red highlights to the hair as indicated. (Henna can color the hair unevenly; it is best applied by a professional.) The color will become softer or darker with each use. To hasten the coloring change, simmer 2 ounces of the chosen herbs in a quart of water for 20 minutes with the pan covered. Let cool, then strain and pour through the hair again and again. Dry with an old towel, because some color will rub off.

An herbal paste will make the most noticeable color change. Use a cup of water to each ounce of herb; then boil, strain, and add kaolin powder or fuller's earth to make a pastelike consistency. One teaspoon of vinegar will help release the dye and maintain the pH balance; 1 teaspoon of glycerin will prevent dryness.

Make the paste before shampooing so it can cool. To apply the paste wear rubber gloves to keep from staining the hands and nails. Apply it in sections, working from the scalp to the ends of all hair strands.

Cover the hair with a plastic shower cap and hot towel and leave for 20 minutes to 1½ hours, then rinse until the water turns clear. Or leave the paste on until it dries, then brush it out, which is best done outdoors.

## HERBAL PILLOW

One of the best beauty aids is a nap or a night of peaceful sleep. Lying back on an herbal pillow allows the fragrance to take you to a pleasant garden scene or a warm summer afternoon. Herbal pillows make thoughtful gifts. They are a great comfort to someone who must spend time in bed or to someone who loses precious sleeping time to insomnia.

Hops are the best known of the sleep-inducing herbs; they contain lupulin, a substance that helps bring on normal, natural sleep by relaxing the muscles. Lupulin is present only in small amounts in the fresh leaves, but the concentration increases as the leaves dry.

Because the fresh, piney fragrance of hops changes with drying to a less pleasant scent, it is best to stuff a hop pillow at least half full with a potpourri of fragrant soothing herbs such as lemon-verbena, rose petals, rosemary, and chamomile. The sleep-inducing qualities of hops can be effective for as long as four years. The hops can be replaced or renewed by adding a few drops of essential oil.

Other suggested mixtures for herbal pillows include eucalyptus, lemon balm, linden flowers, marjoram, and hops mixed with orrisroot (pieces, not powder) or other fixative. Another mix is agrimony, meadowsweet, woodruff, cloves, and crushed dried orange zest mixed with fixative. The flowers of corn poppy (*Papaver rhoeas*), mullein, violet, common mallow, and marshmallow are also said to help alleviate sleeplessness and cure headaches.

Lavender has long been used to calm, relax, and relieve headaches and is said to dispel sadness. However, because many find its scent to clash with that of hops and because some find lavender invigorating rather than soothing, it might be better in a separate pillow mixed with such other herbs as bay, lemon thyme, mint, rosemary, lemon balm, or rose. This mix is excellent for a headache pillow. A pillow made in an hourglass shape will cradle the neck.

Also suitable for herbal pillows are chamomile (it supposedly prevents nightmares), pine needles (refreshing), and marjoram (once used as a sedative). Dill is said to calm fussy babies.

Herbs for pillows should be dried and mixed as for potpourri (see page 114), using spices, fixatives, and essential oils to enhance and preserve the fragrance. For gifts or for guests who may be allergic to orrisroot when used in such proximity to the face, alternative fixatives include angelica root, oakmoss, patchouli, or benzoin.

The herbs for pillows should be crushed a bit to reduce their rustling and smooth their texture. Herb pillows are usually plain, flat muslin bags from 6 to 12 inches square. They shouldn't be stuffed too full—the filling materials need room to rub against each other to release their best fragrance.

These small pillows can be stacked on the bed during the day. Resting the head on them releases the oils and lets them perfume the room. The small pillows can be slipped inside the regular pillowcase at night. Or they can be inserted into decorative outer covers that can be removed and laundered as needed; the fabric should be porous enough to let the fragrance through. It's best to avoid using fancy eyelet, bows, or any decorations that will not be smooth to the cheek.

*Filled with herbs known for their properties of relaxing and inducing sleep, herbal pillows contribute to a good night's rest.*

# HERBS IN DECORATION

*Herbs—both fresh and dried—are naturally decorative. Place scented herbs where they can be touched to release their fragrance. This wreath will release its fragrance whenever the door is opened.*

The colors, textures, and scents of herbs make them lovely and fragrant decorations. Herb flowers and foliage can be arranged as would any cut flowers. They can be dried and used in bouquets, nosegays, and wreaths and to make scented candles. Herb sprigs can be tucked into gift bows, and herb sachets can be used in the desk to scent stationery.

Bringing the cut flowers and foliage of herbs indoors allows you to showcase the best from the garden, to spotlight the blooms that might not be noticed outdoors, and to smell and touch the fragrant foliage. Arrangements of fresh or dried herb flowers and foliage make ideal gifts. Hostesses can use small foliage clusters as table decorations and give them to guests to take home. Dried herb garlands and swags can decorate your front door for the holidays.

*Opposite: Drying does affect the colors of flowers and foliage, as is evident in this mixture of dried and fresh material. Pages 156 through 160 give information on different methods of drying herbs for arrangements.*

# CUT FLOWERS AND FOLIAGE

The subtle blooms and fragrant foliage of fresh herbs can be used alone or to complement other showier annuals or perennials in an arrangement. Herbs share their qualities whether or not they are the focus of a bouquet.

Some of the herbs will root in a vase in plain water, and these can be planted in pots or in the garden to perpetuate the joy.

It's fun to experiment with different foliage, flowers, and seedpods harvested at different stages. The vase should be tall enough for the stems to be well submerged. Woody stems should be split with pruning snips or crushed with a hammer so that they will take up more water. Any leaves that would be underwater should be removed; they can be used for cooking, drying, or potpourri.

Unless otherwise specified (see instructions for cutting and keeping herb flowers on page 158), cold water is best in the vase. If the foliage or flowers wilt prematurely, the stems can be recut and placed in warm (100° F) water. A misting with cool water once a day will keep leaves fresh longer.

# DRIED BOUQUETS

The foliage, flowers, and seedpods of many herbs dry easily for everlasting bouquets or wreaths. They add color, warmth, and fragrance to the winter room and keep the garden scenes of summer alive in the heart. They also make excellent gifts. Flowers best suited to the following methods of drying are listed at left.

One of the easiest methods of drying is to hang bunches of the flowers and stems upside down in a dry, airy place. (In humid climates an air conditioner might be necessary to remove moisture from the air.)

Some herbs will also dry standing in a vase of water; the stems need to absorb about an inch of water as they dry to keep from wilting.

Most seedpods will dry on the plants and can be cut and used at once in dried bouquets. An entire bouquet of seedpods can be gathered in autumn and used alone or saved until summer to combine with colorful flowers.

The color of herb flowers can be better preserved by drying the flowers in silica gel or sand or combinations of drying agents. Sand is the easiest because the flowers can be left in it until you want to remove them. They may take up to three weeks to dry. Clean white sand from a builder's supply is the type to use.

Silica gel works the fastest and gives the best results, but it requires careful timing so that the flowers do not become too dry. This product is more expensive than sand but can

---

## METHODS OF DRYING HERBS

Some herbs can be dried by hanging them upside down in a dry, airy place. Others should be dried in sand, borax, silica gel, or a combination of drying mediums. Still others look best if dried in glycerin and water.

| In Air | Mints with small or crinkly leaves | Geranium |
|---|---|---|
| Allium | Oregano | Love-in-a-mist |
| Artemisia | Rose hips | Marshmallow |
| Bergamot | Rosemary | Rose |
| Butterfly weed | Rue | Sunflower |
| Clary sage | Sage | Violet |
| Clover | Santolina | |
| Coneflower | Sorrel | **In Glycerin and Water** |
| Dusty-miller | Tansy | Bay |
| Goldenrod | Yarrow | Bayberry |
| Hops | | Boxwood |
| Horehound | **In Drying Medium** | Broom |
| Joe-pye-weed | Calendula | Eucalyptus |
| Lady's-mantle | Chamomile | Ivy |
| Lamb's-ears | Crocus | Linden |
| Lavender | Feverfew | |

## CUTTING AND KEEPING HERB FLOWERS

You can lengthen the life of cut flowers by following these simple suggestions for handling them correctly. Reference to warm water means 80° to 100° F; hot water means more than 100° F.

■ Alkanet flowers will continue to open for 10 days after cutting. Keep the plants uncrowded so that they develop long stems. Cut the central stems first and the plant will branch and continue to bloom. Condition cut flowers overnight in cold water.

■ Artemisia flowers and foliage last for 5 to 10 days fresh and indefinitely dried. Cut the flowers when only half the spike is open; cut the foliage anytime after true leaves develop. Split woody stems. Condition for 24 hours in cold water deep enough to cover much of the stems. If the foliage wilts, recut the stems and use warm water.

■ Bergamot flowers last for 5 to 7 days, the buds and foliage up to 10 days. Cut when one-quarter of the blooms on each stem are half open; they will continue to open in water. Condition overnight in warm water.

■ Butterfly weed lasts for 5 to 8 days. Cut when the clusters are half to three-quarters open. Ignore the clear green juice; searing the stem is not usually necessary. If the flowers wilt, recut the stems and place in warm water and they will revive quickly.

■ Clover (pink or red) lasts for 5 to 8 days fresh and retains its color well if dried.

■ Dusty-miller has very attractive silver foliage. Split the stems and condition them overnight in hot water. If the foliage does not become crisp and firm, recut the stems and place again in hot water.

■ Eucalyptus of the silver-dollar, or florist, variety is ideal alone or with other materials. Split the stems and place them in cold water. To permanently change their color, immerse them at least 6 inches in a solution of 1 part glycerin to 2 parts water. Recut the stems once a week and leave them in the solution until they feel pliable and have reached the desired color. (Sometimes the foliage must be placed in the sun to cause the color to change.) After that, no water is needed. The plant material should be blotted between newspapers for several days after drying to remove the excess oil. The above method also works well for bay (it may take 2 to 3 weeks) and ivy (4 to 5 days).

■ Evergreen herbs often need a washing to remove dust or dirt. Use soapy water if needed and rinse in cold water. Split woody stems for 2 to 3 inches and condition in warm water overnight or longer, or submerge them completely for a day if they are cut during cold weather. If you wish, tie them in curves while conditioning; they will stay that way with little straightening. (Adding 1 tablespoon of glycerin per quart of water helps the stems stay pliable. Flowers should not be put in a glycerin solution.) When using evergreens for Christmas decorations, spraying with an antitranspirant spray will reduce water loss, prolong their life, and make them more fire retardant.

■ Goldenrod lasts fresh for 1 to 3 weeks and dries nicely. For fresh flowers, cut the spires at any stage; the florets will continue to open in water. Condition in cold water. For drying, cut the spires when the flowers are fully open, then hang or dry in borax (see page 160).

■ Honesty flowers last fresh for 5 to 7 days; cut them when the clusters are half open and condition in warm water overnight. To dry the silver pods, cut them when they are past the green stage. Hang in bunches for 4 weeks or more. Remove any tannish green covering from each disk with a soft slide of the thumb.

■ Lamb's-ear foliage is velvety silver. Cut the flowering stems at any stage. Split the stems and place in warm water.

■ Lavender blooms last up to 10 days. For fresh flowers, cut when the blooms on half of the spike are open. Cut the foliage separately. Split the stems and condition them overnight in warm water. For dried flowers, cut when the blooms on three-quarters of the spike are open; spread on newspapers to dry. The flowers can be rubbed off the stems and saved for potpourri.

■ Lemon-verbena flowers last for 7 days. Cut when the panicles are one-quarter to one-half open. Split the stems and condition overnight in hot water. Mist with cold water and remove some leaves to make the flowers last longer.

■ Love-in-a-mist lasts for 7 to 10 days. Cut it when the central flower and one or two more are open. Condition in warm water to which sugar has been added (4 teaspoons of sugar per quart of warm water). Cut the seedpods in various shades and stages. Condition the green ones as above; hang the brown ones in bunches.

■ Nasturtium flowers last for only 1 to 3 days, the foliage up to 2 weeks. Break the stems from the plant, then recut and mash. Do not overcrowd. Condition the flowers in cold water, the leaves in warm water.

■ Passionflowers last for only a day. Cut well-developed buds with color showing in late afternoon and condition them overnight in cold water, or cut them when just open and condition for 1 to 4 hours.

■ Perilla has inconspicuous blooms but lovely foliage and fruits. Condition overnight in warm water.

■ Roses last for 3 to 7 days. Cut with sharp shears when the outer petals begin to unfold. Make a slanting cut just above an outside-facing 5-leaved leaflet (this cut benefits the shape of the plant). Then recut just below a node and place overnight in cold water deep enough to cover much of the stem. If the blooms wilt, recut the stems and place in hot water. Dry small half-opened buds in sand, borax, or silica gel (page 156).

■ Rosemary foliage lasts for 2 weeks or more. Cut mature growth anytime. Split the stems and place in cold water; if the stems wilt, recut them and place in hot water.

■ Rue flowers last for 5 to 7 days, the foliage to 12 days. Cut clusters with 3 to 6 open flowers, the foliage at any stage. Split the stems and place in hot water. Use fruits at any stage without conditioning. Dry them for winter.

■ Sage flowers last for 5 to 10 days; flower spikes will dry in the vase. Cut stems when half the spike is open or when dry on the plant. Split the stems and condition in warm water.

■ St. John's wort lasts for 3 to 5 days if the blooms are fully open before cutting. Otherwise it will probably not open in water. Split the stems and place in cold water.

■ Sorrel, or dock (*Rumex*), has inconspicuous flowers but fruits that are good in dried arrangements. Pick them at different stages of development and maturing colors. Let a little foliage remain at the tips of the stems when drying.

■ Sunflowers last for 6 to 10 days if cut when the petals are open but the centers are tight. If several buds are on a branch, cut when at least half the buds are open. Remove unneeded leaves. Split the stems and place in warm water. Wire the stems if the blooms threaten to bend them.

■ Tansy lasts for 1 to 3 weeks and is very useful in fresh or dried arrangements. Cut when the blooms are almost fully open; the buds do not open after being cut. Place in cold water. Flower heads shrink considerably in drying, so gather plenty.

■ Vinca flowers last for 3 to 5 days; buds continue to open for a week. Cut when 2 or 3 flowers are open on each stem. Split the stems and place them in cold water. Remove extra leaves and spent flowers.

■ Violets last for 4 to 7 days. Cut when the blooms are almost fully open; the buds do not open after being cut. Submerge in cold water for 1 hour; keep pushing down gently. Remove carefully, then place the stems in cold water. Wrap loosely in waxed paper until you want the fragrance to escape.

■ Yarrow lasts for 3 to 15 days. For fresh flowers, cut when more than half the blooms are open. Condition in cold water to which salt has been added (2 tablespoons of salt per quart of cold water). For dried flowers, cut when fully open; hang to dry.

*Originally carried by nobility to shield themselves from the stink of the streets, nosegays became favorites for many occasions, including weddings.*

method can be used in dried or fresh arrangements, because water will not permeate the stems.

Glycerin is available in drugstores (but only in small, costly amounts) and chemical supply companies (for a quart or larger amounts).

## OTHER FRESH AND DRIED DECORATIONS

Nosegays and door decorations such as swags, wreaths, and garlands are just some of the arrangements that can be made with fresh and dried herbs. You can also use herbs to scent candles and stationery.

### Nosegay

These clusters of flowers and foliage, also known as tussie-mussies, became popular in the sixteenth century for their aromatic and supposed disinfectant properties; they were carried by both men and women. They soon became a way of sending hidden messages using the language of herbs (see page 164). Still among the most popular forms of bridal flowers, they can be carried or used as table decorations.

To make a nosegay, gather herb flowers and leaves as you would for any fresh arrangement. Start with a central flower, which should stand just a bit taller than each surrounding circle. Encircle the first bloom with contrasting flowers and leaves. Continue until the desired diameter is reached.

Enclose the outer edge of the cluster with large leaves, such as those of lady's-mantle, ivy, scented geranium, or violets, or with loops of grasses. At one time lace surroundings were popular. You can use paper doilies, or purchase sturdier plastic ones that have handles and hold a porous material that keeps the flowers fresh.

Unless you are using such a handle, bind the stems and wrap them

be reused indefinitely. It is available at craft shops, garden shops, and well-stocked hardware stores.

Combination drying mediums use 1 part sand to 2 parts borax, cornmeal, or silica gel. Flowers dried in this medium will take a bit longer than with silica gel and will not look as perfect.

Glycerin and water (1 part glycerin to 2 parts water) is excellent for drying foliage. The glycerin changes the flower color to varying degrees and enhances autumn colors. The resulting foliage lasts indefinitely and is more pliable than fresh. Plant material dried by this

with florist tape (and ribbon if they are to be carried). If the cluster is to be used as a table decoration, wrap it tightly enough to hold the stems in place but not so tight as to prevent them from taking up water. Most nosegays will stay fresh for a week in water.

To dry nosegays for keeping, hang them in a dark, warm place. Or start with dried flowers and foliage such as those mentioned below. To preserve the scents longer, sprinkle the dried arrangement with a little orrisroot or other potpourri fixative and add a few drops of essential oil.

## Door Decorations

A swag, wreath, or garland on your door is a festive holiday decoration. With minor changes these decorations can be a welcoming addition in any season.

**Swag** A swag is the easiest door decoration to make. You will need 24-gauge florist wire, which is strong enough to hold the swag but flexible enough to be wound easily. It comes in short lengths or in spools, called paddle wire; coated with green plastic, it is rust resistant and inconspicuous.

*Swags can be made in almost any shape, and from a variety of materials. The one under construction here is made of fresh bay; it will dry on the swag and can be picked whenever a leaf is needed for the soup pot.*

## HERBS FOR DOOR DECORATIONS

These fresh and dried herbs can be used to make door swags and wreaths, which can be adorned with any of the suggested decorative accents.

**Fresh Foliage**
Artemisia 'Silver King'
Boxwood
Fennel
Germander
Horehound
Juniper, with berries
Lavender
Myrtle
Oregano
Rosemary
Santolina
Southernwood

Tansy
Thyme
Wormwood
Yarrow

**Dried Foliage**
Basil
Bergamot
Burnet
Catnip
Comfrey
Coriander
Costmary
Lemon balm

Mint
Tansy

**Decorative Accents**
Chiles
Dried flowers
Pinecones
Seed heads
Seedpods, such as
 Chinese-lantern or
 milkweed
Spice bags
Whole cinnamon sticks
Whole nutmeg

A mixture of several kinds of herbs makes an interesting swag, but it's possible to use all one kind as well. Fresh herbs are more pliable and less fragile than dried; once in place the fresh herbs will dry and hold their fragrance for weeks. Some of the best choices for fresh and dried foliage are listed on page 161.

Gather the branches into an oblong, asymmetrical diamond shape. Grasp them near the top, with most of the branches hanging down. Turn a few short branches upright to cover the stems of the others, then tie them together firmly with wire. Leave enough wire to make a loop on the back for hanging.

Once the basic outline is established, you can add decorations. See page 161 for suggestions.

For a bow, use at least 3 yards of ribbon, preferably weatherproof for outdoor use. It comes in an array of colors, patterns, and textures. Tighten the center of the bow with wire, then fasten it to the base.

To attach pinecones, wind a circle of wire around each cone near its base (the wire will work its way in as it's tightened), then insert the ends into the swag in the desired position. Or attach several cones or pods together with wires of the desired length, and add them to the base of the swag.

Make indoor swags in any shape that is pleasing or that fits your decor: heart shapes, half circles, fans, or fancy curves. Good sources of ideas are craft shows, craft shops, or catalogs. Have fun experimenting.

It may be more practical to hang the swag beside the door rather than on it, where it could swing when the door opens and closes. A single nail is sufficient; winding the wire tightly around it is the best way to keep the swag secure.

**Wreath**   To make a wreath you will need 24-gauge florist wire (see above) and some type of frame. A wide variety of frames made of Styrofoam, straw, and wire is available in craft shops.

Or you can make a frame from natural materials. Cut long branches of privet pruned from the base of the shrub and put them in water to become more supple, then wind them around and intertwine the smallest end to form a firm circle. A mature grape vine can easily be pruned enough to provide vines for weaving a fine circle, decorative enough in itself to need very few additions.

To decorate the frame for a traditional wreath, begin adding small clusters of dried or fresh herbs and securing them with wire; wind the wire around the frame, adding a new cluster every few inches. Turn the clusters to the sides or top as needed for a full and rounded effect.

Herbal wreaths are decorative indoors as well as out. Hang them on doors, in windows where the light can filter through, or on walls. Use them on tabletops to encircle the base of a candle or serving dishes and punch bowls. To store a wreath for another season, spray with hair spray to help preserve it.

A living wreath of culinary herbs can hang in a sunny spot near the kitchen stove and yield snips to use in cooking all year long. Or it can be used as a centerpiece on the kitchen or dining table.

To give a living wreath for a holiday gift, start making it in fall before the first frost. For each wreath, twist a length of chicken wire into a tube, then form the tube into a circle. Use thin wire or heavy thread to hold the shape. Or use a wire florist frame. Wear gloves while you fill the frame with damp sphagnum moss, taking care not to pack it too tightly.

Take herb cuttings and treat them with rooting hormone. Insert them into the moss-filled tube, with the stems aligned in the same direction. Thyme, sage, and rosemary work well.

Keep the finished wreath flat under fluorescent growing lights or hang it in a sunny window. Mist it at least once daily (more often is better). Periodically take it down and soak the frame in water to which a weak dose of fertilizer has been added. Trim the growing tips of the plants to keep them compact. Once the plants are rooted and well established, the wreath is ready to be given as a gift; include instructions on watering and misting.

**Garland**  Long garlands are traditional favorites to decorate a stairway, mantle, or buffet table or to hang over a doorway or special picture.

To make a garland, cut a long piece of wire or heavy cord to

*A wreath is more substantial than a swag, being made on a rigid frame, but the method of construction is much the same. Search your yard and garden for interesting additions, such as seedpods.*

## THE LANGUAGE OF HERBS

Over the centuries, herbs have been used to convey symbolic meanings. An herb sprig in a gift bow can convey your sentiments without words, although it is only fair to explain your intention if you aren't sure that the recipient will understand it. Here is a list of the language of herbs, and also the meaning of the color of flowers. You might refer to this list when assembling wedding bouquets.

| Common Name | Sentiment |
| --- | --- |
| Allspice | Compassion |
| Aloe | Healing, protection, affection |
| Ambrosia | Love returned |
| Angelica | Inspiration |
| Arbor vitae | Unchanging friendship |
| Bachelor's-button | Single blessedness |
| Basil | Good wishes |
| Bay | Glory |
| Bergamot | Compassion |
| Borage | Courage |
| Burnet | Mirth |
| Calendula | Joy |
| Caraway | Faithfulness |
| Carnation | Alas for my poor heart |
| Chamomile | Patience, humility |
| Chervil | Sincerity |
| Clover, red | Industry |
| Clover, white | Think of me |
| Cloves | Dignity |
| Coneflower | Justice |
| Coriander | Hidden worth |
| Daffodil | Regard |
| Daisy, white | Innocence |
| Dill | To lull |
| Dogwood | Durability |
| Fennel | Strength, worthy of praise |
| Geranium, oakleaf | True friendship |
| Goldenrod | Encouragement |
| Heliotrope | Eternal love, devotion |
| Hibiscus | Delicate beauty |
| Holly | Hope, foresight |
| Hollyhock | Ambition |
| Honeysuckle | Bonds of love |
| Horehound | Health |
| Hyssop | Sacrifice, cleanliness |
| Ivy | Friendship, continuity, marriage |
| Johnny-jump-up | Happy thoughts |
| Lady's-mantle | Comfort |
| Lamb's-ears | Surprise |
| Larkspur | Lightness, levity |

| Common Name | Sentiment |
| --- | --- |
| Lavender | Devotion, virtue |
| Lemon balm | Sympathy |
| Lemon-verbena | Enchantment |
| Mallow | Mildness |
| Marigold | Grief |
| Marjoram | Joy, happiness, blushes |
| Mint | Eternal refreshment, wisdom, warmth, virtue |
| Myrrh | Gladness |
| Myrtle | Love |
| Nasturtium | Patriotism |
| Oak | Strength |
| Parsley | Festivity |
| Peach blossom | I am your captive |
| Pine | Humility |
| Pinks | Bonds of affection |
| Poppy, red | Consolation |
| Rose | Love |
| Rosemary | Remembrance |
| Rue | Grace, clear vision |
| Sage | Wisdom, immortality, health, virtue |
| Salvia, blue | I think of you |
| Salvia, red | Forever mine |
| Savory | Spice, interest |
| Sorrel | Affection |
| Southernwood | Constancy, jest |
| Sweet cicely | Gladness |
| Sweet pea | Pleasure |
| Sweet woodruff | Humility, be cheerful |
| Tarragon | Lasting interest |
| Thyme | Courage, strength |
| Valerian | Readiness, an accommodating disposition |
| Violet, purple | Loyalty, devotion |
| Violet, yellow | Rural happiness |
| Xeranthemum | Cheerfulness under adversity |
| Yarrow | Health |
| Zinnia | Thoughts of absent friends |

| Color | Sentiment |
| --- | --- |
| Blue | Peace, sleep |
| Brown | Home |
| Green | Prosperity, luck, beauty, youth |
| Orange | Success |
| Pink | Love, fidelity, friendship |
| Purple | Power |
| Red | Strength, courage |
| White | Protection, peace, happiness |
| Yellow | Wisdom |

the desired length. Begin with a base of herb foliage, added a cluster at a time, just as if you were making a wreath (see page 162). Clusters of flowers, berries, or other herbs of various colors and forms can be woven in as you work for an overall effect, or added afterward as accents.

## Gift Bow

Sprigs of herbs make attractive additions to gift bows. Choose herbs that hold their shape and scent and wilt gracefully, such as juniper with its berries, boxwood, germander, curryplant, artemisia, and rosemary.

Cut generous stems and place them in water for several hours or overnight. Remove them from the water at the last minute, blot the stems, and dry them with a paper or cloth towel. Cut sprigs just a bit longer than the width of the bow, and insert the sprigs through the center of the bow.

## Pressed Arrangement

Herbs can be pressed and used to decorate stationery or to make pictures for framing. Collect the finest specimens from your garden, then arrange them between waxed paper, paper towels, or blotting paper. Then press them between the pages of a heavy book. Let dry for at least three weeks. When you are ready to make the pressed arrangement, assemble the plant material, stationery or background paper, tweezers, and white glue or rubber cement.

Lay out a pleasing arrangement. Push tiny drops of the glue or rubber cement beneath the leaves, stems, or petals to hold them in place. Press until dry. If the arrangement is to be framed, place it directly under glass or cover it with clear, self-adhesive vinyl contact paper.

## Scented Stationery

You can scent a box of ordinary stationery or notepaper with sachets filled with dried herbs or blotting paper scented with essential oil.

To make a sachet, cut a flat fabric packet to fit the box of stationery, and fill the packet with dried herbs such as lavender or any kind of potpourri.

To scent blotting paper, cut a piece of it and a piece of shirt cardboard to fit the box. Spread a few drops of essential oil on the blotting paper, then cover it with a few layers of cheesecloth (to allow the fragrance to come through but prevent staining the paper). Cover this with a porous print fabric and glue the edges to the back of the cardboard. Place this in the box, replace the stationery, and cover the box. Wait a week or more before using the stationery.

## HERB CANDLES

Burning scented candles fills a room with fragrance. Making them is an easy and pleasant project, ideal to do with children.

Molds can be any container that will hold hot wax, such as salad molds, cupcake pans, glasses, milk or yogurt cartons, or cardboard tubes. Paraffin, beeswax, or even pieces of leftover candles can be mixed in any proportions. Wax crayons will do for color, and string can be used for a wick (although candle wicking, available in various thicknesses at candle-making supply shops, burns better and longer).

Alternatively, you could purchase a candle-making kit, so that the only materials you will have to supply are the herbs. From craft or candle-making shops you can also buy molds in many shapes, including intricate flowers or fruits. Made

of rubber, the molds peel away from the finished candles. Shops also sell beeswax and stearin; the latter makes paraffin candles stronger and less inclined to drip (use 1 part stearin to 9 parts paraffin). The shops also sell dye disks and special oils for candles that will distribute more evenly through the wax than essential oils.

Herbs that can be used in candles include costmary, germander, hyssop, bergamot, lavender flowers, lemon thyme, mint, and rosemary.

*Herbs can be incorporated into homemade candles in a variety of ways—as scent from essential oils or infusions of fresh herbs, as decoration within or on the outside of the candles, or even as the wax itself.*

For a mild fragrance, use up to 1 cup of dried herbs or 2 cups of fresh herbs for each pound of wax.

The berries of bayberry and the leaves of bog myrtle (*Myrica gale*) contain small amounts of wax that can be mixed with other waxes to scent them. Release the wax by boiling the leaves or the berries in water for 15 minutes; let cool, then skim off the wax, remelt, and strain.

To make herb candles, spread newspapers over the work surface, assemble all the materials and herbs, and lubricate the molds with petroleum jelly or cooking oil.

If the mold has a hole in the top, pass the wick through it. Then tie the wick to a pencil or knitting needle and rest this on the rim of the mold with the knot in the center of the candle. Pull the wick taut to the bottom end or anchor it with commercially available sealing compound made for this purpose.

Measure the volume of the molds and melt only enough wax to fill them. As a rule, 12 ounces of paraffin or beeswax plus 1¼ ounces of stearin (see below) will make a total of 1½ cups of melted wax.

Place the wax in the top of a double boiler or in a container over a pan of water, and melt it on the stove over low heat. If you are using stearin, melt it in another double boiler.

**Caution** Wax is highly flammable. Never melt it directly over the heat or leave it unattended.

After the wax has melted, add the herbs. Leaves will give the candles a translucent green color. If you are using flowers, choose a dye disk or crayon to bring out the color. Add the color just before the herb bits. If you are using stearin, add the color to it, then add the colored stearin to the wax.

There are several ways to scent the candles. If you want the pieces of dried herbs and flowers to be part of the candle, stir them into the wax. (Some herbs will sink to the bottom of the candle; others will be evenly suspended.) If you don't want pieces of herbs in the candles, infuse the herbs, dried or fresh, in the wax for 45 minutes, then remove them. Beeswax has a sweet honey scent of its own that complements most herbs.

Stir the wax occasionally as it cools. When it reaches the consistency of almost-set gelatin, pour it into the mold. Reserve some to fill the hollow that will form in the center as the wax contracts. After 15 to 45 minutes, make a small hole in the surface near the wick and fill this with the additional hot wax. You may have to do this more than once. Candles with flat or sunken tops do not burn as well as those whose tops are mounded around the wick.

Allow the candle to set for at least five hours to harden thoroughly. Then remove the mold either by peeling it away or by running hot water over it to loosen the wax. Trim the wick to ½ inch. Polish the surface of the candle with an old nylon stocking or rub it with a cotton ball dipped in vegetable oil.

To decorate the outside of the candle, save a bit of wax, paint this on the back of a pressed herb sprig or flower, press the sprig onto the candle, and paint over the sprig with a little more wax to keep the sprig in place.

To clean the pans used for melting wax, carefully heat them, then pour the unused wax into a container that can be placed in the trash. Never pour hot wax down the drain. Add boiling water to the pan, scrub away any wax residue, and discard it along with the unused wax.

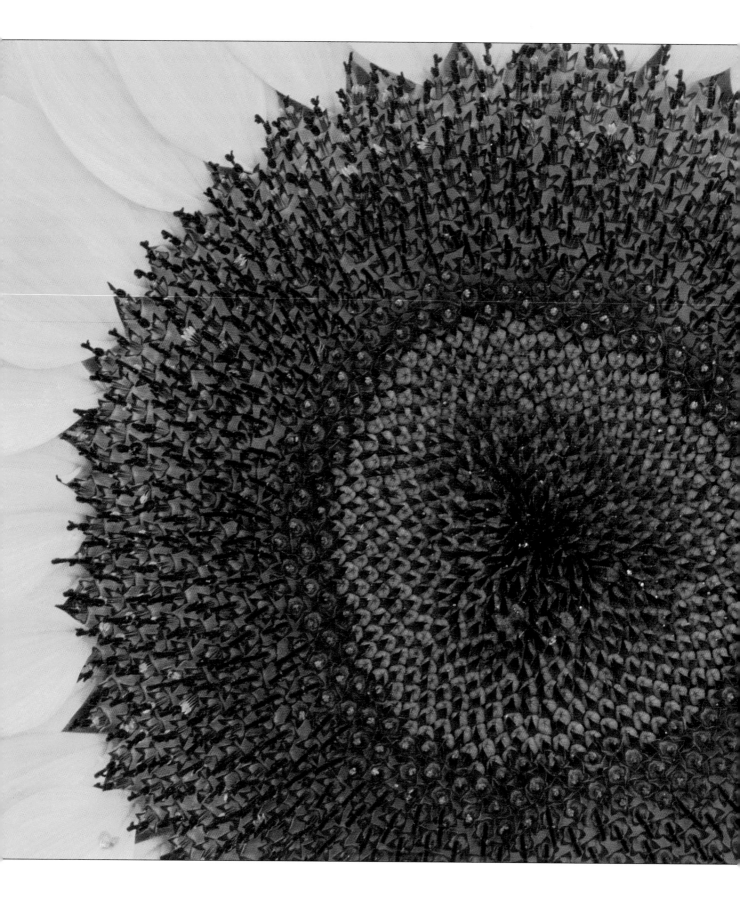

# ENCYCLOPEDIA OF HERBS

*Robust and gloriously yellow, sunflowers are a cheery presence in any garden. For the herb gardener, they offer a wealth of edible seeds (see page 273). This is 'Sun Bright'.*

This alphabetical list of herbs for many uses—culinary, medicinal, dyeing, ornamental, fragrance, cosmetics, and others—will help you identify the plant, grow it in your garden, and use it. Zones and growing requirements are given. The historical uses are also described for some herbs; in many cases their medicinal use has been discontinued for various reasons. In other cases extracts of the herb are used in modern medicine and cosmetic preparations.

## Agrimony, church-steeples
*Agrimonia eupatoria*
*ag-ri-MON-i-a*

■ Zones 3–8
Full sun to light shade
Dye, tea, ornamental

**How to identify**   Agrimony is a perennial of the rose family, wide growing and 3 to 5 feet tall with downy, compound dark green leaves. These vary from 3 inches long at the top to 7 to 8 inches at the bottom; pairs of small leaflets alternate along the stalk with pairs of larger saw-toothed leaflets about 1 to 1½ inches long. Spires of small yellow flowers, each with 5 egg-shaped petals, each petal notched at the end, bloom in July and August. The plant has a delicate apricot scent. It was once used to tan leather.

**How to use**   With its spikes of yellow flowers, agrimony is attractive in wildflower or rock gardens and is a bright spot in the herb garden. The leaves and flowers, fresh or dried, make a pleasant-tasting tea; they should be harvested just as blooming begins and hung upside down to dry.

Agrimony tea was held in high regard as a gargle, especially by singers and speakers who used it to refresh the throat before performances. It was also used to ease sore throats from colds or flu. Cold tea can be used for a lotion to clear the skin or added to a bath to soothe aching muscles and joints. As a dye agrimony yields a buff yellow early in the season, bright yellow toward fall.

**How to grow**   Agrimony is easily grown from seed, cuttings, or divisions; it thrives in dry soil. Plants should be set 7 to 9 inches apart; they will self-sow readily.

**Agrimony**

## Alexanders, horse-parsley, black-lovage

*Smyrnium olusatrum*
*SMIR-nee-um*

∎ Zones 5–10
Full sun to light shade
Culinary

**How to identify**   This celerylike member of the carrot family can be biennial or perennial. It grows 3 to 4 feet high and 2 feet wide with glossy dark green leaves and clusters of greenish yellow flowers.
At one time it was a major culinary and medicinal herb, but today, particularly in North America, it is almost a forgotten plant. It is better known in Europe; it stands erect on sea cliffs in the fiercest gales on the Irish coast, where it blooms in April and May.

**How to use**   All parts are edible, but the tender stems and leaves are preferable. The outer leaves can be used like celery when they are a foot tall. Blanching the stems makes them taste bitter, but they can be eaten raw or added to salads. Leaves, roots, and shoots may also be eaten like asparagus.

**How to grow**   Alexanders can be started from seed sown directly in the garden in early fall where winters are mild, early spring elsewhere. It needs some cold and 2 weeks to germinate. The plant prefers cool weather, moist soil, and frequent feeding and watering. The first winter in cool climates, it should be covered with leaves about a month before fall frost.

## Alkanet, bugloss

*Anchusa officinalis*
*an-CHEWS-a*

∎ Zones 6–10
Full sun to part shade
Dye, ornamental, culinary

**How to identify**   This relative of borage has rough, lancelike dark

Alkanet

green leaves and clusters of deep blue, violet, or purple flowers from May to August. It is small and bushy, growing about 1 to 1½ feet high and wide. It does not do well in Florida or along the Gulf Coast.

**How to use**   These neat, long-flowering plants are an attractive addition to any garden. The flowers, which taste like cucumber, are used to float on and flavor fruit drinks, wine punches, and fruit cups. The roots produce an indelible red dye.

**How to grow**   Alkanet can be started from seed or root divisions in spring, from root cuttings in fall. Seedlings should be thinned to 12 inches apart; they take a year to reach maturity. Root cuttings are started by planting 2-inch lengths of root about 1 inch deep in good potting soil, then setting the pots in a cold frame over the winter. Cutting back the faded flowers encourages more bloom. The plants should be mulched lightly in late fall to avoid frost heaving.

### Aloe, burn plant, bitter aloe
*Aloe vera*
*AL-oh or AL-oh-ee*

▮ Zones 9–10
Partial shade to full sun
First aid, cosmetic, ornamental

**How to identify**   This member of the lily family is one of the most useful and soothing of all plants—a blooming first-aid kit. Aloe has a rosette of thick, succulent, strap-like green or gray-green leaves, the gel from which can ease anything from a burn to a mosquito bite to diaper rash. The leaves are often dappled with gray or white; the leaves of some varieties have spiny edges. In California plants become large bushes 4 feet wide and tall. Other places they stay low and spread along the ground, sometimes sending up single or branched stalks of tubular yellow to orange-red flowers.

**How to use**   This plant grows well indoors on a sunny windowsill, so it is easy to pinch off a piece of leaf whenever needed. The cut end oozes a gel; applied liberally and quickly it will take away much of the pain and irritation of burns, insect bites, and abrasions. Aloe is also used in many lotions to preserve skin tone.

Aloe grows well in almost any garden soil. It is attractive in dry or natural areas of the xeriscape, charming among shrubbery or rocks, an interesting textural contrast in flower or herb gardens. It is also attractive against a wall, especially with Spanish or modern architecture.

**How to grow**   Aloe is practically a no-fail plant. The only ways to kill it are to move it from indoors to bright sun too quickly or to expose it to temperatures below 41° F. In hot climates and when first moving it outdoors, some shade should be provided. It is easily started from root division or offshoots; a single plant will yield a dozen or more yearly. Aloe requires little water yet does not rot easily if located with more thirsty plants. Leaves may

**Left and right:
Aloe**

spot if water falls on them when they are exposed to the sun. The leaves heal over as pieces are broken off; the resulting brown tissue can later be removed. Using the same few leaves helps preserve the beauty of the plant.

## Ambrosia, feather-geranium, Jerusalem-oak
*Chenopodium botrys*
*chen-o-POD-ee-um*

■ Zones 3–10
Full sun to partial shade
Decoration, fragrance

**How to identify** This hardy annual has intensely aromatic foliage, and its flowers on arching stems are prized for dried flower arrangements and wreaths. The leaves are somewhat like those of oakleaf geranium—deeply cut, ½ inch to 2 inches long, dark green on top and reddish underneath. Plants grow 2 to 3 feet tall before the feathery sprays of petalless yellowish green flowers bend the stems into graceful plumes.

Two other Chenopodiums are grown as culinary plants. Good-King-Henry (*C. bonus-henricus*) is a perennial with arrow-shaped leaves; it grows 2 to 3 feet tall in zones 5–8 and prefers sun to partial shade. Goosefoot (*C. album*), or lamb's-quarters, has smooth grayish leaves shaped like a goose foot and is a common weed; it grows 1 to 3 feet tall in much of the country. Both forms are edible. Another form, Mexican ambrosia (*C. ambrosioides*), or wormseed, is made into a strong infusion and used to swab floors and porches to deter insects in tropical countries.

**How to use** Ambrosia and good-King-Henry are interesting plants for the flower, vegetable, or herb garden. The edible leaves can be used in salads and as greens when they are young and tender; the

Angelica

young shoots can be cooked like asparagus. Ambrosia flowers are used mostly in dried bouquets and wreaths. Used fresh, the flowers keep the water sweet. Ambrosia can also be used as a strewing herb and in potpourris.

**How to grow** If anything, ambrosia is too easy to grow and will send up volunteers all over the yard. If this seems a problem, the stems can be cut for drying when the knobby seed heads begin to form. Good-King-Henry can be started from seed or divisions and thinned to 12 inches. Until the plants are 3 years old, only a few leaves at a time should be cut.

## Angelica, archangel, wild-parsnip
*Angelica archangelica*
*an-GEL-i-ca*

■ Zones 3–8
Sun with afternoon shade
Fragrance, tea, flavoring

**How to identify** This moisture-loving biennial is a member of the Umbelliferae, or carrot, family and can grow 5 to 8 feet tall. Many tiny flowers, white or greenish in globe-shaped umbels up to 6 inches across, come the second year from May until fall and have a honey-like scent. Stout, hollow stems are purple at the base. In the garden angelica looks like a giant celery or parsnip plant. Dark green leaves are compound, oval, and toothed, with a fragrance faintly like licorice, a bit like celery. Small, oblong fruit capsules each contain 2 winged yellow seeds. The roots and seeds are used commercially to flavor such liqueurs as Benedictine®; the roots flavor gin and vermouth.

**How to use**  Stems and roots are good raw or in herb butter. Stems can be cooked like asparagus or mixed with rhubarb to sweeten and complement the flavor. Candied

**Anise**

stems are a delicacy often used to decorate desserts. Leaves can be added to salads, soups, or stews or used as a garnish. Dried leaves, seeds, or ground roots are good in breads, cookies, and other baked goods. Steeped dried leaves make a relaxing tea. Angelica can be toxic in large doses.

Angelica leaves used in the bath are said to calm the nerves. The leaves add a pleasant scent to herb pillows. As a dye, angelica mordanted with iron turns wool green.

**How to grow**  Angelica should not be gathered in the wild unless its identity is certain. Poisonous water hemlock looks similar and grows in the same habitat. Angelica is striking but can dominate the garden; it should be put at the very back. It is best to start plants from fresh or refrigerated seed indoors in early spring or outside in late summer. The seeds should be barely covered; they need light to germinate. Plants should be set at least 3 feet apart in final beds by the second spring. They may last several years if all umbels are cut off before they bloom. Potential problems include aphids and red spider mites, especially on the seed heads, and crown rot in wet weather.

### Anise, anise seed
*Pimpinella anisum*
*pim-pi-NEL-a*

▌Zones 3–10
Full sun
Culinary, sachets, mouth freshener

**How to identify**  An annual herb of the carrot family, anise blooms in summer with yellow flowers much like Queen-Anne's-lace. The leaves have long stalks. The lower leaves are bright green and round to heart shaped and toothed; the upper ones are feathery. Seeds are flattened, oval, and ½ inch long with a lengthwise rib. Anise grows 2 feet tall with spindly growth that needs wind protection. The Romans grew anise for flavor, fragrance, and medicine; it was so valued that it was one of the herbs used to pay taxes.

**How to use**   Related to licorice, anise is used for its seed, which adds flavor to eggs, stewed fruit, cheese, spinach, carrots, and cookies. Arabic, Greek, East Indian, and many other cultures use it extensively in cooking. It combines well with cinnamon and bay and complements duck, pork, fish, and game. Fresh leaves are good in salads or as a garnish; dried leaves make a tea that aids digestion. Seeds steeped in warm milk make a soothing bedtime drink. Commercially, anise is used to flavor many liqueurs.

Pliny, a Roman naturalist who wrote about plants in the first century, recommended chewing anise seed to sweeten the mouth in the morning, which he believed helped one look young. Today, anise is used as an ingredient in toothpaste, mouthwash, soap, and perfume. Crushed seeds add fragrance to a sachet.

**How to grow**   Anise grows best from seed in soil that is at least 70° F. Seed should be sown in the permanent location in late spring, thickly enough so that the plants can help support each other. Where summers are short, seed should be started indoors.

Individual plants do not produce much seed. Seed is harvested by cutting the seed heads after they are ripe but before they open; the seed head should be inserted into a bag to catch the seeds as they scatter. The seeds should be allowed to dry completely, then stored in airtight containers.

## Anise-hyssop, giant-blue-hyssop, fragrant-giant-hyssop
*Agastache foeniculum*
*a-GAS-ta-she*

▌Zones 4–9
Sun with afternoon shade
Ornamental, cut flower, tea, garnish

**How to identify**   This sun-loving ornamental is perennial from zone 7 south, annual elsewhere. It grows 20 inches to 5 feet tall, and its many flower spikes bloom in shades of blue, yellow, red, pink, or white from midsummer to fall. The fragrance of the foliage varies with the color and ranges from peppermint and spearmint to anise and licorice. Leaves, seeds, and blooms look similar to those of its mint cousins.

**Anise-hyssop**

**How to use** This fine addition to the flower garden is excellent for color and for cut flowers and dried arrangements. Bees, birds, and butterflies are attracted to it. Leaves and flowers can be used in fruit salads and for teas and other drinks. The tea is used in China as a mouthwash and hangover remedy. The dried leaves, seeds, and flowers can be added to sachets and potpourris for filler and fragrance.

**How to grow** Seed should be started early indoors and transplanted after all danger of frost is past, or old clumps can be divided; plants are not wide spreading. Anise-hyssop self-seeds freely. Plants should be set 1 to 2 feet apart in fertile, well-drained soil; they should be fed and watered as needed to maintain good foliage color.

### Arnica, mountain-tobacco, mountain-daisy

*Arnica montana*
AR-ne-ca

▌Zones 2–8
Full sun to light shade
Tincture for external use only

**How to identify** A perennial of the daisy family, arnica is native to mountainous regions of Europe and Siberia and has naturalized in some parts of North America. It has round stems and toothed, entire, opposite bright green leaves, slightly hairy on the upper side and attached directly to the stem. Flower stalks bear 1 to 3 fragrant white or yellow-orange daisylike blooms 2 to 3 inches across. The plant grows to 2 feet tall with a lanky habit.

The helenalin in this plant may cause a rash on sensitive people, who should avoid all contact. Although the plant today is considered poisonous if taken internally, it has been one of the best-known and most popular healing herbs since the Middle Ages.

**How to use** A bright-blooming flower, arnica is lovely where it grows wild in some mountainous areas. All parts are used for an ointment that is famous for healing sprains and bruises, reducing pain and swelling, and relaxing the muscles. A homemade salve can be made by heating an equal weight of flowers and vegetable oil for several hours, then straining and cooling before applying. Owners of fine racehorses use arnica salve extensively for bruised legs, but it should be used with care on humans, and never on broken skin.

Flowers should be gathered in July and dried quickly; leaves can be harvested before or after flowering. Roots can be gathered in fall by lifting the plant, then resetting the remainder.

**How to grow** Arnica can be started from seed, cuttings, or divisions and planted in well-drained but moist soil, preferably acid.

### Artemisia, southernwood, sagebrush, mugwort, wormwood

*Artemisia* species
ar-te-MEEZ-ee-ah

▌Zones 4–9
Full sun
Ornamental, moth guard, crafts, dried bouquets

**How to identify** Most artemisias are perennials of the daisy family. Finely cut, lacy silver foliage varies with cultivars. So does the height—from dwarf to 5 feet tall. Flowers are yellow and inconspicuous in August. Wormwood (*A. absinthium*), a spreading perennial, yields armloads of branches for cutting. A choice cultivar is the 4-foot-tall 'Lambrook Silver'. *A. ludoviciana* 'Silver King' is taller. Landscapers often use the low-growing *A. schmidtiana* 'Silver Mound'. The only annual form, sweet wormwood (*A. annua*), has feathery green foliage, almost like asparagus, and a Christmas tree form. It grows tall and makes an attractive filler at the back of the garden. It turns golden brown in fall, has a long-lasting aroma, and is used to make wreath bases. The sagebrush of the western states is *Seriphidium tridentatum*, formerly *A. tridentata*; an oil from it is used to make scented candles and soaps.

**How to use**  Its feathery texture and downy foliage make artemisia a fine landscape shrub or background for brighter flowers. The odor is said to repel bees. The tall, robust, silver-backed, green-leaved mugwort, *A. vulgaris*, is heavily aromatic and is the only culinary artemisia. It is often added to German dishes.

All artemisias dry well for wreaths, crafts, and bouquets. Leaves are aromatic and soothing for the bath and discourage moths in closets. A decoction of southernwood (*A. abrotanum*) and barley is an effective wash for acne. Artemisias make a yellow dye for wool.

**How to grow**  All artemisias are easy to grow from seed or plants, usually self-sow, and transplant easily. Some spread from roots and can become invasive.

**Arugula, rocket**
*Eruca vesicaria*
e-RU-ca

▌Zones 9–10
Full sun to light shade
Culinary

**How to identify**  This mustard cousin has deeply cut dark green leaves growing in a basal rosette. The leaves taste peppery but not bitter. This is not the same plant as sweet rocket (*Hesperis matronalis*), although the young leaves of this plant are edible.

**Artemesia schmidtiana**

**Arugula**

**How to use**   The tender, young fresh leaves of arugula add zest to a salad. Arugula can also be cooked with other greens, chopped on potatoes, or mixed in marinades, sauces, or pastas.

**How to grow**   The seed of this cool-season annual should be sown outdoors as early as the ground can be worked. It germinates in 4 to 6 days and grows to maturity in 45 to 60 days, but harvest can begin as soon as the leaves are 4 inches long and can continue for weeks if the plants are kept cut. They will bolt in hot weather and the leaves then become bitter. As far north as Connecticut it can be sown in fall for a late harvest up to Thanksgiving. All but protected plants will freeze at 25° F.

**Basil 'Genovese'**

## Basil, common basil, sweet basil

*Ocimum* species
*OS-i-mum*

▌Annual
Full sun
Culinary, ornamental, cosmetic

**How to identify**   A tender, tropical plant of the mint family, basil is one of the most important culinary herbs. The fragrant, opposite, oval leaves are up to 3 inches long and can vary in scent from lemon to cinnamon to licorice, in color from bright green to deep red-purple, in form from glossy to velvety, from ruffled to smooth edged, and in width from 3 inches for the lettuce leaf basil to less than 1 inch in the dwarf purple bush variety. Leaf and stem surfaces are dotted with tiny oil glands that release fragrance if touched or even moved by a breeze. Flowers are tiny and white or purplish and are borne in whorls of six on mintlike spikes. Plants are bushy and grow 1 to 3 feet tall.

**How to use**   The plants are attractive in herb or flower gardens or in containers, especially the purple-leaved forms or the cinnamon basil with its light lavender flowers enclosed in dark purple bracts. Basil is one of the main ingredients in pesto, tomato sauce, Italian and Thai cooking, vinegar, and salads; it is used as a garnish and as a flavoring for veal, lamb, fish, poultry, pasta, cheese, vegetables, and eggs. It combines well with lemon, garlic, and thyme. A mint, it is considered good for digestion.

Rinsing the hair with a basil infusion adds luster, and basil is widely used in cosmetics. Dried leaves add fragrance in sachets and potpourris.

**How to grow**   Basil is easy to grow from seed started indoors, or outdoors after the last frost; it will not germinate in cold ground. It can also be grown from cuttings. It prefers fertile soil and mulch. Frequent use will keep it trimmed and bushy. Leaves cut before the flowers open provide the best flavor. Plants can be brought indoors before winter and kept on a sunny windowsill.

## Bay, sweet-laurel, bay-laurel
*Laurus nobilis*
*LAR-us*

▮ Zones 7–10
Full sun to afternoon shade
Ornamental, culinary, herbal arts, dye

**How to identify**   This is a semi-hardy evergreen tree appropriate for container culture. It has shiny gray bark and alternate, glossy dark green leaves up to 3 inches long and 1 inch wide. Small clusters of greenish yellow blooms are tucked tightly into the leaf axils in spring. The fruit is a dark purple to black one-seeded berry, ½ to 1 inch long; it attracts birds. Bay may grow 10 feet tall in the southern United States, up to 60 feet in its native Mediterranean habitat. It provides the laurel leaves that were worn by the Greeks and Romans as a symbol of reward and glory.

Bay should not be confused with the sweetbay of the South, which is *Magnolia virginiana*, nor with the native redbay (*Persea borbonia*), nor the California bay (*Umbellularia californica*). These 3 trees are sometimes used as substitutes. Sweetbay is not as aromatic as true bay, the flavor of which is closest to redbay. California bay tastes stronger and somewhat gamey. Bayberry (*Myrica pensylvanica*) is an altogether different plant.

**How to use**   Bay makes a lovely, valuable small tree where it is hardy. It can be easily pruned for a formal shape, a clipped hedge,

Top and bottom: Bay

or a topiary design. If grown in a container, it can be placed on a sunny patio or porch in summer.

Young leaves have the most flavor. With a bay wreath on the wall, cooks can pluck off leaves as needed to enhance fish, game, soup, stew, tomato sauce, or a Spanish, Creole, or French dish. Commercially the essential oil is used in many meats, sausages, canned soups, and baked goods.

Bay leaves dry nicely although to a lighter color. They can be used fresh or dried in wreaths, added to bath bags or lotions, or put into a canister of flour or rice or used in the dog's bed to repel insects. Bay is thought to help digestion, rheumatism, and aching muscles and joints. It contains eugenol, which can have narcotic effects, and the oil may cause a rash in some people. Prunings add fragrance to a wood fire. Bay leaves make a pale green dye.

**How to grow**   This plant is difficult to start from seed or cuttings.

Green shoots cut in fall have the best success rate but still take 6 to 9 months to root, so buying plants from a nursery is recommended. Bay grows slowly but steadily. Container plants can be placed in a cool, sunny spot in winter; humidity can be added by misting the leaves or placing the pot on a tray of wet stones, although watering should not be frequent. Plants should not be fed until spring. Terminal buds should be pinched in spring to force lateral branching. Plants should be watched for scale infestation.

### Bayberry, bog myrtle, wax myrtle, sweetgale

*Myrica* species
*my-RI-kah*

▮ Zones 2–10
Full sun to partial shade
Ornamental, crafts

**How to identify**   Bayberry is an evergreen shrub or tree, except for the semievergreen northern *M. pensylvanica.* Of the 50 species, some will grow 30 feet, but most grow 9 to 12 feet tall. Large clumps

**Bayberry**

or thickets are found in moist woodlands and on the sandy shores of ponds and swamps. Grayish bark, waxy branchlets, and small, alternate, narrow, delicately toothed dark green leaves that are dotted with resin glands make them easy to recognize. The leaves give off a distinctive fragrance when crushed. The flowers grow on inconspicuous yellowish catkins, with male and female flowers separate and usually on separate plants, so two or more plants are needed for berry production. The female catkins are globular, the male more elongated. The berries are small, gray, and covered with an aromatic resin.

**How to use**   This broadleaf evergreen does well in poor, sandy soils and tolerates salt along the coast. It is a fine ornamental for the shrub border or for massing.

The early American settlers made candles from the fragrant berries even though it takes a large quantity of the tiny berries to make a usable amount of wax. Bayberry wax can also be combined with other wax. If the berries are boiled in water, the wax will float to the surface and can be skimmed off when it hardens.

Bayberry is also used in soaps and ointments. Henry David Thoreau used it to remove pine pitch from his hands. A bayberry tea was used for sore throats and nasal congestion, and poultices from the roots were considered effective in healing ulcers, cuts, bruises, and insect bites. An infusion of bark is astringent and recommended for lotions or baths. The berries dry well and are decorative in dried bouquets or wreaths.

**How to grow**   Seed can be started when it is fresh in moist, peaty soil with a pH of 5.0 to 6.0—fairly acid.

**Bayberry**

When transplanting, the seedlings should be cut back severely. Old, leggy shrubs can be renewed by cutting back to the ground.

### Bergamot, beebalm, oswego-tea, monarda
*Monarda didyma*
*moh-NAR-dah*

▌ Zones 4–9
Full sun to partial shade
Ornamental, teas, and potpourris

**How to identify**   This annual, biennial, or perennial is easy to grow except in very hot climates. It prefers moist soil; the wild form (*M. fistulosa*), with lavender flowers, is found in moist woods and along stream banks.

A member of the mint family, bergamot has characteristic square stems and also has a citruslike fragrance. Cultivars for the garden include brilliant scarlet, pink, violet, salmon, mahogany, or white. The flowers' unique shape comes from 2 tiers of asymmetrical, tubular blossoms arranged in a whorl around a button of bracts; flowers bloom for a long period in July and

**Bergamot 'Cambridge Scarlet'**

August. Leaves are opposite, ovate, textured, and dark green, 3 to 6 inches long. Fruit nutlets resemble seeds. Plants grow 3 to 4 feet tall. Native Americans introduced this plant to the colonists; it made a popular tea to replace the black tea taxed by the English. The Shakers used this plant medicinally. Horsemint (*M. punctata*) is a wild cousin that has whitish green blossoms with purple and pinkish bracts.

**How to use**   This is an attractive plant for the flower or woodland garden and ideal where you can see it visited by butterflies and hummingbirds, which prefer the forms with scarlet or deep red flowers. Bergamot adds a lemony orange flavor to fruits, salads, teas, and meat dishes. It can be used with mint. Wild species have a stronger flavor. The flower is attractive when added to apple jelly or fruit punch. Bergamot is also useful in potpourris, lotions, baths, herb wreaths, and dried or fresh arrangements. A sprig tucked in the brim of a garden hat or into the hair is said to help keep away mosquitoes and gnats.

**How to grow**   Bergamot spreads by underground runners, like mint, but not enough to be a nuisance. It takes a season to become established, needs ample water, and blooms best in sun. Plants set 2 feet apart will fill in. They should be mulched in cold winters to prevent heaving. Cutting back right after the first bloom is over may prompt a second bloom in early fall. Bergamot leaves for drying should be stripped from the stems.

## Bloodroot, redroot, Indian-paint

*Sanguinaria canadensis*
*san-guin-nar-EE-ah*

■ Zones 2–10
Full sun to partial shade
Ornamental, dye

**How to identify**   This lovely perennial wildflower is found in the woods and meadows and along wet banks, blooming in early spring with delicate, slightly cup-shaped white flowers 1 to 2 inches across with 7 to 16 whorled petals. The plant grows 6 to 14 inches tall. The yellow-green leaves are quite distinctive in texture, round to heart shaped and deeply lobed. Each flower is encased in a leaf as it unfolds; the leaves enlarge after bloom.

The root is an orange-red rhizome. The sap, also orange-red, which oozes forth wherever a leaf or flower is broken off this plant, was used by Native Americans both medicinally and for painting. It is caustic for either purpose and not recommended today.

**How to use**   This is a lovely little plant for wildflower or naturalized gardens or rock gardens or planted among ground covers under trees and shrubs that leaf out in late spring. A double-flowered cultivar, 'Flore Pleno' ('Multiplex'), blooms later and lasts much longer.

As a dye, bloodroot colors fabrics orange with no mordant, an attractive rust color with a mordant of alum or cream of tartar, or reddish pink if tin is used. The root should be used fresh in fall for dyeing.

**How to grow**   Bloodroot can be started from seed or from divisions of the rhizome in early fall. Plants should be set 6 to 8 inches apart in soil to which peat moss has been added. Bloodroot prefers rich, moist, acid soil. The double variety can be propagated only by division.

**Left: Bergamot
'Croftway Pink'
Right: Bloodroot**

### Borage, talewort, cool-tankard
*Borago officinalis*
*bor-RAY-go*

▮ Annual
Full sun to light shade
Culinary, ornamental, bee plant

**How to identify**   Blue buds in loose, drooping clusters open to reveal pink stars ½ inch in diameter, which continue from midsummer until frost. Like the flowers of its cousin anchusa, borage flowers turn blue as they mature. Leaves grow from a rosette and are hairy, oblong ovate, gray-green, and up to 6 inches long. The stems are hollow. The plant sprawls somewhat, growing 2 to 3 feet tall.

Ancient soldiers supposedly drank borage wine to calm their fears, give them courage, and lift their spirits. Borage has been known through the ages as an antidepressant, an herb of gladness, a comfort for sorrow, and a bringer of joy. Borage contains considerable potassium as nitrate of potash, which stimulates the adrenal glands.

**How to use**   Borage is a delight in an informal herb garden. It attracts bees and is said to be a good companion for strawberries. Older leaves can be coarse, so the plant should be placed accordingly, or a succession of young plants can be relied upon. Borage stems and fresh young leaves lend a crisp cucumber flavor to salads. They can be sautéed or steamed like spinach or added raw to drinks, pickles, salad dressings, and cream cheese, and to cheese, poultry, and vegetable dishes. The chopped leaves are good on cucumbers and in soups. The blossoms can be used in salads, as a garnish, candied, or spread over sliced tomatoes. Borage blends well with dill, mint, and garlic. The leaves make poultices that are cooling to skin irritations and swellings.

**Left and right: Borage**

**How to grow**   Borage grows easily and quickly from seed started indoors, or outdoors after all danger of frost is past. It needs rich soil and about 2 feet to spread. In most climates, once you have borage, you will have it forever, though it is not a nuisance. It is drought resistant and adaptable to poor soil.

## Boxwood, box, boxtree
*Buxus sempervirens*
*BUX-us*

▮ Zones 5–8
Full sun to light shade
Ornamental, woodworking

**How to identify**   Boxwood includes several evergreen shrubs with small, elliptical to round leaves up to an inch long; they are opposite, dark green on top and pale green underneath. Clusters of inconspicuous yellow-green flowers from April to June turn into horned green capsules of shiny black seeds. Boxwood makes large rounded mounds if left unclipped. It can withstand intense shearing and still look vigorous and green.

The American colonists brought plants from the Old World and used them for the tightly clipped lines of knot and ribbon gardens. Boxwood was once considered medicinal and used to treat epilepsy, leprosy, and toothaches, but it is considered of little use by pharmacologists today. The wood, however, is as highly prized now as it was when the plant was named for its use in making decorative boxes. The wood has also been used for making flutes and other musical instruments, chess pieces, and for fine inlay work.

**Caution**   The leaves of boxwood are poisonous and have caused animal deaths.

**How to use**   Dwarf forms of boxwood are almost indispensable for edging formal herb gardens. Their compact form also takes well to the

**Boxwood**

special shapes of topiary. Boxwood also comes in varieties that are weeping, pyramidal, with variegated leaves, or as small trees 20 feet tall in optimum conditions. The variety 'Suffruticosa' is one of the best to edge beds and formal gardens. Littleleaf boxwood (*B. microphylla*) grows less than 6 feet tall with smaller leaves. Korean boxwood (*B. microphylla* var. *koreana*) is the hardiest form of this species. *B. microphylla* 'Winter Green' is one of the best varieties for retaining the green color in winter.

**How to grow**   Boxwood is usually started from plants and may need some coddling until it becomes established. Once settled in, it takes minimal care. It grows in acid or alkaline soil but needs good drainage and fairly constant moisture. The root system is shallow, so that mulching is especially important, and any cultivation should be done with great care. Young plants should be protected from intense

sun the first summer and from drying winter winds. Spraying with an antitranspirant coating helps guard against moisture loss. Heavy snow that might bend down or break the branches should be swept off.

## Broom, dyer's broom, Irish or Scotch broom
*Cytisus scoparius*
*SIT-i-sus*

▮ Zones 5–8
Full sun
Ornamental, insecticidal, wildlife, dye

**How to identify**   This stiffly branched shrub grows to 10 feet and is often found in open woods and along sandy coastal areas and roadsides. It has spread like a weed in the Northwest. It blooms profusely as early as April and continuously through May and June with delicate but brilliant cascading pealike yellow flowers borne singly or in pairs along the branches. Hairy brown seedpods follow. The

**Broom**

small leaves are sparse, alternate, ¼ to ½ inch long, upper ones single, lower ones compound to 3 leaflets.

**How to use**   Broom can be used as accent plants, added to the shrub border, or grown on the edge of a woodland or on a bank for erosion control. As a legume, it adds nitrogen to the soil. It is a reliable bloomer and charming and graceful all year.

Broom was once used as a medicine but is considered unsafe today. The branches, once used for thatching, can be woven into baskets, or cut from the base of the plant, tied to a stick, and made into a serviceable broom. The plant tops can be used as a yellow dye for wool.

**How to grow**   Broom grows best in poor-to-average, slightly acid, well-drained soil. It is known as a dry soil plant and will thrive where many plants barely survive. It can be started from seed, grafts, or cuttings taken in August. The seed has a hard shell; it should be nicked, then soaked in boiling water for 3 hours before planting. It will still take 20 to 30 days to germinate. Broom should be transplanted carefully; it has a scant root system. Pruning after bloom keeps it full at the base. This broom has naturalized on the West Coast, and can become a pest there. Plant it cautiously along the coast of Northern California, Oregon, or Washington.

### Bugleweed, ajuga, carpenter's-herb, middle-comfrey

*Ajuga reptans*
a-JOO-ga

▮ Zones 3–10
Full sun to moderate shade
Ornamental, medicinal, dye

**How to identify**   This common ground cover, a member of the mint family, grows from rosettes of spoon-shaped, wavy-edged bronze

Top: Broom
Bottom: Bugleweed

**Bugleweed**

leaves. The plant spreads by creeping runners and blooms in spring with dark-blue-flowered spires less than a foot tall. The glossy leaves change color subtly with the season, remain nearly evergreen even in the North, and make a neat carpet all year long.

**How to use**  Bugleweed is an excellent ground cover for sun or shade, dry or moist soil. It spreads quickly and crowds out weeds. It is also good for edging walks. It should not be used in rock gardens, where it will crowd out its neighbors. Hybridized varieties are available in many shades and forms, from those with deep burgundy leaves to a velvety variegated form of green, white, and pink, and with deep blue, purple, red, or white blooms.

Bugleweed was once used to treat coughs, ulcers, rheumatism, and hangovers. Probably its most au-thentic cure was for healing cuts; the plant contains tannin, and plants with tannin are known to slow bleeding. The common name carpenter's-herb derives from this use. Bugleweed makes a black dye for wool.

**How to grow**  The plants should be set 6 to 12 inches apart. By the end of a single season there will be many more to transplant to new locations. With little care bugleweed gives rewarding results.

**Burnet, salad burnet, pimpinelle**
*Sanguisorba minor*
*san-gwi-SOR-ba*

▌Zones 3–10
Full sun to light shade
Culinary, landscaping, tea

**How to identify**  This neat, low-growing perennial, a member of the rose family, has gracefully arching stems of small, toothed, opposite leaves. Flower stems shoot up to 3 feet in May and June and have small pink to purple tufts of flowers. The lower ones are male, the middle rows have both stamen and pistil, and the upper rings are only female and not very showy. The flavor is that of both melon and cucumber, but cucumber predominates. A taller variety known as greater burnet (*S. canadensis*, or Canadian burnet), which grows up to 5 feet, has become naturalized in bogs, thickets, and roadsides in the Pacific Northwest to Alaska and in some eastern and central sections of North America.

**How to use**  Burnet grows well in large containers as long as it has 5 hours of sunlight a day. The plant is attractive in flower or herb gardens and makes a graceful edging. Tender young leaves add cucumber flavor to salads months before cucumbers are available. They also make delicious vinegars, marinades, herb butters, and beverages, and are attractive as a garnish. The leaves can be stripped from the stems and frozen; dried leaves do not have much flavor. Chewing burnet leaves is said to aid digestion. The seeds are good in vinegars, marinades, and cheese dishes, and for flavoring French dressing.

**How to grow**  Seed or root divisions can be planted in late fall or early spring in light, well-drained soil. Burnet is slow to germinate and become established, so there will not be a large harvest until the second year. Seedlings should be thinned to 12 inches apart; vigorous plants should be divided each year. Large plants do not transplant well. The plants can be trimmed back as needed to encourage tender new growth; leaves can be harvested until covered by the snow.

**Butterfly weed, pleurisy-root**
*Asclepias tuberosa*
as-KLEE-pee-as

▌Zones 2–10
Full sun
Ornamental, butterfly plant

**How to identify**  This perennial herb of the milkweed family grows wild in many areas. It reaches 3 feet tall and branches at the top.

Top: Burnet
Bottom: Butterfly weed

## Butterfly weed

The lance-shaped leaves are alternate, dark green on top, pale green underneath. Bright clusters of pumpkin orange flowers, 3 to 5 inches across, bloom from July to September. Then narrow seedpods mature and release silky milkweed hairs on the winds of autumn. The root is large, deep, and tuberous and allows the plant to withstand dry conditions. Unlike other members of this family, butterfly weed does not have milky sap.

**How to use**   This is an excellent ornamental plant for the back or middle of the flower border, mixed with shrubs in a foundation planting, or used in wildflower or cut-flower gardens. Swallowtail and monarch butterflies hover over its flowers throughout the summer. Blooms are bright, have long stems, and are long lasting in bouquets.

Native Americans and early settlers mixed the dried and powdered root of butterfly weed to make a paste to heal sores. They used a tea made from the root for respiratory problems, including pleurisy, whooping cough, and pneumonia. The shoots were cooked like asparagus, the flowers were made into a sugar, and the young pods were eaten. Butterfly weed is poisonous in large doses, however, and internal use is not recommended today. It is also considered a rare and protected plant in some states.

**How to grow**   Butterfly weed is easily started from stem and root cuttings, or fresh seed planted in fall. It germinates in 3 weeks at warm temperatures, but seedlings will not bloom until their third year. Plants should be set 10 to 12 inches apart; the spot should be marked, because the plant is late to come up in spring. Once started, the plant self-seeds readily. Full sun is essential. Butterfly weed is adaptable but does best in light, sandy, well-drained soil of medium fertility. The plants can be moved the first year; after that, transplanting is difficult because of the long taproot.

## Calendula, pot-marigold
*Calendula officinalis*
*kah-LEN-deu-lah*

∎ Annual
Full sun
Ornamental, culinary, dye

**How to identify**   Calendula, one of the brightest of the herb flowers, has large, flat, daisylike blooms 2 to 4 inches across with several rows of ray petals in brilliant shades of yellow and orange. The blooms close up at night. The long, narrow, alternate leaves are light green and have smooth to finely toothed edges and wide, rounded ends. Leaves and stems are covered with fine hairs

**Calendula**

and give off a distinctive odor when bruised. Dwarf varieties are available, but most grow to 18 inches.

**How to use**   Calendula is neat and colorful in the garden, and the flowers are lovely in fresh arrangements. They also dry well for winter bouquets or herbal wreaths. The flowers are edible and add color and mild flavor to salads, butters, teas, cheese, custards, sandwiches, liqueurs, stews, soups, and rice. At one time calendula was used so much in cooking that it was almost considered a vegetable, hence the common name pot-marigold. It was also used as a food color and a substitute for saffron. The petals can be dried by spreading them on paper so that they do not touch, and turning them frequently until crisp. They should be stored in an airtight container.

The ancient Romans believed that the flowers bloomed on the first day of every month, hence the name calendula. During the American Civil War and World War I, calendula was used to slow bleeding and speed healing of wounds. A calendula rinse brings highlights to blond and brown hair and makes a stimulating herbal bath. Calendula makes a yellow dye.

**How to grow**   Calendula grows easily in all but very hot or humid climates. Fresh seed can be sown indoors for earliest bloom or outdoors as soon as the ground can be worked; it germinates in 10 days at 50° to 60° F. In zones 8 to 10, the seed can be sown in fall. Seedlings should be spaced about 10 inches apart. Spent flowers should be removed. Overwatering may cause the roots to rot.

## Caraway
*Carum carvi*
*KAR-um*

▮ Zones 3–9
Full sun to light shade
Culinary

**How to identify**  This cousin of anise and dill is usually biennial with a basal rosette of finely cut, ferny leaves; it stands about 2 feet tall when in bloom. It looks a bit weedy in the garden, and several plants are needed to get much seed. Leaves die back in winter but return in spring. White or pink flower clusters usually bloom the second spring or early summer. The oblong seeds, pointed on the ends and with 5 distinct, pale ridges, ripen about a month later.

**Caraway**

**How to use**  The seeds are most often used in rye bread and with sauerkraut. They can also be added to baked goods or to German pork dishes or Hungarian stew, and are good with many vegetables, especially pickled ones. The seeds can become bitter with cooking, so they should be added in the last 15 minutes. Crushed seeds release more flavor. Crushed seeds steeped in milk or water are said to relieve indigestion. Chopped leaves can be used in tossed or fruit salads, and the long taproots can be cooked like parsnips.

**How to grow**  Caraway is easily started from seed or cuttings. Seed can be planted outdoors in early spring or fall. Like its carrot cousin, caraway doesn't mind cold, damp ground. It thrives best in fertile soil with constant moisture. It should be transplanted with the utmost care. Plants die out after going to seed but self-sow freely. Seed heads should be checked for aphids. Seeds suspected of harboring hidden insects can be scalded with boiling water before drying and eating. This also destroys the viability; seeds intended for planting should not be scalded.

## Cardamom
*Elettaria cardamomum*
*el-et-TAR-ee-a*

▮ Greenhouse plant
Partial shade
Culinary, fragrance

**How to identify**  Cardamom is a spice rather than an herb. This member of the ginger family grows 6 to 12 feet tall in the jungles of India and Guatemala, where rainfall can be 150 inches a year. The plant has ferny dark green leaves on simple canes that come from a thick rhizome. The flowers are small and white with yellow lips and hang in long clusters. Ribbed seedpods can be white, green, or black, and have 3 cells, each with 4 to 6 small light brown seeds.

**How to use**   The contents of each seedpod, up to 18 seeds, make only ¼ teaspoon when ground, and every seedpod must be snipped by hand, so it is no wonder that cardamom is one of the most costly spices, second only to saffron. The essential oil found in cardamom seed is a stimulant similar to ginger, but the oil is even more expensive and hard to find. The seeds taste like mild ginger with a touch of pine and can be used whole, shelled, or ground when green, or after roasting. Seeds keep their flavor best if they are stored in their pods until you're ready to use them.

Cardamom can be used in cakes, cookies, biscuits, breads, waffles, coffee or chocolate drinks, fruit punches, honey, and marinades or with legumes, vegetables, curries, or poultry. It is widely used in Arabic, East Indian, Scandinavian, and African cooking and is one of the main ingredients in *garam masala*, a mixture of Indian spices that is a bit sweeter and more fragrant than curry powder.

Chewing on cardamom seed relieves indigestion and sweetens the breath. The leaves can be used between linens and blankets, and the leaves or seeds can be added to a bath for an invigorating soak. Seeds can be added to potpourris. Clove-studded pomander balls can be rolled in ground cardamom for a rich and long-lasting fragrance.

**How to grow**   Plants are available from some herb nurseries. Cardamom can be grown outdoors in a container in a shady spot, then wintered over indoors and misted frequently to maintain maximum humidity. Plants start easily from root divisions or seed in spring.

**Cardamom**

## Catnip
*Nepeta cataria*
*NEP-e-tah*

▮ Zones 3–10
Full sun to light shade
Tea, cat toys, dye

**How to identify**   This perennial has grayish green leaves and grows to look like a small bush, up to 3 feet tall and wide. The leaves are opposite, about 2 inches long, ovate with a heart-shaped base and scalloped edge. Downy white fuzz covers leaves and the square stems characteristic of the mint family. The flowers—white and pale pink with purple dots inside the corollas—are fairly inconspicuous; the odor verges on rank.

**How to use**   *N. grandiflora* has strong spikes of lavender blue flowers and is an attractive border plant. *N. ×faassenii* (formerly *N. mussinii*), with lavender blue spires, is a 12-inch-tall edging plant that can be clipped.

Catnip has been used for centuries as a pleasant-tasting tea; pregnant women should refrain from using it. Leaves can be added to salads.

Plants came from Europe with the colonists and escaped into the countryside. If you have this plant growing on your property, your cat may identify it for you. Most catnip is grown for cats' delight, either fresh in the garden or dried in cat toys. Cats may chew on the leaves, which releases the aroma. Goldfinches eat the dried seed well into winter. The entire plant can be used for a soft yellow to gold dye.

**How to grow**   Catnip is so easy to grow that it can become a weed. It can be started easily from cuttings, layering, divisions, or transplanting. It has the most aroma when grown in full sun, larger and more tender leaves in partial shade. The branches can be cut all summer after the flower buds form.

## Chamomile, Roman chamomile, English chamomile
*Chamaemelum nobile*
(formerly *Anthemis nobilis*)
*kam-e-MEL-um*

∎ Zones 3–9
Full sun to partial shade
Tea, fragrant ground cover

**How to identify**   This fragrant perennial is a member of the daisy family, of Peter Rabbit stories, and of English lawns. Ferny gray-green to bright green foliage stays low until bloom, then grows to 1 foot and is covered with single white daisies with a fresh apple scent in late spring through summer (the name comes from Greek roots that mean "groundapple"). In many places, however, the plants will freeze in winter and weeds will take their place in the lawn. The milder German, or sweet false-chamomile (*Matricaria recutita*), an annual, grows 2 to 3 feet tall, has a sweeter fragrance, and has a hollow in the center of the yellow disk flowers. True chamomile is preferred for tea. A wild form (*Anthemis cotula*), known as stinking chamomile, mayweed, or dogfennel, has an unpleasant odor and flavor.

**How to use**   Chamomile can be planted between stepping-stones or as a lawn substitute where the

**Chamomile**

ground does not freeze hard for long periods. *Anthemis tinctoria*, or dyer's chamomile, has bright yellow daisylike flowers that are lovely in the border or for cutting. The flowers yield a yellow dye. Chamomile is favored as a companion plant, especially for onions and cucumbers.

Blossoms can be dried for teas. Chamomile is useful as a fragrant strewing herb, in potpourris, in hair rinses and perfumes, and as a soothing bath. People allergic to ragweed should approach chamomile tea or flowers with caution.

**How to grow**   Chamomile is easy to grow from seed sown in spring or from divisions or offshoots. Creeping stems root as they grow; the plant particularly favors moist areas. It will die out where summers are very hot or winters are very cold. Shade in the South and mulch in the North are beneficial.

## Chervil, French chervil, gourmet-parsley
*Anthriscus cerifolium*
*an-THRIS-kus*

▌Hardy annual
Light shade
Culinary, wines

**How to identify**   Chervil belongs to the carrot family, with foliage resembling finely cut parsley, but it has a delicate anise aroma and flavor. Chervil grows into mounds about 1 foot high and 1½ feet wide. Long, lacy leaves, curly or plain, shoot up from the center. Clusters of small white umbrella-like flowers borne on stalks bloom in summer. The variety 'Crispum' has curly leaves but tastes the same as the species. Woodland chervil, or cowparsley (*A. sylvestris*), is a perennial hardy in zones 3 to 10. It grows up to 6 feet tall with a flavor and uses similar to the species.

**Top and bottom: Chervil**

**How to use**   Chervil makes a dainty edging. It needs less light than many herbs and therefore is good for windowsill gardens. The leaves and stems can flavor soups, stews, veal, oysters, fish, vegetables, cheese, creamy sauces, and eggs; they should be added at the very end of cooking. The French use chervil extensively, especially with parsley, thyme, tarragon, shallots, marjoram, pepper, and lemon and in béarnaise sauce and vinaigrette or in a butter baste for chicken. It can be added to salads or used as a garnish. The leaves should be cut 3 inches above the ground. Because chervil loses flavor in drying, it should be dried quickly in a conventional or microwave oven or used in herb butter or stored in the freezer. Frozen chervil should be finely minced before it defrosts.

**How to grow**   Seed should be sown in place outdoors in early spring and again in fall, in successive plantings for a constant supply. Germination takes 10 days with light. Chervil prefers cool weather and bolts in the heat. Seedlings should be sprinkled several times a day or covered with cheesecloth and kept damp; they should be thinned to 9 to 12 inches apart. Harvesting can begin when the leaves are half grown, about 6 to 8 weeks. The harvest can be prolonged by providing some summer shade and pinching off flowers, although a few flowers should be left to self-sow.

### Chicory, blue-sailors, coffeeweed, succory, witloof
*Cichorium intybus*
*si-KOH-ri-um*

▌Zones 3–10
Full sun
Ornamental, culinary

**How to identify**   This perennial is often found growing at the edge of the roadside with ragged blue daisylike flowers. The leaves of wild chicory are sparse and much like those of dandelion; plants usually grow about 2 feet tall. Cultivated varieties have larger, glossy leaves and flower stalks 3 to 4 feet tall. Most of the flowers are blue, but a few varieties have white or pink blooms.

**How to use**   The magnificent blue of the chicory blossom makes

Chicory

it worthy of being planted in the flower, vegetable, or wild garden. The flowers open and close so precisely with the morning sun that Linnaeus, the Swedish botanist famous for his classification of plants, included chicory in a floral clock he planted at the university town of Uppsala, Sweden. Chicory was cultivated in Egypt 5,000 years ago.

The leaves can be used fresh in salads or cooked like or with spinach and other greens. They are not good dried or frozen. The root has long been used with or as a substitute for coffee; it has no caffeine. The witloof (white leaf) variety is best to force in winter to produce endive. Popular salad greens such as radicchio are actually forced leaves of special varieties of chicory. Bruised leaves are good as a poultice for swellings.

**How to grow** Seed should be sown directly in early spring in soil to which compost has been added. Too much nitrogen will result in abundant leaves and less bloom and root. For Belgian endive, the roots should be dug carefully from older plants in fall and stored in a warm, dry place for at least 3 months of dormancy, then planted in a container at least 18 inches deep filled with equal proportions of soil, sand, and peat moss. The roots should be watered, then placed away from light at about 55° F. As each root sends up a shoot, it should be covered with an inverted flowerpot with the hole plugged for complete darkness. In 3 weeks the pale leaves will form cone-shaped buds 6 to 8 inches long. The buds are sliced off for eating—they have a pleasantly bitter flavor. The roots are discarded, and a new batch of roots is started. Planting the roots in stages ensures a continual supply of endive.

## Chives
*Allium schoenoprasum*
*AL-ee-um*

▌Zones 4–9
Full sun
Ornamental, culinary, crafts

**How to identify** This onion relative is a hardy perennial that belongs in every herb garden. It is a neat edging plant, growing in low clumps that multiply and have cloverlike pink to lavender flowers 1 inch across in spring.

**How to use** Chives planted near the kitchen door provide easy snipping. Planted around roses, carrots, apples, grapes, or tomatoes, they seem to help repel insects and inhibit plant diseases.

Chives have been added to foods for some 5,000 years and came to America with the colonists. The leaves can be used fresh or frozen;

Chives

they do not store or dry well. Chopped leaves flavor salads, soups, creamy sauces, vegetables, fish, and poultry as a milder and prettier substitute for onion. In cooked dishes they should be added at the very last minute. Flowers can be added to salads or vinegars.

**How to grow**   Chives are easy to start from seed but germinate slowly and require darkness and a temperature of 60° to 70° F. Plants or divisions are easier. The stalks should be cut back after bloom. Plants or part of a clump can be potted up in late summer; the leaves should be clipped to ease the transplanting, and the pot should

**Garlic chives**

be left outdoors for a month or more of dormancy and freezing. Then it can be brought indoors to force on a windowsill. Or new plants can be purchased for indoors in winter and set out in spring. Chives, like all the onion family, prefer rich, well-drained soil and plenty of water. Spears should be cut flush with the soil; new leaves will regrow with no yellow tips. Potted plants should be fed once a month; garden plants should be fed bonemeal plus a well-balanced food in spring, after flowering, and again in September. Clumps should be divided every 3 to 5 years or more often if needed.

## Chives, garlic or Chinese
*Allium tuberosum*
*AL-ee-um*

▌Zones 3–10
Full sun
Ornamental, culinary, crafts

**How to identify**   This hardy perennial is an ancient plant that is much taller than regular chives, up to 30 inches, has flattened leaves, and blooms in late summer with large globular white flower clusters.

**How to use**   Garlic chives are attractive in flower borders or as a companion plant in the vegetable garden. The leaf tips can be chopped for a mild garlic substitute in salads, soft cheeses, and cottage cheese, on baked potatoes, or as an attractive garnish. Fresh flowers can be used in salads. The knobby green seed heads can be used for flavoring or for rubbing the salad bowl for a trace of garlic flavor. Seed stalks should be cut before they fall to the ground and sprout. They can be stored upside down in a paper bag until used.

**How to grow**   Seed can be sown directly in early spring or late summer, or clumps can be divided. If seed heads mature, volunteer plants will appear the following year. Garlic chives prefer well-drained fertile soil and frequent watering to keep the leaf tips from yellowing. They are heavy feeders and should be fed as for regular chives. Clumps should be divided and shifted to new soil every 3 years to keep them neat and the soil undepleted. Garlic chives can be potted up and brought indoors for the winter.

## Clover, red clover

*Trifolium pratense*
*tri-FOL-ee-um*

▮ Zones 2–8
Full sun
Tea, cough syrup, soil improver

**How to identify**   This is a standard hay crop in much of the country but has escaped to grow wild in fields, meadows, and vacant lots. Clover has 3 rounded leaves and grows up to 2 feet tall with egg-shaped purplish pink blooms.

**How to use**   As a legume that will absorb nitrogen from the air and store it in nodules on its roots, clover is an excellent green manure crop to grow on vacant ground and plow in to improve the soil. It also is good for the compost pile. It draws bees but frustrates them because they cannot get to the nectar easily, so some effective bee plants should be located nearby.

The dried flower heads make a palatable tea, but it is much improved in flavor when mixed with mint. The flowers are easily gathered and spread out to dry.

**How to grow**   Clover can be grown from seed planted in spring in prepared, well-drained soil or dropped among grasses into cracks of soil made by raking. It should be kept moist until germination; it is not drought tolerant. If the plants are allowed to go to seed before

they become established, they often die, so blooms should be picked or animals should be allowed to graze the patch to prevent this early blooming.

## Comfrey, knitbone, blackwort, ass-ear

*Symphytum officinale*
*SIM-fi-tum*

▮ Zones 3–10
Full sun to partial shade
Ornamental, dye, bee plant, compost activator

**How to identify**   Comfrey, a perennial member of the borage family, comes up early in spring with a large rosette of fuzzy dark green leaves, each 15 to 20 inches long

**Red clover**

**Top and bottom:
Comfrey**

and 3 inches wide. The plant can grow 1½ feet tall by mid-May, then it sends up flower stalks that may reach 3 feet tall. The smaller leaves growing up the stalk are alternate. Flowers are creamy yellow, pink, or blue, bell shaped, and borne in pendulous whorls about an inch long. The bees work them constantly. If the plant is not cut back, the tall stalks simply fall over and new vegetative growth begins to repeat the cycle several times a season.

**How to use**    This plant makes an interesting addition to flower, vegetable, herb, or wild gardens. A related species with variegated leaves (*S. officinale* 'Variegatum') is difficult to find but worth the search. Comfrey leaves can be cut back and used for mulch or added to the compost pile. The plant is an excellent green manure crop. Flowers bring bees from early spring through fall.

Using comfrey to ease world hunger was the focus of the Henry Doubleday Association, named for English founder Henry Doubleday and begun in response to the Irish potato famine in the 1840s. As late as the 1970s, comfrey was hailed as a wonder food as well as a cure-all medicine. It was added to soups, sandwiches, tomato juice, salads, and tea and was used like a cabbage leaf to encase ground foods. The tea was given to sick people and animals; the name *comfrey* comes from Latin words meaning "knit together." In 1978, however, research found that rats fed a diet containing 33 percent comfrey leaves and roots developed cancer, so internal use is no longer touted.

Comfrey contains allantoin, which pharmacologists currently add to ointments and lotions. It is used in creams to soothe and soften the skin. Adding it to a warm bath was once reputed to restore virginity, a reminder not to rely on all old herbal cures. The leaves produce yellow, orange, and brown dyes, depending on the mordant.

**How to grow**   Divisions can be started with at least one piece of the root and leaf bud, or plants can be started from seed or cuttings. Comfrey is very easy to grow. It does best in moist, rich soil but tolerates poorer conditions. Clumps can be divided by the end of the first year and could soon cover a large area. Comfrey is difficult to eradicate; a small piece of root left in the ground will start a new clump. Plants should be set 3 to 6 inches deep and 3 feet apart, well away from small or delicate plants. Comfrey looks best if the flower stalks are clipped back to no more than 2 inches from the ground after bloom.

## Coriander, cilantro, Chinese-parsley
*Coriandrum sativum*
cor-ee-AN-drum

▌ Self-seeding annual
Full sun to light shade
Culinary, bee plant

**How to identify**   The leaves of this robust parsley cousin are the part of the plant referred to as cilantro. They grow from multiple stems from the base, similar to parsley, 12 to 30 inches high. Leaves are bright green and glossy. Flower stalks grow to 2 to 3 feet from spring to late summer. Stems are slender, erect, and finely grooved. The brownish yellow seeds have a musty odor that becomes pleasantly citruslike as they mature. Only the dried seed from the pinkish white flowers is referred to as coriander.

**How to use**   Coriander is one of the bitter herbs used for Passover. The ancient Romans used it as a

**Coriander**

meat preservative. It is often interplanted with caraway, and it is thought to help the growth of anise. Coriander honey is so delicious that some people mix small quantities of oil of coriander into clover honey. The root is cooked and chopped in Thai dishes. The tender young leaves, seeds, roots, or all three are minced in Chinese, Mexican, and many other ethnic dishes; they have a fragrance and flavor that combine strong sage and citrus. The leaves should be used fresh—sparingly at first; the flavor is strong. The leaves can be stored in the refrigerator for a week or more in a plastic bag to contain the moisture. Dried leaves have little flavor.

Coriander can be mixed in potpourris and is grown commercially for perfumes and cosmetics. To collect the seed, the whole plant is cut after the seeds ripen, then hung over collecting papers or upside down in paper bags. Tossing handfuls of the seed heads into the air on a windy day or in front of a fan will separate most of the chaff. Seeds infested with insects can be scalded as for caraway, then dried carefully and stored in airtight containers.

**How to grow** Coriander, like parsley, has a taproot, so it is best sown in place in the garden after all danger of frost is past, or in fall in mild climates. To speed up the slow germination, seeds can be washed in dish detergent, then rinsed and dried partially before they are sowed. Seedlings should be thinned to 2 to 4 inches apart. They should not be overfed or the plants will have less flavor.

## Costmary, alecost, bibleleaf

*Tanacetum balsamita* (formerly *Chrysanthemum balsamita*)
*tan-a-SEE-tum*

▌Zones 4–9
Full sun to moderate shade
Culinary, potpourri

**How to identify** A leafy perennial of the daisy family, costmary has leaves that are bright light green and oblong, the upper ones 5 inches long, the basal ones up to 12 inches. There are 2 small lobes at the base of some leaves; all leaves have serrated margins. Leaves dry to a leathery texture and are sometimes found in old Bibles, where they still smell faintly of balsam. Fresh leaves combine the fragrance of lemon, balsam, and mint with a sweet flavor. The tiny yellow button flowers bloom in clusters in late summer. Plants grow 3 to 4 feet tall and spread quickly by underground runners. Feverfew (*T. parthenium*), painted daisy (*Chrysanthemum coccineum*), and pyrethrum (*T. cinerariifolium*) are all close relatives often used in flower borders for their showy blossoms and insecticidal properties.

**How to use** American colonists used the bitter mature leaves of costmary to flavor ale, hence the common name alecost. Young leaves have a minty flavor and are good used sparingly in drinks, chilled soups, and green or fruit salads, and as a garnish. Astringent and antiseptic, the leaves are used in lotions; the strong stems can be woven into herb baskets. Dried costmary is used as a strewing herb, and dried leaves can be added to sachets and potpourris.

**Costmary**

**How to grow**    Costmary is best started from divisions or plants; it produces little or no seed. It should not be mulched, since it spreads aboveground. It can become leggy and weedy looking if not clipped. If the flower stalks are allowed to develop, they may need staking. (Costmary rarely blooms in the shade.) The plants should be divided in spring and the outer portions reset for the most vigorous growth.

## Cress, garden, curly cress, peppergrass
*Lepidium sativum*
*le-PID-i-um*

▌Hardy annual
Full sun to light shade
Salads, mixed greens

**How to identify**    Plants resemble slender, upright mustard greens with deeply cut, lacy leaves. The curly variety has cupped leaflets like parsley.

**How to use**    All types of cress have a distinctly peppery, biting flavor, like strong mustard greens, so they are best mixed with other greens. The leaves should be used before they grow more than 6 to 8 inches or they will be too strong. Plants can be cut back halfway when they are only a few inches tall, as soon as 3 weeks after planting. They are good added to cream cheese or used instead of or with lettuce on sandwiches.

**How to grow**    Seed can be sown directly in the garden or in a container in early spring or late summer through fall. Small successive sowings can be made every 2 weeks except in hot weather, when the plants soon bolt to flower without making enough leaf growth to harvest. Cress can be seeded between cabbage or other cole crops; it will be out of the way before they spread too far.

## Cress, water-
*Nasturtium officinale*
*nas-TUR-shum*

▌Usually grown as an annual
Full sun to light shade
Culinary

**How to identify**    In the wild this delicious member of the mustard family grows in thick mats of floating stems that are anchored to the banks of cool, clear, flowing brooks. Rounded dark green leaves with slightly scalloped edges are ready for harvest 60 days after planting.

**How to use**    Watercress is high in vitamin C, iron, and iodine, and has a crunchy texture and pleasantly tangy flavor similar to garden cress but more mild. Plants will grow in

**Garden cress**

a glass of water or a pot set in water on the windowsill in winter. The leaves can be added to sandwiches, salads, soups, pasta, potatoes, fish, poultry, or sauces or used as a garnish. The Chinese often add watercress to stir-fried dishes. Watercress is best eaten raw or added to dishes at the very last moment of cooking. It can be stored in the refrigerator wrapped in a damp cloth and placed in a plastic bag for use within a few days.

**How to grow**   Watercress can be started from seed indoors, or outdoors in early spring and again in early fall. It often dies out in hot weather. Watercress takes 50 to 60 days to mature from seed. The first leaves are very tiny. Sometimes it can be started from cuttings from a fresh bunch from the grocery store. It needs cool, clean, running water to thrive, but that can be simulated in the garden by planting it in a 10-inch trench and adding water every morning, or planting it near a dripping faucet or in a pot that sits in water with the water changed

often. Lime and humus should be added to the soil, and the roots should be kept wet at all times.

## Cumin
*Cuminum cyminum*
*KOO-min-um*

▮ Zones 5–10
Full sun
Culinary

**How to identify**   Cumin is an annual member of the carrot family, a native of the Upper Nile region. Its leaves resemble fennel, but it grows only 6 to 12 inches tall. The seeds are the part used; it takes 4 months of warm weather for them to ripen. Pink or white flowers in flat clusters are followed by yellowish green-brown seed heads that weigh down the plants, so it is best to plant them thickly so that they can support one another.

**How to use**   The small, dainty plants make an attractive edging for flower or herb beds. The seeds, prized since Old Testament times, should be harvested before they dry, either by pulling the whole

**Watercress**

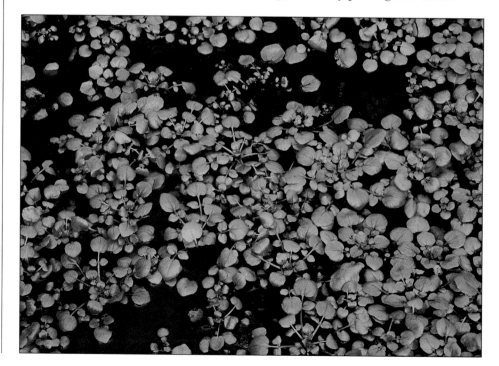

plant or cutting just the seed heads. The seeds do not develop flavor until dried. Rubbing the seed heads between the hands, then passing them through a sieve separates the chaff from the tiny seeds. For the best flavor, the seeds should be parched in the oven just before use. Ground or whole, the seeds have a strong, spicy flavor; they are part of the mixture sold commercially as curry. Cumin is good in spaghetti or chile sauce and wherever caraway is used, including breads, cookies, soups, sausage, game fish, rice, vegetables, and egg dishes, in marinades and gravy, or with roasts. It is a major herb in Mexican and Indian cooking.

**How to grow**   In zones 5 and 6, seed should be started indoors in late March, 3 or 4 seeds in a 6-inch pot. The seeds, which stay viable for 3 years, take 1 to 2 weeks to germinate. Seedlings should not be set outdoors until nighttime temperatures stay above 55° F. The roots should not be disturbed in moving. Clumps of seedlings should be set 4 inches apart. For outdoor planting in warmer climates, seed can be sown as thickly as 16 to 20 seeds per foot. Seedlings should not be thinned. Plants should be watered when the soil is dry.

## Curryplant
*Helichrysum italicum*
(formerly *H. angustifolium*)
hel-i-KRY-sum

▌Tender annual
Full sun
Landscaping, culinary

**How to identify**   This member of the daisy family has a delightful, spicy aroma, although it does not taste like curry. The plants are shrubby and feathery, with needle-like silvery white foliage. They

Top: Cumin
Bottom:
Curryplant

grow slowly and rarely exceed a foot in height and spread. Clusters of tiny yellow flowers bloom only where summers are long and dry. Curryplant is native to the Mediterranean region.

**How to use**   Leaves deter moths, keep the musty smell from garden sheds, add fragrance to potpourris, and can be used as a strewing herb. They should be replaced every year for the greatest effectiveness.

**How to grow**   Purchasing plants is recommended; growing curryplant from seed takes skill and patience. It does best in well-drained, even dry, soil. It can be brought indoors to a windowsill for the winter.

**Dandelion**

### Dandelion, telltime, blowball

*Taraxacum sp.* (formerly *T. officinale*)
*ta-RAX-a-cum*

▌ Zones 2–10
Full sun to part shade
Culinary, bee plant, dye

**How to identify**   Almost everyone knows this weedy perennial member of the daisy family, with its whorl of long, deeply toothed dark green leaves. These inspired the French to call it *dent de lion,* or "lion's tooth." Each plant sends up hollow stems with bright yellow flowers, primarily in a flush in spring that colors lawns and meadows bright yellow. This is followed by an airy globe of wispy seeds that blow far and wide, partly because each seed has its own parachute of down. Seeds that land in a welcoming spot sprout in only 3 days. The thick roots grow deep, and if the top is broken off, 2 plants appear where before there was one.

**How to use**   Colonists brought dandelions with them from the Old World, and Native Americans quickly adopted the plant as a tonic and medicinal tea. Later settlers took it to the Midwest as a bee plant. Before World War I, dandelions were planted for coffee, 4 pounds of seed to the acre. By the second fall this would yield 4 to 5 tons of roots, which were dried and sold for dandelion coffee.

All parts of unsprayed plants are edible. The leaves are a good source of vitamins A, B, C, and D plus iron and calcium. Young leaves can be used in salads or cooked mixed greens. Washed flowers can be dipped in batter and fried as a vegetable, or they can be used to make dandelion wine. Roots can be dried and added to coffee like chicory or to hot chocolate. Flowers can be minced to add color to butter or vinegars or used as a garnish. Boiled, the flowers yield a yellow dye; the whole plant yields a magenta color.

**How to grow**   The best greens for salad are from plants on which the flowers have not been allowed to bloom. Plants can be cut back to the ground as many as 5 times a season, and can be covered with a cloche and harvested for winter greens. Dandelion is considered a helpful companion when planted with fruit trees.

## Dill, dill weed
*Anethum graveolens*
*ah-NEE-thum*

▮ Annual
Full sun
Culinary

**How to identify**   A member of the carrot family, dill has feathery, almost threadlike blue-green foliage. A single, long, hollow stem rises from the root. Tiny yellow flowers have side petals rolled inward and grow in large, flat clusters up to 8 inches across. The seed is ribbed and flattened and about ¹⁄₁₆ inch long. Plants grow 3 feet or more, depending on soil and climate.

**How to use**   The Egyptians mentioned dill in their writings 5,000 years ago. Most dill raised for commercial use today comes from India. The leaves are usually called dill weed, the seeds dill. Tender young leaves can be harvested anytime and chopped into salads, soups, potatoes, or fish dishes or used as a garnish. The yellow flowers are attractive scattered over a salad or relish plate. Seeds are good fresh or dried in pickle recipes; whole clusters are often added to each jar of dill pickles. Seed heads should be cut as they begin to ripen—2 to 3 weeks after bloom—and hung upside down in paper bags until the seeds ripen, dry, and drop. The dried seeds

should be stored in airtight containers. Seeds make a classic vinegar or can be used instead of caraway seed in rye bread. Leaves can be frozen or dried but are best used fresh; they are excellent with asparagus and good with cream cheese for a vegetable dip.

**How to grow**   Plants grow easily from seed sown in place in early spring just before the last frost, or in late summer. A permanent spot should be selected for them at the side of the garden so that they can reseed without disturbance. Seed takes 1 week to germinate; seedlings take 6 weeks to mature. Once the plants start to bloom, there may

**Dill**

be a scarcity of tender leaves for dill weed, so if the plants are grown mostly for foliage, it is best to make successive plantings or keep cutting off the flower heads from some of the plants.

### Elecampane, horseheal, yellow starwort, wild-sunflower
*Inula helenium*
*IN-yu-la*

▌Zones 3–8
Full sun to partial shade
Ornamental, flavoring, medicinal

**How to identify**   This tall, bold plant grows wild in damp roadside ditches and pastures with a 3- to 6-foot stalk rising from a basal rosette of large, pointed, finely toothed leaves. The lower leaves can be 2 feet long; upper leaves clasp the stem. All are bristly on top, velvety on the underside. From July through September the plant blooms with loose bunches of bright yellow daisylike flowers with the same color centers (one variety has contrasting black buds), some up to 4 inches across, like small sunflowers. The roots are large and long and are yellow on the outside and white within; the roots have a strong odor of violets.

**How to use**   Elecampane is a striking accent in the back of herb or other gardens. The flowers are lovely either fresh or dried in arrangements.

Ancient Romans used elecampane to soothe the stomach after banquets, "to expel melancholy, and to cause mirth," according to Roman scholar Pliny. In medieval times elecampane was the main herbal addition in a digestive wine. It was brought to North America mostly to heal scab on sheep and various ailments of horses. The root is a traditional flavoring for sweets and can be candied for a treat that is said to lift the spirits. The same candy can be used for a coughdrop or throat lozenge. A tea is made by simmering the roots in water. The roots are harvested in fall after 2 hard frosts from plants that have been growing for at least 2 seasons.

**How to grow**   Seed can be planted in spring or fall. Seedlings should be transplanted when they are 3 inches tall into humusy soil that stays moist; they should be spaced 2 to 4 feet apart. The offshoots from the roots can be divided in spring or fall. Roots should be divided every 3 years to renew the plants.

**Elecampane**

## Eucalyptus, blue gum, fevertree, silver-dollar

*Eucalyptus* species
yoo-ka-LIP-tus

▌ Zones 8–10
Full sun
Ornamental, cosmetic, crafts

**How to identify**   The genus includes 500 to 1,000 species of fast-growing evergreens; all but four are native to Australia, where three-fourths of the trees are eucalyptus and some trees grow to almost 500 feet, the tallest of the broadleaf evergreens. All eucalyptus can be grown as indoor tub plants in cold climates and placed outdoors only in summer. They are treasured for their smooth or peeling bark, weeping form, highly ornamental and fragrant foliage, interesting seed capsules, and puff-like flowers of cream, pink, yellow, orange, or red. The leaves of young trees vary in oil content and are more rounded in shape than those of mature trees.

**How to use**   Several species offer quick shade and screening or are attractive accent plants in favorable climates. All can be planted as interesting and aromatic houseplants.

The trees provide timber, firewood, and volatile oil that is used extensively in coughdrops, tannin, fibers, and dyes. The trees are used as windbreaks for orange groves and to attract bees for honey and pollination. They have been planted all over the world to stop erosion, dry up swamps, and purify the air.

Eucalyptus tea made from the fresh or dried leaves can be consumed or breathed from a vaporizer for bronchitis, asthma, colds, coughs, congestion, and respiratory ailments. The distilled oil can also be used, but with care and always diluted; it is quite potent, and large doses cause nausea, diarrhea, or muscle spasms. An infusion can be added to bathwater as a stimulating astringent, used as an antiseptic skin lotion, or mixed with alcohol and used as an aftershave. The dried leaves can be added to potpourris or used as strewing herbs. The oil is part of many commercial or homemade air fresheners and deodorants; 1 teaspoon of oil in 1 cup of warm water makes a strong insecticide for both people and animals if it is rubbed on the skin. The oil is also used in some moth-repellent mixtures. The leaves can be preserved for arrangements by immersion for a few days in a

**Silver-dollar eucalyptus**

mixture of 1 part glycerin to 2 parts water; they will then last indefinitely in wreaths and dried bouquets or as permanent indoor plants.

**How to grow**   Eucalyptus grows easily from seed. A few species need prior cold treatment for 3 to 4 weeks. Otherwise, the seed should be sown in early summer in partial shade and the seedlings transplanted when they are 2 to 3 inches tall. They will grow 6 to 12 inches the first year and must be brought to a sunny window indoors before frost. Overwatering them as houseplants can cause leaf blister. The plants are very drought resistant outdoors.

**Fennel**

## Fennel, sweet-fennel
*Foeniculum vulgare* var. *dulce*
*fo-NIK-cu-lum*

∎ Annual
Full sun
Culinary, dye

**How to identify**   This tall, feathery member of the carrot family is ferny like dill but has bright green instead of blue-green foliage. Fennel grows to 4 feet tall. It has a strong anise or licorice aroma and flavor. The flowers are yellow, small, and inconspicuous but grow in showy clusters.

**How to use**   Regular fennel and bronze fennel (*F. vulgare* 'Purpurascens') are attractive toward the back of the flower border. Bronze fennel is more ornamental. Florence fennel (*F. vulgare* var. *azoricum*) is coarser and best grown in the vegetable garden. Milder than other fennels, Florence fennel has a large bulb at the base of the stem. Sold as *finocchio* in markets, the bulb is good cooked as a vegetable or used for coleslaw. Florence fennel can be blanched like celery once the bulb reaches egg size. It should be harvested 2 to 3 weeks later or as needed; it will hold for weeks in cool fall weather.

Fennel tastes less like licorice than it smells, somewhat like a nuttier anise. The leaves can be used fresh in salads, as a garnish, or chopped with fish, sausage, poultry, rice, pickles and pickled vegetables, beans, breads, eggs, and cheese. Fennel is used to take away the objectionable odor and flavor of oil in fish. The stems can be eaten like celery or chopped into fruit salads or cold fruit soups. Seeds are good in butters, cheese spreads, and salad dressings. Fennel tea is made by pouring boiling water over bruised seeds.

The leaf tips can be cut as soon as the plants are 6 inches tall. The tips will keep for a week or more in the refrigerator if they are wrapped in a damp cloth and placed in a sealed bag to hold in the moisture. Or they can be frozen or dried. The stems and bulb should be used before the flowers form.

Fennel's cleansing and medicating virtues are tapped in cosmetics; the seeds can be ground for steam facials. Chewing the seeds is supposed to suppress the appetite; an early Greek name for fennel meant "to grow thin." Flowers and leaves make a yellow to brown dye.

**How to grow**   Seed should be sown in place in early spring for flowers in late summer, or sown in late summer for flowers the following year. Florence fennel, which grows 2 to 3 feet tall, should be planted in July; otherwise the culture is the same. Plants may reseed themselves. Seedlings should be thinned to 10 to 12 inches apart. Fennel may need staking, especially in a windy spot. It is quite drought resistant once established.

## Fenugreek, Greek-hayseed, trigonella

*Trigonella foenum-graecum*
*tri-go-NEL-a*

▮ Annual
Full sun
Culinary, dye

**How to identify**   Fenugreek is among the oldest herbs and was once among the most widely used. A member of the pea family, fenugreek looks much like clover in its early stages, but it grows 1 to 3 feet tall with hollow stems and 1- to 2-inch oval leaves in groups of 3 arranged alternately on the stem. Fragrant yellowish white flowers bloom for many months beginning in early summer and are followed by upright pointed seedpods in the

**Florence fennel**

leaf axils. The first seeds mature and turn brown about 4 months after planting, 2 to 3 months after flowering.

**How to use**   A tea made of fenugreek seeds seems to protect seedlings against damping-off and was once considered beneficial to the entire garden. The dried seeds have a sweet, nutty flavor and are usually used whole to enhance chutneys, curries, meats, poultry, and marinated vegetables, and in the Middle Eastern candy halvah. Too much fenugreek, however, can make food bitter. Seeds can also be sprouted for a nutritious addition to salads. Seeds should be harvested when ripe but not open. The entire plant should be uprooted and hung upside down in a paper bag until the seeds dry. Then they can be separated from the chaff and stored in airtight containers. The leaves can be eaten as greens.

This herb was one of the principal ingredients of Lydia Pinkham's famous Vegetable Compound, hailed as "the greatest medical discovery since the dawn of history" when it came on the market in 1875.

Fenugreek was first a fodder crop and is still used to add sweetness to animal feed. It is sometimes mixed with stored grain to repel insects. Seeds were used for medicine from earliest times and produce a mucilage that is used in poultices and ointments. Today an extract or oil flavors candy, butterscotch puddings, ice creams, and imitation maple syrup. Fenugreek seeds make a yellow dye when mordanted with alum.

**How to grow**   Seed should be sown thickly outdoors in rich, well-drained soil that has warmed to 55° F. Seedlings should be thinned to 4 inches apart.

### Feverfew, wild-chamomile

*Tanacetum parthenium*
(formerly *Chrysanthemum parthenium*)
*tan-a-SEE-tum*

▌ Zones 5–10
Full sun
Ornamental, medicinal, crafts, dye

**How to identify**   Sometimes mistaken for chamomile, feverfew is much more upright in habit and grows 2 to 3 feet tall. The small, daisylike flowers have flat yellow centers and short rays; they bloom in tight, flat clusters. True chamomile has a dome-shaped, daisylike center and leaves that look more feathery. Feverfew can be grown as a biennial or perennial. The leaves

**Feverfew**

are strongly scented, somewhat bitter, alternate, 4 inches long, and a bit more deeply cut than garden chrysanthemum leaves.

**How to use** Feverfew is easy to grow; the flowers are fragrant and showy in perennial borders, rock gardens, window boxes, and herb gardens during summer and fall. This herb seems to keep away harmful insects, perhaps because its roots contain the natural insecticide pyrethrum. Feverfew also keeps bees away from a garden, so it should be distanced from plants that need bees for pollination, such as squash and cucumber, or from plants grown especially to attract bees.

Feverfew has little culinary use except to flavor wines and pastries. The Italians serve it with fried eggs. It gains its name from its traditional medicinal use. In the seventeenth century, herbalist John Parkinson thought it helpful in treating opium overdoses. Cotton Mather, the famous preacher and scholar who helped found Yale University, used it to relieve toothaches. Feverfew can, however, cause mouth ulcers, in which case use should stop immediately. (The recommended dosage is no more than 3 or 4 small leaves a day.) The leaves have a bitter flavor, alleviated by mixing with food. Leaves may be frozen; they lose some potency when dried. Leaves can be steeped in alcohol and then dabbed on the skin when working outdoors to keep away small biting insects. Flower heads can be dried, ground, and used as a safe insecticide. The flowers are good fillers for fresh or dried bouquets. Fresh leaves and stems make a greenish yellow dye.

**How to grow** Clumps can be divided, or seed started in early spring, or cuttings taken from October through May. Seed should be

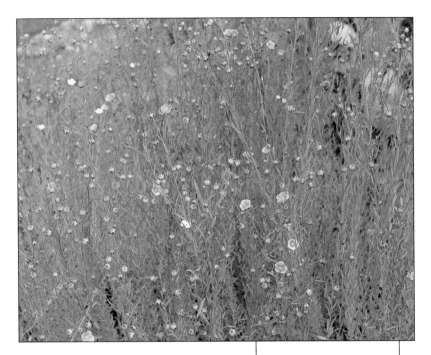

Flax

sown indoors 2 weeks before the last frost date in your area, or outdoors in early fall in mild climates. Transplants can be set in the garden in June, or seedlings thinned to 9 to 12 inches apart. Feverfew self-seeds readily. It thrives in dry places and has larger and fernier foliage when grown in partial shade.

## Flax, linseed, lint-bells
*Linum* species
*LY-num*

∎ Zones 2–9
Full sun to light shade
Ornamental, crafts, oil

**How to identify** The flax grown commercially is an annual (*L. usitatissimum*) that thrives and sometimes escapes cultivation especially in the Pacific Northwest and in Canada. But a very similar perennial garden plant (*L. perenne*) grows over much of the country. Both have erect, slender stems and alternate, needlelike blue-green leaves; the plants grow 1 to 3 feet tall, branching at the tip into several flower stems. The flowers are about ½ inch across, with 5 petals;

they form a cloud of delicate bloom that continues for many weeks.

**How to use**   As a garden plant flax graces the flower border or herb garden with its feathery foliage. *L. perenne* has blue flowers; the variety 'Album' has 1-inch white blooms. *L. flavum* grows 15 inches tall and has waxy yellow flowers all summer. Scarlet flax (*L. grandiflorum* 'Rubrum') is a 14-inch annual with silky inch-wide red flowers. It often self-sows. All forms are best planted in masses.

Flax was one of the first plants used for anything other than food; *usitatissimum* means "most useful." Fibers spun from the stalks are the source of linen; such fibers were found among the remains of Swiss lake dwellers 10,000 years ago. The Egyptians wrapped their mummies in linen.

Flaxseed is a traditional additive to hearty bread, but it should be used carefully and in small amounts. Immature seed can be poisonous. Flax contains 30 to 40 percent linseed oil, plus mucilage, wax, tannin, protein, and gum. Commercially it is used as linseed oil in paints, varnishes, and linoleum, and as a fiber and as livestock feed and birdseed. The delicate yet sturdy stalks can be woven into dried herb baskets. Ground seed mixed with water or water and butter was once used as a poultice for festering sores.

**How to grow**   Seed should be sown directly in the garden in light, well-drained soil in early spring or late fall, or seed can be started indoors and the seedlings set outdoors 4 inches apart. Though they look delicate, the plants are very hardy and easy to grow. They should not be fed until they are ready to bloom. Roots are very shallow, so cultivation should be done with utmost care; mulching is preferable to control weeds. Winter mulch is beneficial in cold climates.

## Garlic
*Allium sativum*
*AL-ee-um*

▌Zones 4–10
Full sun
Culinary, medicinal, insecticidal

**How to identify**   This perennial of the lily family forms large, coarse, flat-leaved plants that grow 1 to 3 feet tall. In midsummer they send up stems tipped with spectacular, aromatic globes made up of many small pinkish white to lavender pink flowers. Tiny sterile bulbils form after the flowers. The edible underground bulbs include about 5 cloves. Elephant garlic bulbs are larger and usually have 7 to 10 cloves, sometimes as many as 15 cloves.

**How to use**   Garlic is a favored companion plant for deterring insects, fungi, and hungry deer from

**Garlic**

cabbage, eggplant, tomatoes, roses, and fruit trees.

Eating garlic was once supposed to impart strength, speed, and endurance. The ancient Romans took it into battle. It is the principal ingredient of Four Thieves Vinegar, popular in France because it was reputed to have saved from the plague four criminals condemned to bury the dead in Marseilles in the early 1700s.

Garlic is one of the most popular of the culinary herbs. Natural foods stores carry descented garlic tablets for various medicinal purposes.

**How to grow** The cloves should be separated from the head and planted 3 to 4 inches apart (1 foot apart for elephant garlic). In warm climates the cloves can be planted from spring until late summer, just deep enough to cover the tips. In cold climates the cloves should be planted about 2 inches deep in fall. Like all alliums, garlic needs fertile soil and 2 to 3 feedings per season. Plants that do not bloom the first season will live over the winter in all but the far north and bloom by midsummer the second season. Removing the flowers directs the plant's strength to root development.

Garlic should be lifted, allowed to dry thoroughly, then hung in a cool, dark, dry, airy spot; refrigeration encourages mold. Braided bulbs are decorative as well as handy to use.

### Geranium, scented
*Pelargonium* species
pel-ar-GOH-nee-um

■ Zones 9–10
Full sun to partial shade
Ornamental, tea, sachets

**How to identify** Scented geraniums belong to the same family but not the same genus as common geraniums. Varied leaf forms as

**Scented geranium**

well as scents of rose, apple, orange, ginger, lemon, lime, coconut, apricot, strawberry, and peppermint make scented geraniums fascinating plants to grow or collect. Many have lovely flowers as well. Leaves are opposite and often frilly, ferny, velvety, or slightly sticky to the touch and give off a distinctive fragrance when brushed or rubbed. Each bloom has 5 petals and bears a long, pointed, storklike fruit from which the genus gets its name.

**How to use** These make ideal potted plants that can be set out in summer especially where they will be brushed against to release the scent. Upright varieties can be trained into standards. Apple and peppermint geraniums are pendulous and ideal for hanging baskets or high window boxes. Some forms, such as the coconut-scented geranium, make good ground covers.

Leaves of rose, mint, or lemon geranium can be used to flavor sugar, tea, jelly, punches, vinegars, puddings, and stuffings. Apple jelly with rose geranium leaves is a time-honored favorite. Scented geranium leaves make a lovely garnish. Dried leaves add scent and bulk to sachets and herb pillows, and can be used as strewing herbs. Fresh leaves are attractive in finger bowls, as the border in nosegays, and in herbal baths and steam facials.

**How to grow**  Because the seed germinates very slowly and the resulting plants are quite variable, it is better to start with plants or cuttings. More than 60 different varieties can be ordered from nurseries specializing in geraniums. The plants do best in sandy, well-drained soil. They can be kept in the pot the first year to see what they do and where they thrive and look best. The second year they can be planted in the ground for the summer, then repotted for the winter or cuttings taken. (Cuttings of lemon geranium take up to 3 months to root.)

Scented geraniums need more water during active growth than in winter. Blooms are encouraged by undersized pots, and root rot is less of a danger where excess moisture does not remain on the roots.

### Germander, garlic-sage
*Teucrium chamaedrys*
*TOO-kree-um*

▮ Zones 5–10
Full sun to partial shade
Ornamental

**How to identify**  A perennial of the mint family, germander comes in as many as 100 varieties; it has a slender, 4-sided stem and small, opposite leaves with serrated margins. The plant grows in neat tufts rising 6 to 18 inches from creeping roots. It has a rich, piney fragrance. Upright stems are woody and will bear shearing. Tubular flowers, speckled pink to mauve with upper and lower lips, grow in whorls of about 6 where the leaves join the stem. They bloom in late summer. The variety 'Prostratum' grows only 5 to 8 inches tall but spreads 3 feet wide.

**How to use**  Germander is now mostly used as a small, neat hedge, an edging or ground cover plant, in rock gardens, or between stepping-stones. It is ideal for knot or ribbon gardens.

Sage-leaved germander (*T. scorodonia*) has crinkly, downy leaves and a hoplike odor; it has been used as a substitute for hops in making beer. It can become a weed in the garden and should be controlled like mint. Tree-germander

**Germander**

(*T. fruticans*) has silver foliage
and blue flowers and is attractive
as a potted plant. It can grow very
tall and wide in hot, dry climates.
Cat-thyme (*T. marum*), which resembles thyme, attracts cats. Germander can be used as a strewing
herb. It was once used to cure gout
and rheumatism.

**How to grow**  Seed takes 30 days
to germinate. Plants start easily
from cuttings, layering, or divisions. They should be set 12 inches
apart in fairly rich, well-drained
soil. The plants benefit from mulch
in harsh winters, especially if the
snow cover is light. Germander is
almost evergreen except in the
far north. It should be sheared back
every spring to encourage new
growth and keep it dense.

### Ginger, gingerroot
*Zingiber officinale*
*ZING-i-ber*

▌Zones 9–10
Light to moderate shade
Culinary, ornamental

**How to identify**  This herbaceous
tropical perennial grows from
the familiar aromatic, tuberous rhizome used in Asian cooking. It is
knotty and branched and may be
whitish or tan. In northern states it
can be grown as a potted plant and
set outdoors in summer. Except in
tropical climates you may never
see the dense, conelike spires of
yellow-green flowers, each with
one purple lip. The leaves are
grasslike but branched, much like
some of the palm leaves used by
florists. They shoot up directly from
the root and can grow 3 to 4 feet
tall in tropical climates. This plant
is not to be confused with several
other ornamental gingers, though
their leaves and flowers may be
somewhat similar.

**How to use**  The Greeks used
ginger 4,000 and more years ago

**Ginger**

for something resembling gingerbread. The fresh rhizome is a
staple in stir-fried Asian dishes.
Ginger adds a zesty flavor and is
said to aid digestion. Partly used
rhizomes can be stored in vinegar
or wine, or wrapped in a damp
cloth and kept refrigerated, or
frozen in a plastic bag and grated
as needed. Fresh ginger will last for
several months. The tender shoots
are used in Japanese cooking.

**How to grow**  A portion of the
fresh rhizome, purchased at a grocery store, can be pressed flat into
the top of a pot filled with 12 inches
of moist, porous soil. The pot

should be sealed in a plastic bag and kept at 75° to 85° F until growth begins, then the bag removed and the pot set in a warm, sunny spot and watered sparingly to prevent root rot. Once the plant develops a root system, it can be moved to light shade in the garden; it thrives in heat and humidity. It should be fed occasionally. When the tops die down at the end of the season, signaling the onset of dormancy, part of the rhizome can be removed for cooking and the remainder left to start the plant the following year. The rhizomes from young shoots have the most flavor.

**Goldenrod**

## Goldenrod, Blue Mountain tea
*Solidago* species
*sol-i-DAY-go*

▮ Zones 3–10
Full sun to light shade
Crafts, tea, dye

**How to identify**   There are 130 species, native mostly to North America, of this well-known plant that grows by the roadside or in open fields and woods, 3 to 7 feet tall, with branching spires of mustard yellow flowers from July through September. The leaves are alternate, lance shaped, and simple, with toothed or smooth edges; when crushed they have an anise-like aroma something like French tarragon.

**How to use**   Though a common weed to many, goldenrod is much prized in European gardens. Some named varieties offer larger flowers; dwarf plants 1 foot tall are attractive at the front of the border. Wild goldenrod works well in the back of a flower bed, a wild garden, or the edge of a wooded area.

Native Americans used goldenrod for a wide range of ailments. The Pennsylvania Dutch and the col–onists after the Boston Tea Party used it for a tea so pleasant tasting that it was exported to China.

Goldenrod is still wrongly blamed today for the misery of hay fever sufferers when the plant at fault usually is ragweed (*Ambrosia*), which blooms at the same time. The pollen of goldenrod is carried by bees, whereas that of ragweed is wind-borne.

Goldenrod has had medicinal uses that include a tea for colic or for stomach upset. The Chinese have used it to treat flu, sore throat, and measles. Tea or crushed fresh leaves can be applied to wounds or insect bites. The flowers dry beautifully for winter bouquets, but they

Goldenseal

need good ventilation when drying or they will turn black and musty. Small sprigs of dried goldenrod are decorative in wreaths. As a dye plant goldenrod produces various shades of yellow.

**How to grow**   Wild plants transplant easily, although seed and plants are available from nurseries. Goldenrod grows best in poor soil.

## Goldenseal, ground-raspberry, eyeroot, yellowroot
*Hydrastis canadensis*
*hy-DRAS-tis*

▌Zones 3–8
Deep shade
Ornamental, medicine, dye

**How to identify**   This native American herb, sometimes called poor man's ginseng, is found in the same moist, rich woodlands as is true ginseng, especially in the Ozarks and the Appalachians. Goldenseal is a low-growing peren-nial with erect, hairy stems 6 to 18 inches tall. The palm-shaped leaves have 5 to 7 lobes and are hairy and prickly like raspberry leaves. The fruit resembles a single red raspberry; it is borne just above the leaf. Flowers are solitary and greenish white, ¼ to ½ inch across and appearing in April or May. The root is a knotted rhizome with bright yellow flesh, up to 2 inches long and covered with yellow-brown bark.

**How to use**   With patience and care, goldenseal can be grown in wild, woodland, or rock gardens. It can also be grown under grape arbors or lattice or wherever there is enough shade.

Used by the Cherokee Indians and then the settlers, goldenseal leaves and roots were considered an almost magic cure-all and have been used to treat almost every known ailment. Goldenseal was once famous as an eyewash and is used in some manufactured eyewashes and eyedrops today. Goldenseal is said to increase the power of other herbs when used in combination with them. It was once cultivated in Oregon and Washington State. During the early 1900s, growers dug as much as 300,000 pounds of the root each year. The plant is now in danger of extinction. It contains hydrastine and berberine, which are mildly antiseptic, antibiotic, and astringent.

Goldenseal capsules are available in natural foods stores. The powdered root should have a sweetish, licorice odor and a bitter flavor. The root produces a permanent dye from pale yellow to orange. In combination with other plants such as indigo, it produces green on wool, cotton, and silk. It is also used as a pigment in watercolors and oil paints.

**Caution**   Goldenseal has a cumulative effect and should be used only in small doses for a short time and never by pregnant women. Large amounts can overstimulate and cause convulsions, burning skin, miscarriage, or overproduction of white blood cells.

**How to grow**   Seed can be sown in spring or fall. Plants or roots should be placed 8 inches apart in moist but well-drained soil to which generous amounts of leaf mold, peat moss, bonemeal, and/ or compost have been added. Plants should be protected from sun and wind and should be mulched in winter. Roots large enough to dig take 3 years from plants, 5 years from seed. The growing spot should be marked before the top growth dies.

The leaves and stems for infusions should be gathered after they dry on the plant. Roots should be harvested in late fall after several hard frosts, then dried slowly and stored in airtight containers. The small rootlets can be replanted ¼ inch deep. It takes about 16 plants to make a pound of powder.

### Honesty, moneyplant, moonwort, satinpod
*Lunaria annua*
*loo-NAR-ee-a*

▌Zones 3–10
Light shade
Ornamental, dried bouquets

**How to identify**   The leaves of this plant are usually alternate, oval to heart shaped with scalloped edges, and slightly fuzzy. One variety has a variegated leaf. Honesty may be hard to identify the first summer after planting, but it will thrive between and beneath annuals, and once everything else in the garden turns brown, honesty is still green. In early spring when the fruit trees bloom, honesty sends up stalks of sweet-scented flowers, mostly lavender and a few white, that look much like dames rocket or wild phlox. The individual flowers have 4 petals and are about an inch across; the stalk grows up to 2 feet tall. Before all the flowers have faded, some of the unique flat, ovalish seedpods form, each with a few seeds inside and a soft spine at the tip. These are green but not showy all summer. In fall, when wind rubs away the outer dry tan layer, a satiny, silvery coin remains.

**How to use**   This is the "white satin flower" described in *Gerard's Herbal* of 1597 and in Shakespeare's plays. The plant is easy, carefree, and delightful in the garden in light shade, under fruit trees, or at the edge of a woodland. It has 2 showy seasons, spring and fall, and is neat and obedient in between. Unripe seeds and roots have a hot, mustardy flavor and can be eaten in salads. The seedpods are highly prized for wreaths and dried arrangements.

**How to grow**   Seed can be planted in spring, early summer, or fall outdoors in light shade and average soil. Seed takes 10 to 20 days to germinate. The plants self-sow readily and tolerate poor and dry soils.

## Hops
*Humulus lupulus*
*HEU-mew-lus*

▌Zones 3–10
Full sun
Culinary, medicinal, ornamental

**How to identify**   This herbaceous perennial of the hemp family grows 15 to 30 feet in a season and dies back to the ground each winter. The opposite leaves are hairy, heart shaped, and bright green, and have 3 to 5 coarsely toothed lobes. The variety 'Aureus' has golden yellow leaves. Annual forms include Japanese hops (*H. japonicus*) and a variegated form (*H. japonicus* 'Variegatus') with leaves splashed with white.

The male flowers of hops are tiny and greenish yellow in loose bunches 4 to 8 inches long. The inconspicuous female flowers are borne on separate plants. Both bloom in July and August. The female blooms are pale greenish, in pairs, and mature into greenish pink fruiting cones, called strobiles. These are covered with yellow glands containing the bitters that give beer its pleasantly bitter taste and also preserve it. Drinks flavored in the old way with costmary and ground ivy came to be called

**Left and right: Honesty**

**Left and right: Hops**

ales; those using hops took their name from the German *bier*.

**How to use**   Hops can be trained to cover trellises, arbors, or fences for quick shade or screening. In containers or in the open, plants can grow as small weeping trees. They quake in the breeze and have a refreshing, pinelike fragrance.

The English once considered hops a wicked weed that caused melancholy, and Henry VIII prohibited its use. It became an important commercial crop by the 1800s. Most of the hops grown in the United States come from the Northwest.

The tender, young growth can be snapped off in 6-inch pieces in spring and eaten raw in salads. Or the shoots can be steamed or boiled like asparagus and served with butter or cream sauce. Lemon juice can be added to preserve the color. The shoots are a great favorite in

Belgium and France. The flowers are also edible and can be added to salads or used as seasoning.

Hops have been used medicinally and are still used today in pillows for their sleep-inducing qualities. Abraham Lincoln and King George III slept on such pillows. But some consider the aroma too strong in such concentrated doses, so hops might be used in combination with other herbs. Flowers can be dried for wreaths and dried arrangements, and the vines can be woven into herb baskets. The Scandinavians use the fibers from the vines to weave a coarse cloth.

**How to grow**   Hops will grow anywhere except in the desert. Seed, cuttings, or root divisions can be started in early summer. Cuttings and root divisions will give the desired female plants. Male seedlings can be removed once their sex can be determined. Plants should be set 6 feet apart. They need rich, humusy soil, excellent drainage, and plenty of water. They also need strong support (they twine from left to right), ample room, and good air circulation. Once established they can grow 6 to 12 inches a day, as much as 30 feet a year. The growth should be cut back as it dies in fall and removed to a hot compost pile to prevent possible mildew, aphids, and mites.

After the second year, half the shoots can be harvested every spring to thin the plant. By the third and following years, the strobiles can be gathered when they are amber brown and partly dry. Their stickiness is a measure of the essential oils—the stickier the better. The strobiles should be dried in a dark place and used as soon as possible.

## Horehound, white horehound
*Marrubium vulgare*
*ma-ROO-bee-um*

▌Zones 3–10
Full sun
Candy, crafts, bee plant

**How to identify**   This perennial of the mint family is a handsome plant, with crinkled silver white leaves. It is sometimes found growing wild, especially in California and Oregon. When mature it has whorls of white flowers above each of the upper pairs of leaves. The barbed seeds catch on clothes and animal fur and can travel far, so the seedlings can spring up anywhere in the garden or beyond.

**How to use**   Horehound can be sheared for a gray-green edging or border. It is thought to discourage flies. Silver horehound (*M. incanum*, formerly *M. candidissimum*) has a more erect habit. It is harder to locate but is superior as a garden plant.

Horehound

Horehound leaves have a menthol-like flavor. Horehound was once popular in England for flavoring ales. It gets its common name from its use as a treatment for dog bites. The plant should not be confused with black horehound (*Ballota nigra*), which is a strong-smelling weed and may be toxic in large quantities; it has lavender flowers but is otherwise very similar in appearance to *M. vulgare*.

Horehound candy is more of a coughdrop and throat lozenge than a treat. The leaves are best used fresh and can be cut anytime. The most flavor is achieved by cutting only the top third of the plant. The leaves are then removed from the stems, chopped and dried, and stored in airtight containers. Although claims for other uses abound, horehound is most valued for soothing coughs, hoarseness, and sore throats. Horehound coughdrops are available in most drugstores, or you can make your own lozenges or an infusion. Flowers can be dried for wreaths, and fresh branches last a long time in cut-flower bouquets.

**How to grow** Horehound grows so easily from seed that it may become a nuisance. Seed can be sown directly outdoors. Cuttings or root divisions should be taken or seedlings transplanted while they are still small. Plants should be set 1 foot apart in the garden. Horehound thrives in poor, dry soil; the down on the leaves reduces moisture loss. Plants may not bloom until the second year. Flowers should be cut before they set seed. Trimming the plants in spring keeps them bushy.

## Horseradish
*Armoracia rusticana*
(formerly *Cochlearia armoracia*)
ar-mor-A-see-a

▮ Zones 3–10
Full sun
Culinary

**How to identify** Horseradish is a perennial of the mustard family, usually started from root cuttings developing into a bold plant, 2 to 3 feet tall and wide. Leaves are dark green, coarse, and abundant, most of them growing directly from the ground and about 1 foot long. In late spring the plant sends up stalks bearing small, faintly scented, fairly showy, mustardlike white flowers; the seeds almost never mature.

**How to use** This herb should be planted at the side of the vegetable garden where the plow or tiller can work around it. The tender leaves can be added to tossed salads. Sticklike pieces of side roots, about 2 inches long, added to homemade pickles will keep them crisp. The roots can be dug anytime they are large enough, but they have the best flavor in late fall.

The roots should be peeled or scrubbed and scraped before storing. The entire root can be stored in sand, in the ground, or in the vegetable drawer of the refrigerator until needed. Or the root can be grated and frozen in ice cube trays, so that only as much as needed can be defrosted. Alternatively, the root can be diced and ground in a blender with enough vinegar or

**Horseradish**

mayonnaise to moisten and sugar to taste. This mixture will keep for months in the refrigerator and makes a fine gift. It can be mixed with mustard, spread on roast beef, and used to season fish dishes. It is good with grated raw beets and sour cream. Horseradish adds vitamin C as well as zip to the diet.

Horseradish was once used as an herbal diuretic for flushing the system. Only in recent centuries has it been used for seasoning.

**Caution**   Touching your face or eyes while grinding horseradish will cause pain that makes onion tears seem mild.

**How to grow**   Horseradish is easy to grow, and plants spread abundantly, since every bit of root left in the ground starts a new plant. Roots can be started indoors in a gallon pot in winter or outside directly in the garden in early spring. Compost should be worked deeply into the soil, and lime should be added if necessary; horseradish prefers an almost neutral pH. The root pieces can be set vertically or at a slant with the large end to the top and about 4 inches below the soil surface and 12 to 18 inches apart.

Side shoots and roots can be harvested when the leaves are about a foot tall; care should be taken when removing them not to disturb the bottom roots, which usually branch deep into the ground. This procedure can be repeated 6 weeks later.

**Hyssop**
*Hyssopus officinalis*
*his-SOP-us*

▮ Zones 3–7
Sun or partial shade
Culinary, ornamental

**How to identify**   This pretty, compact perennial member of the mint family grows wild through much of the United States. It has narrow dark green leaves, a spicy mint fragrance when crushed, and flower spikes of white, pink, or blue. It blooms mostly in July and August and grows 2 to 3 feet tall.

**How to use**   Hyssop is a neater, showier, and less aggressive mint. It can be sheared as low as 6 inches for edging, hedges, or knot gardens. Its flower spikes combine well with roses and other flowers both in the garden and in fresh or dried arrangements. Bees love it so much that beekeepers once rubbed their hives with the leaves to convince the swarms to stay; it adds a pleasant flavor to honey. It attracts butterflies and hummingbirds as well and is said to deter whiteflies and cabbage moths.

**Hyssop**

As far back as the seventh century, hyssop was strewn on the floors of sickrooms and kitchens to cleanse the air. The volatile oil from hyssop is one of the key ingredients in such liqueurs as Benedictine®.

The minty leaves and flowers are good in drinks and in green and fruit salads, and they add a piquant, slightly bitter flavor to chicken soup or stuffing, game meats, lamb stew, cheese omelets, rice, and tomato sauce; they can also be dried for herbal teas. Hyssop is relaxing for herbal baths and cleansing for steam facials. It is popular for potpourris, and the oil is used in many perfumes and soaps. It was once used as a cure for head lice.

**How to grow**   Hyssop grows easily from cuttings, root divisions, and seed sown indoors about 6 weeks before the last spring frost. Clusters of 2 or 3 seedlings each should be transplanted to stand 12 to 18 inches apart. Hyssop will grow only 12 to 15 inches and produce only a few flowers the first year but will be much more vigorous the second season and thereafter. It is almost evergreen well into the winter even in the North. It should be sheared back in spring to encourage new growth. Young divisions can replace old plants that have become woody. The green, not the woody, parts should be harvested and hung to dry. Hyssop does not do well in the house.

## Juniper, horse savin
*Juniperus communis*
*ju-NIP-er-us*

∎ Zones 3–9
Full sun
Ornamental, flavoring, cosmetic

**How to identify**   A commonly used evergreen shrub, juniper comes in many forms, from a low ground cover to a fairly tall tree. Needlelike leaves are narrow, ⅛ to

Juniper

¼ inch long, concave, sharply pointed, with a white band above, and in whorls of 3 along the stems at almost right angles. Yellow male and green female flowers are on separate plants from April through June but are so inconspicuous that they are seldom noticed. The ½-inch berries ripen over 3 years from green to bluish or purple and are usually covered with a waxy white coating. The bark is reddish brown. Juniper is an endangered species in some states.

**How to use**   There are forms and varieties of juniper for ground covers, rock gardens, foundation plantings, screening, hedges, and windbreaks. They will hold the soil on steep banks. Some have variegated foliage and some range in color from bluish green to reddish purple. The more open the exposure, the stronger the plants' aroma. Plants of both sexes are necessary for berries.

The Dutch word for juniper is *jenever*, from which the name *gin* is derived. Juniper has been used in folk medicine and witchcraft. Native Americans made a tea from the twigs for relief of colds and stomachache, and they wrapped sore limbs in steaming bundles of branches.

Juniper berries can be used in meat marinades or added to stews and sauces in place of bay leaves. The berries are quite strong, and a few go a long way. They combine well with parsley, fennel, garlic, or bay. The ripe berries should be picked in fall. They are best used fresh; drying reduces the oil content. Juniper clippings can be added to the outdoor grill to give meat a delicious smoky flavor.

The cleansing, pungent aroma of juniper makes an invigorating and energizing bath for aching muscles.

**Juniper**

Branches can be used in fresh bouquets or as strewing herbs to freshen the air.

**Caution**   Repeated consumption of juniper can cause kidney damage, convulsions, or personality changes; pregnant women and those with kidney problems should avoid internal use.

**How to grow**   Plants are usually started from nursery stock and grow easily in sandy or light loamy soil. Juniper can be grown from seed, but without 30 to 120 days of cold treatment the seed may take 2 years or more to germinate.

## Lady's-bedstraw, yellow bed-straw, curdwort, cheese rennet

*Galium verum*
*GAL-ee-um*

∎ Zones 3–6
Full sun to part shade
Ornamental, dye

**How to identify** This perennial member of the Madder family grows to 3 feet tall with inch-long needlelike leaves in whorls of 4 to 8 around the erect, nearly square stems. Lady's-bedstraw has ferny foliage and small bright yellow flowers in dense, elongated clusters. The entire plant has a honey-like fragrance. It grows wild in much of southern Canada and the northeastern United States.

**How to use** The plants sprawl naturally and are attractive in a rock or wild garden or as a ground cover. They can be staked if upright growth is preferred.

This herb was traditionally used to stuff mattresses and pillows; the heat of the upper body and head releases the soothing scent that is supposed to help one relax and sleep. It was also traditionally used in footbaths, as a curdling agent and coloring for cheese, and as a hair dye.

Lady's-bedstraw is an attractive cut flower or can be hung to dry for winter bouquets or wreaths. The leaves produce a yellow dye, the roots various shades of red depending on the mordant.

**How to grow** Seed or root divisions can be started in spring or fall. Plants should be spaced 1 foot

**Left: Lady's-bedstraw**
**Right: Lamb's-ears**

apart. This herb will adapt to a wide range of soils, can be root-pruned to keep it in bounds if necessary, and should be divided every 2 to 3 years.

## Lamb's-ears, wood betony
*Stachys byzantina*
*STAK-is*

▌ Zones 3–10
Full sun
Ornamental, crafts, medicine

**How to identify**  The grayish white leaves of this perennial have a soft, downy texture much like a furry animal's ears. The plants provide an attractive color and texture accent in the garden; they spread to make a thick cover 12 to 18 inches tall. Leaves are 3 to 6 inches long and 1½ inches wide, opposite, with smooth edges, and covered with soft woolly hairs. The handsome flower spikes are also woolly and gray with small mintlike lavender flowers; kept cut back the plants will continue to bloom from midsummer until frost. Wood betony (*S. officinalis*) has showier flower spikes and smooth rather than fuzzy foliage. The entire plant is strongly aromatic.

**How to use**  Lamb's-ears delights all of the senses and is attractive in the front of the shrub or flower border, near paths or patio for touching, or in rock gardens. The leaves were once used as bandages and poultices, the juice to treat wounds, the tea as a gargle for sore throats and for diarrhea. Large doses can irritate the stomach. The flowers can be used in wreaths and dried arrangements.

**How to grow**  Lamb's-ears is easily started indoors from seed or outdoors from root divisions. Plants should be set 12 to 18 inches apart in average, well-drained, moderately moist soil; they will fill in the spaces. Clumps should be divided every 2 to 3 years or when the center of the patch begins to die out.

## Lavender, English, true lavender
*Lavandula angustifolia*
*lah-VAN-deu-lah*

▌ Zones 5–10
Full sun
Ornamental, fragrance

**How to identify**  This lovely perennial member of the mint family grows like a compact bush to 30 inches in height. It has slender blue-green to gray leaves and

**Lavender**

spikes of lavender to blue flowers. At the base of each individual flower is a small, shield-shaped yellow bract. Leaves are opposite and up to 2 inches long. Lavender has been a favorite perfume herb through the centuries. There are dozens of related species and varieties that divide into 2 groups. The winter-hardy ones include 'Munstead', which grows to 15 inches and is similar to the species in leaf and flower; 'Hidcote', which grows to 12 inches and has brilliant purple flowers, the deepest color of all the lavenders; and 'Rosea' and 'Jean Davis', both of which grow to 12 inches and have pale pink blooms. The tender French, Spanish, spike, and woolly lavenders perish at 20° F but make excellent indoor plants in sunny, cool windows and with not too much water. They can be set outdoors in pots for the growing season.

**How to use**    Lavender is most attractive in the garden as a border or among flowers or shrubs, and along paths or in the rock garden.

The flowers can be added in small amounts to salads and used to flavor vinegars and jellies. Oil of lavender on a ball of cotton will freshen a room or keep moths out of woolens. Lavender is excellent for adding to the bath or to lotions for the skin. Dried flowers are used in bouquets and wreaths. Lavender was burned in hospitals to cleanse the air. Just smelling lavender is said to ease headaches. Lavender is grown commercially for a large perfume, soap, and scent market. It is the favorite herb for scenting linens and storing blankets, and for sachets in drawers and closets.

**How to grow**    It is best to buy plants and set them out after all danger of frost is past. Lavender is slow to start from seed or cuttings. Seed should be fresh; it needs a long, cool period for germination, and the soil should have lime and plenty of humus (although poor soil seems to intensify the fragrance). Seedlings may grow only a few inches the first year. If the flowers are cut the first year, the plant will

**'Hidcote' lavender**

grow better and bloom more pro-fusely the second spring. Even the hardy lavenders should be winter-mulched in all but the South.

Old woody growth should be pruned in spring, and the bush should be trimmed after harvesting the flowers. No more than a third of the top growth should be taken at one cutting. Flowers air-dry eas-ily but need storage in complete darkness to preserve the color.

## Lemon balm, sweetbalm
*Melissa officinalis*
*me-LIS-ah*

▌Zones 4–10
Full sun to light shade
Ornamental, culinary, bee plant

**How to identify**   Lemon balm is an easy-to-grow, fast-spreading, delightful perennial member of the mint family. The opposite leaves are textured dark green with scal-loped edges; the plant grows up-right and loosely branched to about 2 feet tall. It has interesting but not showy white flowers from July through September. Golden lemon balm has variegated gold and green leaves; it does not grow as tall nor is it as hardy as the species.

**How to use**   Planted along walks and patios, lemon balm releases its lemony-minty scent when brushed against. The plant is a pleasant addition to any garden and an ex-cellent one for bees (*melissa* is the Greek word for "bee"). The leaves can be used like mint to flavor and garnish tea or wine, by themselves or in combination for herbal teas, chopped into salads or salad dress-ings, in orange marmalade, or with fish. Lemon balm can serve as a mild substitute for lemon-verbena. Leaves can be dried, or frozen up to 2 months. Fresh sprigs placed in a pitcher of water will keep the water fresh and lemony tasting.

**Lemon balm**

Balm is said to lift the spirits. Fresh leaves rubbed on the hands or hair will leave a lemony scent for hours; they also make a relaxing bath. Add dried leaves to sachets.

**How to grow**   Lemon balm is easy to start from seed, cuttings, or divisions. It has the most intense scent when grown in poor soil. It takes more shade and moisture than most kitchen herbs. Seedlings planted in April will yield a few sprigs by mid-June and be 18 inch-es tall by the first winter. The plant self-seeds readily. Established plants can be cut back 3 times dur-ing a growing season. A potted plant or new cuttings can be grown on a windowsill in winter.

## Lemongrass
*Cymbopogon citratus*
*sim-bo-PO-gon*

▮ Zones 9–10
Full sun to light shade
Ornamental, tea, culinary

**How to identify**   Lemongrass is a tropical perennial grown as an annual in most of the United States. It forms a 3- to 5-foot-tall clump of flat green blades about ¼ inch wide. In northern gardens or in greenhouses, lemongrass forms erect clumps of wide-bladed grass with saw-toothed edges (which can cut the skin if not handled carefully), but it seldom produces stems thick enough for cooking. Flowers, not common except in the tropics, are grasslike spikes. The closely related citronellagrass (*C. nardus*) is the source of the well-known insect repellent citronella.

**How to use**   Lemongrass can be grown as a potted plant or an accent plant. It needs long, hot summers and much moisture to grow stems large enough to use in Asian cooking. The thick lower stems are peeled and the tender cores bundled and steamed or chopped and added to other foods. The leaves can be harvested and chopped anytime for tea, at the end of the season for drying. The leaves can be used to flavor fish stock, poultry sauces, stir-fried dishes, and curries (the leaves should be removed before serving).

**Left: Lemongrass
Right: Lemon-
verbena**

Dried leaves can be added to dried orange and lemon zest for a delicately scented potpourri. Lemongrass leaves should be dried in the dark to preserve the color.

**How to grow**   Lemongrass is usually started from a side shoot planted in warm, fairly acid, sandy soil after all danger of frost is past. It responds well to nitrogen fertilizer. Plants should be protected from cool winds. The potted plant, or a side shoot of the clump, will not produce new growth indoors in winter but should survive enough to be set out again when the weather warms.

## Lemon-verbena

*Aloysia triphylla* (formerly *Lippia citriodora*)
*a-LOY-see-a*

▮ Zones 7–10
Full sun
Culinary, fragrance, crafts

**How to identify**   Although this plant is a member of the verbena family, it does not at all resemble the creeping annual. It can grow 6 feet tall as a woody shrub even in a container, up to 15 feet tall where it is native in Chile and Argentina. The light green leaves are lance shaped with either slightly toothed or smooth margins fringed with hairs; the leaves are 2 to 4 inches long in whorls of 3 or 4. The flowers are tiny, tubular, and white to lavender in airy clusters of spikes at the branch tips; they appear in late summer and fall.

**How to use**   This tender perennial is usually grown in containers except in the southern states. It has the most authentic lemon fragrance of all the lemon-scented herbs and makes an attractive garden or houseplant with its tall, airy silhouette. It can also be trained as a standard or small tree. The leaves can be cut once a week in mid-summer of the first year and used fresh or dried for tea, and for cooking and baking wherever a touch of lemon is desired. The leaves are tough, like bay leaves; they should be minced well or removed before serving. Sprigs make an attractive garnish.

The leaves can be rubbed on the hands, face, or hair for a lemony fragrance. Dried in the dark and stored in airtight containers, they hold their scent for years and are popular for sachets and potpourris. They can also be used as strewing herbs and in dried bouquets, wreaths, nosegays, lotions, scented baths, herb pillows, scented ink, soaps, and perfumes. The long, limber stems can be woven into wreaths or used in fresh or dried arrangements. Fresh leaves can be used in finger bowls or rolled in damp guest towels, heated in the microwave on high for 30 seconds, and passed to dinner guests.

**How to grow**   It is best to buy plants or propagate tip cuttings taken from new summer growth. A plant that will be brought indoors for the winter should be kept in a pot outdoors in summer; the long taproot makes transplanting difficult. The pot can be sunk below the rim for the outdoor growing season so that it will not dry out, then brought indoors to a sunny window before frost. The leaves will fall off; watering should be reduced accordingly and the stems cut back to encourage new growth. New leaves may start in March but can appear later, so the plant's demise should not be assumed until late summer. The leaves should be checked carefully for whiteflies and red spider mites. Plants should be repotted or new plants started from cuttings every 2 to 3 years.

## Licorice

*Glycyrrhiza glabra*
*gli-sir-RYE-za*

▮ Zones 3–8
Full sun
Wildflower, sweet root

**How to identify**   Wild licorice (*G. missouriensis*) is found mostly in the Midwest. Both European ( *G. glabra*) and wild licorice are hardy shrubs or herbs of the pea family. They grow erect, from 3 to 7 feet tall, with palmlike compound leaves, each with 9 to 17 pairs of narrow leaflets. The leaflets are yellow-green on top, lighter and slightly damp and sticky on the underside. The pealike flowers, purple or lavender on the European, yellow on the wild, are borne in midsummer on spikes. The seedpods are smooth or nearly so on the European, brown and prickly burrs on the wild plant.

**How to use**   The licorice root contains a glycoside called glycyrrhizin that is 50 times sweeter than sugar but quenches thirst instead of increasing it as sugar does. The name means "sweet root," and pieces of the root can be chewed in moderation (see below).  Some people believe that chewing licorice root helps overcome an overeating or smoking habit.

Licorice has uses as a mucilage for cough remedies. It is, however, not recommended as a home remedy in excessive amounts, even of the candy; it can increase salt and water retention and deplete the potassium in the body, causing lack of energy, weakness, abnormal heart activity, and kidney failure. Pregnant women or those with serious health problems should avoid using it.

Licorice is used commercially to sweeten and mask the bitter taste of other medicines, to increase their potency, and to keep pills from sticking together. It adds its own flavor and brings out other flavors in pastries, ice cream, root beer, and brewed beer. It is used in toothpaste, eyedrops, and shampoo and as a wetting and foaming agent in fire extinguishers and insecticides. It is used in composition board and insulation. Ninety percent of the licorice raised commercially is used to flavor tobacco products.

Native Americans chewed a piece of wild licorice root to ease toothaches and made an infusion of the leaves to ease earaches.

**How to grow**   Licorice grows easily from seed or plants in deep, fertile, moist soil. In the wild it grows mostly in bottomlands. Plants should be set 1 to 1½ feet apart. The roots can be harvested at the end of the third year by digging a trench beside them and pulling the roots into it. The pieces

Licorice

of root remaining in the ground will grow back. In fact, they are hard to eliminate and can be invasive. The top growth can be used for compost or mulch. The roots should be dried carefully for 6 months and then stored in airtight containers. Older roots, from fruiting plants, are usually woody. So are those in very cold climates.

## Lovage
*Levisticum officinale*
*le-VIS-ti-cum*

■ Zones 2–9
Full sun to partial shade
Culinary, medicinal

**How to identify** This hardy perennial is a celery cousin and a giant in the garden. Lovage leaves are pale green, stems are hollow and ribbed, flowers are tiny and yellow in flat clusters 1½ to 4 inches across in June and July. The basal leaves are seldom more than 2 feet tall, but the flower stalk can shoot up 5 to 7 feet.

**How to use** The leaves have a strong celery flavor. Leaves and stems can be chopped in salads, used fresh or dried in soups, stews, potato salad, rice, stuffing, tomato sauce or juice, or cooked as a side dish like asparagus. The seeds are good, whole or ground, in pickling brines, biscuits, cheeses, salads, and salad dressings. Lovage is particularly good in low-salt and no-salt diets. Leaves and curls taken from the stems make an attractive garnish; the plant is robust enough to provide plenty for such use. The leaves can be harvested as needed. They should be dried in the dark and stored in opaque containers, because light will yellow them. One of the best ways to preserve lovage is in herbed salt (see page 83). Roots can be dried to make tea. The seeds can be collected when they first begin to brown.

**Top and bottom:**
**Lovage**

**How to grow**   Lovage can be started from plants or divisions or, with patience, from seed planted in fall. Lovage needs rich, moist soil and feedings with liquid fertilizer or manure tea often enough to keep the mature leaves dark green. Where summers are hot it should receive afternoon shade. Plants should be given plenty of room on the north side of the garden so that they won't shade other plants. Lovage grows only 2 feet the first year but can reach 4 feet by June of the second. In the third spring the plant should be dug up before growth starts and the root system split in half and replanted; otherwise, the roots tend to become knotty and unproductive.

### Love-in-a-mist, fennelflower, black cumin, nutmegflower

*Nigella damascena* or *N. sativa*
*ni-JELL-la*

▮ Zones 3–10
Full sun
Ornamental, culinary

**How to identify**   This member of the buttercup family has delicate, threadlike, alternate, glossy dark green foliage that forms a lacy green wreath around each of the dainty blue, white, or pink to lavender flowers, each bloom about one inch across. Bulging green seedpods with triangular black seeds ripen by late summer, about 4 months after planting. Seeds of black cumin (*N. sativa*) are much more aromatic than those of love-in-a-mist (*N. damascena*). Plants of both grow 12 to 15 inches tall and are not long lived.

**How to use**   The delicate blooms and foliage are a lovely addition to flower or herb gardens. They are good cut flowers. The aromatic seeds of black cumin are used as a seasoning in the Middle East and India and are called Four-Spice in France. The seeds can be placed among clothes to repel insects.

Seed heads can be cut when they turn brown; they should be dried in a shady, airy place. The seeds can be collected by rubbing the pods between the palms. Each plant produces only a few seeds; peppery or nutmeg or lemon-carrot flavored, they can be added to curries or cakes or used in rye bread instead of caraway seed. The dried foliage can be used for strewing. The seedpods are decorative in wreaths and winter bouquets.

**Love-in-a-mist**

**How to grow** Seed can be sown outdoors starting in March, in fall where winters are mild. Seed takes 10 to 20 days to germinate; succession sowing will extend the blooming season. Seedlings resent transplanting but it can be done with care. Seedlings should be thinned to 6 to 8 inches apart. The plants like cool weather and self-sow easily.

## Madder

*Rubia tinctoria*
*RU-bee-a*

▮ Zones 7–10
Full sun
Dye plant

**How to identify** This perennial grows up to 4 feet with 4-sided, jointed, viney, succulent stems covered with short prickles, which help them cling. Without support they often sprawl on the ground. The leaves are also prickly, 2 to 4 inches long, lanceolate, and borne in circles of 4 to 6. The flowers, which do not develop until the third year when the plant is grown from seed, are tiny, greenish white to pale yellow, and bloom in terminal clusters in early summer.

**How to use** Madder root was used to color the fabric used to wrap Egyptian mummies. It is a traditional dye used for the woods of violins. One of its constituents, alizarin, prompted nineteenth-century chemical researchers to develop a technique for synthesizing dye from coal tar at less expense and thus replace dye plants with dye chemicals. However, for those using natural dyes, madder is one of the most important dye plants. Depending on the mordant used, the roots yield shades of red, pink, lilac, purple, rose, orange, brown, or black. The reddish brown roots are cylindrical, fleshy, and fibrous, up to 3 feet long with

Top: Love-in-a-mist seeds
Bottom: Madder

many branches. The best roots are dug from plants 3 to 6 years old.

When swallowed, madder colors milk, urine, and bones in animals and people and beaks, bones, and feet in birds. It was thus used, before X-ray technology became so sophisticated, to study bone growth. The plant is dangerous to pregnant women, because it causes uterine contractions. It was once used for a medicine but is now obsolete. As a facial, it is said to remove freckles and blemishes. Madder is used as animal feed. The stalks are good for scouring pots and pans.

**How to grow**   Seed sown in spring takes 10 days to germinate, the plants up to 3 years to become established. Plants from root or

**Marjoram**

shoot divisions take 2 years. Madder needs plenty of sun and space.

## Marjoram, sweet marjoram
*Origanum majorana*
*or-RIG-ah-num*

■ Zones 4–10
Full sun
Culinary, crafts, dye

**How to identify**   This tender perennial grows only a foot tall but at least that wide by the end of the season. Often grown as an annual, it has opposite, ovate, fuzzy pale gray-green leaves ¼ to 1 inch long and tiny white or pink blossoms in spherical clusters in August and September. Marjoram has knotty clusters of green seeds that distinguish it from other oreganos. All are closely related, but some of the others are stronger in flavor. See Oregano on page 246.

**How to use**   *O. majorana* is a good edging or hanging basket plant; there are also variegated varieties and a creeping golden marjoram that make delightful ground covers. The plant has a sweet, pungent fragrance and is one of the most frequently used kitchen herbs. With oregano and basil, it is one of the 3 main herbs used in Italian cooking. Dried leaves have a more intense flavor.

Crowns of marjoram leaves were once put on the heads of newly married couples as a symbol of happiness, and plants were placed on graves to give peace to the departed. Marjoram is an excellent strewing herb. In a bath it helps relieve aches and pains. The dried leaves can be added to sachets. The dried flowers can be used in wreaths and winter bouquets. Marjoram gives a green color to wool mordanted with alum, an olive color if mordanted with chrome.

**How to grow**   Marjoram is slow to start from seed and is usually grown from purchased plants or from cuttings or layering of plants wintered over indoors. It can be planted outside after the soil warms in full sun and with good air circulation. It prefers neutral soil, so lime should be added if necessary. It should be watered sparingly and trimmed often enough to keep the plant in shape. The leaves can be harvested for drying just as the first flowers are forming by cutting back the plant severely. After frost, the plants can be sheared back and potted up to bring indoors for winter use and spring planting. Although the leaves will become much lighter in color indoors, their fragrance will fill the kitchen with every snipping.

## Marshmallow, mallards, schloss-tea
*Althaea officinalis*
*al-THEE-a*

∎ Zones 6–8
Full sun to light shade
Ornamental, culinary

**How to identify**   This species is related to hollyhock (*Alcea rosea*, formerly *Althaea rosea*) and has similar upright growth, 4 feet tall or more, with large, showy, 5-petaled lavender to pinkish white flowers that bloom from July to October. The leaves are heart to maple-leaf shaped, alternate on the stem, toothed, and grayish green. Round, downy seed capsules contain many flat seeds packed side to side in a circle. Marshmallow grows wild on the edges of salt- or freshwater marshes from Quebec to Virginia and as far west as Arkansas.

**How to use**   Many named varieties of annuals, biennials, and perennials have been developed for garden use in a wide range of colors, with double as well as single flowers and from dwarf to very tall. Most of them are closely related to hollyhock.

The tender tops and young leaves of marshmallow can be added to salads or cooked with soups or stews. The leaves should be harvested before the plant blooms. In Middle Eastern cuisine the root is boiled, then fried with onions and butter. Washed roots of this plant

**Marshmallow**

**Marshmallow**

known as a confection; indeed the first marshmallows were medicinal and made from the root of this plant before gelatins and other modern products were known. However, the marshmallows sold in stores today bear no trace of the plant.

**How to grow**   Marshmallow grows easily from seed, cuttings, or root divisions, the latter best done in fall. Plants should be set 2 feet apart in sandy, moist soil.

## Mint
*Mentha* species
*MEN-tha*

∎ Zones 2–10
Full sun to partial shade
Culinary, tea, crafts

**How to identify**   The mint family, to which so many herbs belong, is characterized by square stems, opposite leaves, and whorls of tubular, 2-lipped flowers. Many herb catalogs list 20 or more actual mints, including apple, berga-mot, blue-balsam, Corsican (which forms a low mat of tiny leaves), grapefruit, orange, lime, pineapple, and several spearmints and pep-permints. All are slightly distinctive in appearance, fragrance, and fla-vor and most are so easy to grow that they can become invasive. All are delightful even if only mixed in the grass for their fragrance when walked on or mowed.

All mints except Corsican mint (*M. requienii*) and pennyroyal (*M. pulegium*) are hardy and perennial throughout the United States. Pennyroyal is hardy to 5° F or can be grown as an annual.

**How to use**   Pennyroyal is an ex-cellent flea repellent. All mints can be grown as ground covers in wild gardens. Corsican mint is ideal in rock gardens or between stepping-stones. It is the least rampant of the mints.

were once given to teething babies, who sucked them happily because they were sweet as well as cooling. Crushed leaves seem to lessen the pain and swelling of a bee sting or an insect bite. (The name *althaea* comes from the Greek word mean-ing "to heal.") Marshmallow prep-arations soften and soothe the skin, and an extract boiled from the plant makes a gargle for a sore throat. Some druggists sell dried roots. A poultice made from the roots was once used to treat bruis-es, sprains, and aching muscles. Roots can be gathered in fall from plants at least 2 years old. Lateral rootlets should be discarded and the main one washed, peeled of its corky bark, then dried whole or in pieces.

Charlemagne regarded this plant so highly that he ordered its cultiva-tion. The young leaves and tops are still eaten in France as a spring tonic. Marshmallow is now better

**Orange mint**

Because mints are invasive, they should be isolated from other plants by sinking them into the ground in bottomless containers or planting them in small areas surrounded by buildings or walkways; you can also mow around the edge of the planting to control it. Mints should also be isolated so that they don't cross-pollinate; bees love the flowers.

Mints make ideal garnishes, teas, additions to fruit salads, and juleps, and can be used in a wide variety of vegetable and meat dishes and baked goods. Only the top tender leaves should be used for cooking; old leaves are too pungent. Mint is better fresh than dried and is best stored by freezing as is or chopping into ice cubes.

Mint has long been used for a variety of home healing remedies and is considered one of the safest of the healing herbs. It repels some insects, and peppermint, spearmint, orange mint, and pennyroyal are said to repel mice and rats. Mint is so prolific that it can be strewn with abandon. Use it in the bath, cosmetics, sachets, soaps, and bouquets.

**How to grow**    Mint is so easy to grow that you might as well save your sunniest spots for fussier plants. It prefers moist, slightly acid soil and will die out in arid conditions. Some mints produce no seed at all; in any case propagation by cuttings or divisions is better so that new plants will be true to variety. Too much organic matter added to the soil will encourage rust. Several wilts and insects may bother mint but as a rule only if cultural problems have weakened it first. It can be harvested to a stub or mowed and will grow back more vigorously. Otherwise, the woody growth should be pruned back as needed or at least twice a year. Plants should be mulched where winters are extremely severe. Mint is one of several herbs that are best moved to new ground every 4 to 5 years.

### Mustard
*Brassica* species
*BRA-si-ka*

▌ Annual
Full sun
Culinary

**How to identify**   The genus *Brassica* includes cabbage, broccoli, cauliflower, collards, Chinese cabbage, kale, kohlrabi, brussels sprouts, rape, rutabaga, turnip, and mustard greens. The herb members of this genus are white (sometimes called yellow) mustard (*B. hirta*), black mustard (*B. nigra*), and brown mustard (*B. juncea*), all of which are grown to make the condiment that is essential to hot dogs and many other foods.

Mustard grows 2 to 6 feet tall with bright green alternate leaves of various shapes, the lower ones pinnately lobed, coarsely toothed, and up to 8 inches long, the upper ones less lobed. The flowers are 4-petaled yellow blooms borne on wide-spreading branches. Long, slender pods begin to form on the lower stems while flowers still bloom above. The pods elongate and turn from green to brown when ripe; each contains 4 to 8 yellow seeds. Black mustard is hottest in flavor; the brown is easiest to harvest.

**How to use**   Mustard self-sows easily; it is not uncommon to find a field in early summer where cows stand up to their shoulders in yellow mustard flowers. All parts of the plant are edible.

As a companion plant mustard is said to aid the growth of beans, grapes, and fruit trees, although no evidence other than usage supports this belief. Mustard reduces cabbage aphids on collards and brussels sprouts and keeps flea beetles away from collards as well. It also inhibits cyst nematodes and root rot.

The young leaves are rich in nutrients; they are tangy in salads or boiled and chopped with bacon or salt pork and onions. The Chinese use several varieties of brown mustard steamed or stir-fried. But for the most part the plants are grown for the seeds used in pickles, chutney, and the sandwich spread of the same name.

The seeds can be harvested by spreading the plants on a screen or tray covered with cloth or hanging

**Mustard**

them upside down in brown paper bags. When the seeds have turned brown but before they split open (after about 2 weeks of ripening), they can be pounded out, then winnowed and stored whole or ground in airtight containers. It may be easier to gather seed from wild mustard than to grow your own, because a large patch is needed to produce sufficient seed.

Mustard plasters have been a time-honored treatment for congested chests as well as rheumatism, toothache, and soreness or stiffness. A mix of powdered mustard seed and water, with optional rye flour and egg white to tone it down, is spread over a cloth that is then applied to the chest. This plaster feels warm and should not be left on too long, for it can cause blisters on the skin. The skin should be washed after the plaster is removed; for extrasensitive skin castor oil can be applied before the plaster. An infusion of black mustard seed makes a footbath said to relieve sore and aching feet.

**How to grow**   Plants are easily grown from seed sown directly outdoors in successive plantings during early spring and late fall. Seedlings should be thinned to 9 inches apart. They will live over the winter and bloom by early summer of the next year; new seed will be ready by fall. Mustard can become a problem weed if the seed is left to ripen and drop.

### Nasturtium, Indian-cress
*Tropaeolum majus*
*tro-pee-O-lum*

∎ Annual
Full sun to light shade
Ornamental, culinary

**How to identify**   Spurred flowers in many shades of yellow, orange, and red are bright as jewels. Flat, alternate, round leaves with

smooth, slightly wavy edges are 2 to 7 inches in diameter. Leaves and flowers have a unique fragrance that stays on the hands after picking. Both leaves and flowers are edible, with a peppery-sweet flavor. Small, rounded, turban-shaped buds and seedpods can be pickled by pouring boiling cider vinegar over a jar full of them. Thus prepared, they make a spicy substitute for capers.

**How to use**   Nasturtiums are ideal plants for containers or hanging baskets; the compact varieties, which grow only 8 inches tall, work best. They need 4 hours of sunlight

**Nasturtium**

a day to bloom indoors. Vines that grow 8 to 10 feet in a season make a ground cover in warm climates.

The flowers begin to bloom about 3 weeks after the seeds sprout and continue until frost. Nasturtiums make excellent cut flowers when bunched in a vase; their stems are too soft for much arranging. As companion plants for cucumbers and other vegetables or planted beneath fruit trees, nasturtiums are often considered effective as trap plants, luring aphids to themselves.

The Spanish explorers took this plant home from Peru in the sixteenth century, and it gained favor throughout Europe as a culinary herb. Tender young leaves or flowers can be added to salads or chopped in cream cheese for sandwiches. The flowers can be stuffed with nut butters or soft cheeses for an elegant appetizer.

An infusion of the leaves was once thought beneficial in treating bronchitis and urinary infections. It is said to have a cleansing and antiseptic effect. The infusion can also be used in hair rinses.

**How to grow**   Nasturtiums are so quickly and easily grown that they are ideal for children's projects. The large seeds can be soaked overnight in warm water for better germination, then planted outdoors after all danger of frost is past. They should be planted 1 inch deep and 6 to 12 inches apart depending on variety. Seedlings will emerge in 5 to 7 days. The leaves can be harvested in 3 weeks or as soon as there are enough to spare a few. In rich, moist soil they may produce more leaf than flower. They bloom better in poor, dry soil. One variety, *T. tuberosum*, produces edible tubers.

### New Jersey tea, wild-snowball, redroot
*Ceanothus americanus*
*see-a-NO-thus*

▌Zones 3–7
Full sun to light shade
Ornamental, tea, dye

**How to identify**   This low, thorny, somewhat scraggly deciduous shrub grows wild from Canada to South Carolina and westward. It has finely toothed, downy, oval, usually alternate leaves, dark green on top, hairy and light green underneath. The plant belongs to the buckthorn family; the seedpods look like acorns with horns and 3 distinct lobes that separate when dried into 3 nutlets. The flowers resemble white lilac, and a number of western cousins includes one

**New Jersey tea**

called wild-lilac. Another is called soapbloom; when rubbed in water, the fresh flowers produce a fine lather that makes the skin soft and lightly fragrant.

**How to use**   This 2- to 3-foot shrub is attractive between the middle and back of a flower border or shrub planting or in a wildflower garden or woodland.

The colonists learned from Native Americans to make a passable tea from the green or dried leaves of this plant. Native Americans also used this plant medicinally. At one time the bark was used in commercial preparations to prevent hemorrhaging after surgery. The roots of some species can be used as a dye to give wool a cinnamon color.

**How to grow**   The scraggly habit of this plant can be controlled by cutting it close to the base in late winter. The plant is short lived and may need frequent replacement. New plants are best started from summer cuttings; the long, fibrous roots are difficult to transplant.

Top and bottom: Nicandra

## Nicandra, shooflyplant, apple-of-Peru

*Nicandra physaloides*
*nye-KAN-dra*

▌Annual
Full sun to light shade
Ornamental, fly repellent, crafts

**How to identify**   A member of the nightshade family, this plant grows as tall as 5 to 6 feet but is often smaller, with as wide a spread to the succulent, nearly horizontal branches. It will stay smaller in containers. The leaves are oval, deeply lobed, and 4 to 6 inches long. Blooming begins when the plant is only a foot tall with lovely cup-shaped flowers of delicate lavender blue with white centers. These stay open only part of the day and are quickly replaced by 5-sided,

winged, round green seedpods that grow to about an inch in diameter and turn tan and papery as the seeds inside ripen.

**How to use** This is not the showiest of plants until winter, when the dried pods capped with snow can be the prettiest sight in a withered garden. However, it is a neat and cheering plant to appreciate beside the back door, next to the compost pile, or near the dog run or chicken coop. Although nicandra has no noticeable odor, it has been known to reduce the local fly population from hundreds to a swattable few. The flies crawl on the leaves, but once the blooms begin, the flies simply vacate the area. There is no information to explain this effect.

The fresh foliage, flowers, and seedpods are attractive fillers in fresh flower arrangements, and the dried seedpods are excellent in dried bouquets and winter wreaths.

**How to grow** Seeds may germinate erratically. It is not uncommon for one plant to be 6 inches tall when other seeds planted at the same time suddenly sprout. Nicandra grown for the first time should be seeded indoors so that it is sure to be recognized. It self-sows reliably but does not become invasive. It takes the same care as its cousin tomatoes and looks much the same when it first sprouts. It transplants easily even when quite large. Plants should be set outdoors after all danger of frost is past and spaced at least 3 feet apart. Lettuce or other small plants can be grown between them early in the season.

## Oregano
*Origanum vulgare*
*or-RIG-ah-num*

∎ Zones 3–10
Full sun
Culinary

**How to identify** Several species of the genus *Origanum* are called oregano, most with small, opposite leaves and a low, spreading habit. A few are erect and as much as 2 to 3 feet tall. Each has its own flavor. All of the oreganos used for cooking have white flowers.

**How to use** Oregano is said to be a good companion plant to beans. Spreading varieties make a good edging or ground cover and look attractive cascading over a stone wall.

Used in the cuisine of many cultures, oregano is good with cheese, eggs, breads, beans, meat, shellfish, and vegetables such as eggplant, zucchini, and potatoes. Oregano has long been used principally as

**Greek oregano (*O. vulgarum* ssp. *hirtum*)**

a medicine, said to relieve colic and indigestion. The tea was used to treat chronic coughs and asthma. A drop of oil rubbed on an aching tooth or gum can ease the pain. The oil mixed with olive oil was used for aches, sprains, and rheumatism. Oregano is recommended for baths to relieve aching muscles and is used in some cosmetics. The flowers are an attractive addition to bouquets and wreaths, fresh or dried. Wild oregano makes a purplish dye for wool, reddish brown for linen.

**How to grow**   Oreganos are fairly easy to grow, usually starting with cuttings, plants, or divisions. *O. vulgare* ssp. *hirtum* (formerly *O. heracleoticum*) has the best flavor, although even this plant varies from seedlings. Seeds are tiny and germinate in 4 days. Spreading varieties can suffer from root rot in damp seasons and locations. Oregano tolerates dry soil and neglect, grows among rocks and in gravel in nature, and is highly suited to hanging baskets. Leaves should be checked for red spider mites, aphids, and leafminers. Sprigs can be snipped when the plant is 6 inches tall. Constant harvest makes the plant bushier. Varieties should be grown separately or, better yet, the foliage should be harvested before the flowers go to seed so that varieties do not cross-pollinate.

### Mahonia, Oregon-grape, hollygrape, hollyolive, mountain-grape

*Mahonia aquifolium*
ma-HON-ee-a

∎ Zones 5–8
Shade to partial sun
Ornamental, dye

**How to identify**   One of the hardiest of the broadleaf evergreens, mahonia has lustrous, leathery,

Mahonia

spiny, holly-shaped leaves that are dark green in summer and in fall turn bronze-red, gold, crimson, or purple, depending on the variety. There are 100 species of mahonia and many hybrids. Mahonia is still sometimes considered one of the 500 species of barberry, since it belongs to that family. Mahonia grows 3 to 6 feet tall and spreads up to 5 feet wide. The plant bears bunches of fragrant bright yellow flowers in spring that are followed by deep blue to purple fruit in June and July.

**How to use**    This is a choice shrub for shrub borders and foundation plantings. It can be pruned to a desired shape and height. Some mahonias are hosts to wheat rust fungus and therefore cannot be shipped to wheat-producing states. *M. aquifolium* is immune to this rust and no danger to crops.

The ripe berries have a bitter, not unpleasant flavor. High in vitamin C, they can be used fresh or dried in preserves or made into a syrup.

The wood is often used for treasured small wooden objects. The roots and also a combination of leaves and stems make yellow, tan, and brown dyes. The fruit, mordanted with alum, gives wool a purplish blue color. Native Americans used the roots to make yellow dye for the reeds for their baskets.

**How to grow**    Mahonia can be started from seed, cuttings, or divisions. It increases by underground stolons. It does best in light shade and well-drained soil but is adaptable to other conditions. It is subject to leaf-spot disease, powdery mildew, and rust.

**Orrisroot**

Orrisroot

## Orrisroot, Florentine iris, German iris
*Iris germanica* var. *florentina*
EYE-rus

■ Zones 3–10
Full sun to partial shade
Potpourri, fixative, cosmetic

**How to identify**    This perennial iris looks much like the bearded iris of spring gardens. It has sword-shaped light green leaves 1½ to 2 feet tall and white flowers that bloom in May and June with a touch of blue to lavender in the veins and a yellow beard.

**How to use**    The flowers are a lovely addition to any garden. The ancient Egyptians discovered that the rhizome of orrisroot when dried takes on a sweet, heady violet odor. Roots for drying should be dug in fall (small pieces can be replanted). The larger ones should have the skin removed with a knife or potato peeler, then the roots chopped into coarse pieces and allowed to air-dry for several days. The maximum scent is achieved by storing the dried root for 2 years before using. Orrisroot makes long-lasting sachets and potpourris—about 1 tablespoon of orrisroot for each quart of dried flower petals.

Florence, Italy, has been the center of commercial orrisroot production for the perfume industry since the Middle Ages. Orrisroot has been used to flavor liqueurs and as a base for dry shampoos, tooth powders, and face powders. Allergic reactions to this plant can vary from a rash to hay fever, stuffy nose, red eyes, or asthma. Although it was once used for medicinal purposes, it is now considered too strong to be taken internally.

**How to grow**   Like any iris, this one demands good drainage, prefers fertile soil, and benefits from the addition of bonemeal. The tubers should be spaced 1 to 1½ feet apart at soil level and the stubby roots buried. Good air circulation between the plants will help prevent root rot. Orrisroot can be planted anytime, but spring to early summer is best. The stalks should be cut back after flowering. Roots should be left for 3 years before harvesting.

## Osage-orange, hedge-apple, bois d'arc

*Maclura pomifera*
*ma-KLOO-ra*

▌Zones 5–9
Full sun
Roach repellent, dye

**How to identify**   Although this tree can grow to 60 feet, it is more commonly found about 15 feet tall and rather shrubby in the fencerows of the Midwest. A relative of the mulberry, it is thorny with bright orange inner bark in winter, yellow foliage in fall, and an open, irregular, rounded top habit. Leaves are alternate, smooth, glossy dark green and 5 inches long. Inconspicuous flowers are followed by crinkly skinned, solid light green fruits almost as large as a grapefruit.

Osage-orange

**How to use**   This tree is so thorny that it is not considered choice for landscaping, especially in a small yard. It is an excellent barrier or windbreak plant, but it should not be located near paths or driveways where it could tear clothing or scratch cars. Osage-orange is also a good wildlife- and erosion-control plant; it is available as such from some state forestry departments. Quail are fond of the seeds.

Osage-orange is native to Texas and the surrounding states, where the Osage Indians prized the elasticity of its wood for their bows. The plants were used for miles of hedges before barbed wire replaced them in the middle of the nineteenth century. Even today they provide some of the densest, most durable, decay-resistant wood for fence posts. Trees seldom grow large enough for commercial importance, but the wood is beautiful for woodworking.

The great benefit of this tree to the homeowner is the ability of the

**Parsley**

trees, so both types must be grown for fruit production. If space is limited, 3 trees can be planted in the same hole. The tree, which grows quickly, can be started from seed or plants, is adaptable to many soils, and can withstand heavy pruning, fairly cold winters, summer drought, and high winds.

## Parsley
*Petroselinum crispum*
*pe-tro-SEL-ee-num*

▌Zones 3–10
Sun or light shade
Culinary

**How to identify**   This well-known and much-used herb is a biennial member of the carrot family. It is often grown as an annual; it blooms and then dies out the second year. Plants are neat and attractive at all stages, with flat or curly dark green leaves and a compact habit, growing to 12 inches high and 18 inches wide. Flowers are tiny, yellow-green, and borne in large, flat clusters.

**How to use**   As an edging, a container plant, or blended with other herbs, flowers, or vegetables, parsley adds color and texture to the garden. The universal garnish, it is rich in vitamin A, several of the B vitamins, calcium, and iron, and has more vitamin C per pound than oranges. Its gentle flavor blends well with many foods. Used after eating garlic, it cuts garlic aftertaste and sweetens the breath. The entire plant can be cut 2 inches above the ground and it will regrow, or the outer leaves can be harvested and the center left to keep growing. Parsley can be used dried or fresh; it keeps for weeks in a plastic bag in the refrigerator or freezer.

Parsley root can be somewhat of a laxative. An infusion of the leaves and stems is claimed to be soothing and cleansing in the bath. The oil

fruit to repel roaches and waterbugs. Fruits should be gathered in fall (they can stain cloth, so old clothes should be worn). Six of the fruits tucked into closets and behind the stove can keep a large house free of roaches for as long as 2 years. The inedible fruits when drying give off a subtle, daffodil-like fragrance.

The fruits make striking and nearly permanent additions to wreaths or dried flower bouquets. They can be sliced (they ooze a sticky white liquid), holes poked in the center for wires, and oven-dried for about 4 hours at 200° to 250° F. The bark of the root produces a yellow dye.

**How to grow**   Female and male flowers are borne on separate

is used in perfumes, soaps, shampoos, skin creams, and lotions.

The ancient Greeks fed parsley to horses to give them the stamina to win races. Pregnant women should not use large quantities of parsley because it can irritate the kidneys.

**How to grow** Seed can take as long as 5 weeks to germinate. Pouring boiling water over the seedbed right after planting will soften the seed coats and hasten the sprouting. So will presoaking the seeds in warm water for 24 hours, or freezing them in ice cubes for 3 weeks while the outdoor soil warms up to 50° F. Seedlings should be transplanted while small, because they develop long taproots. Cutting off the flower stalks makes the foliage last longer and taste better. Parsley may develop crown rot or be attacked by nematodes or various worms. It is a favorite of the striped larva of the anise swallowtail butterfly, which rarely does the plant any permanent damage. For winter use, seed can be sown in pots in midsummer and brought indoors, or small plants can be potted up and the foliage cut back drastically to ease the transition.

## Passionflower, maypop, apricotvine
*Passiflora* species
*pass-i-FLOR-a*

▌ Zones 7–10
Full sun to light shade
Ornamental, medicinal

**How to identify** This genus includes a large group of vines that climb by tendrils and have unusual, exquisitely beautiful white to lavender flowers from summer until frost. Some species, such as the crimson red one with recurved petals, at first bear little resemblance to the more familiar one with purple blooms. All are perennial woody vines with trailing stems as much as 30 feet

Top: Passion-
flower
(*P. jamesonii*)
Bottom: Passion-
flower
(*P. alatocaerulea*)

long and edible berries that are an important commercial fruit in tropical countries. Passionflower is native to the southeastern United States.

**How to use** Passionflowers are good house- and greenhouse plants. Outdoors they grow quickly to give cover to porches, arbors, and fences. Native Americans used the leaves for poultices to heal bruises and injuries. Juice from the berries was used for bathing eyes; the leaves and flowers were used as a sedative and painkiller. A tea made from the flowers is considered calming when sipped and also makes a soothing bath to relieve tension. Flowers and berries can be dried.

**How to grow** Plants can be started from seed or cuttings in deep, fertile, well-drained soil.

**Pepper 'Thai Hot'**

Ample water and frequent misting are beneficial. Weak or crowded branches should be pruned in late winter. These shallow-rooted plants should be mulched rather than cultivated. In colder, marginal areas, plants should be located on a south-facing wall. Plants may be bothered by thrips or mealybugs.

### Pepper, hot or chile, cayenne
*Capsicum* species
*KAP-si-kum*

▌Zone 10
Full sun
Ornamental, culinary, insecticidal

**How to identify** This genus includes peppers that are shrubs or small trees in the tropics but are usually grown as annuals in most of the United States. They are prized for their edible fruits, which vary greatly in color, shape, size,

and sizzle. The leaves are pointed, oval, and alternate with one large and one to three smaller ones at each node. Flowers are star shaped and dainty white to purplish with veinlike markings; they are about ½ inch across, followed by the fruit, which may be mild and sweet, such as bell peppers, to hot, such as jalapeños.

**How to use**   Many pepper varieties are grown as ornamentals. The fresh or dried fruit of hot peppers can deter insects on vegetables and flowers; the fruit is blended in water that is then strained and used as a spray. Ground cayenne pepper sprinkled on tomato plants and the silk of corn ears can kill caterpillars and worms.

Native Americans noticed that food flavored with chile peppers did not spoil as quickly and seemed to be digested more easily than un-spiced food. A doctor on Christopher Columbus's second cruise described the plant, and the Spanish and Portuguese explorers took it to many ports where it soon became popular. Pepper plants, especially the fruit, contain capsaicin, a substance that reddens the skin by causing increased blood circulation wherever it touches. (The name means "to bite.") For this reason, it is an important ingredient in liniments for treating bursitis, rheumatism, and other similar ailments. Extracts are antibacterial.

Chili peppers fall into 2 categories—*C. frutescens* or *C. annuum*. The former is a perennial with small, pungent fruit. The latter is an annual (or short-lived perennial) and includes both bell peppers and hot chiles.

Ground black pepper used at the table is not in the genus *Capsicum*. Red, or cayenne, pepper is. (Paprika is the mildest form of cayenne

**Pepper 'Red Cayenne'**

and the highest in vitamin C.) Cayenne comes from *C. annuum* var. *annuum;* tabasco peppers belong to *C. frutescens*. Chili powder, on the other hand, is actually a combination of peppers, herbs, and spices.

**How to grow**   Seed should be planted early indoors. It germinates and grows slowly at first and it should not be set outdoors until all danger of frost is past. Transplanted seedlings should be set at the same depth as in the pot and 12 to 18 inches apart. They should be mulched and kept well watered. Fruits are ready to be harvested when they turn bright red all over. The stems should be cut ¾ inch from the pepper, and the peppers should be dried at once. Or the entire plant can be pulled just before a killing frost and hung upside down in a dry, well-ventilated place until all the peppers are dry. Dried peppers can be ground in a food processor; the dust should not be inhaled.

## Perilla, purple perilla, summer-coleus, beefsteak-plant

*Perilla frutescens*
*pe-RILL-a*

▮ Zones 3–10
Full sun to partial shade
Ornamental, culinary

**How to identify**   Perilla grows 2 to 4 feet tall with branching burgundy stems; it resembles 'Dark Opal' basil. The leaves are large, 2 to 6 inches long, a glowing deep red with fringed edges and white hairs on top and purple ones underneath. The stems are square; perilla belongs to the mint family. The plant blooms with spikes of pinkish green flowers in late summer. Both leaves and round seeds have a spicy fragrance much like that of cinnamon.

**How to use**   The plants are very ornamental in herb or flower gardens or among shrubs. The purple leaves look especially attractive in combination with gray-leaved plants such as artemisia and santolina. The Japanese use the leaves and seeds in making tempura. The salted seeds are tasty alone or served after sweets. The Japanese also use them as a salty center for certain candies. They use the purple variety of perilla to dye their pickled plums. The green-leaved perilla, which they call *shiso*, is used for cooking and flavoring. A quick-drying oil from the plant at one time had economic value in the manufacture of paint.

**How to grow**   Perilla starts easily from seed or plants. For better germination the seeds can be mixed with moist peat moss in a plastic bag and stored in the refrigerator for a week. Seed germinates in 10 days. It can be started indoors in March in the North, outdoors in the South and West. Seedlings transplant easily and should be set 9 to 12 inches apart after nighttime temperatures average 55° F. Plants should be pinched at every 6-inch growth interval to keep them bushy. Unpinched, they become leggy. They may not set seed in cool climates; otherwise they self-sow so freely as to almost be a weed.

## Pipsissewa, wintergreen, rheumatism-weed, groundholly

*Chimaphila umbellata*
*ki-MA-fil-a*

▮ Zones 4–9
Part sun
Ornamental, ground cover

**How to identify**   This woodland evergreen ground cover grows 3 to 10 inches tall with glossy bright green leaves in whorls around the

**Perilla**

stem rising from a pale yellow rhizome. The leaves of one variety, *C. maculata*, have prominent white veins. The fragrant, inch-wide, nodding pink or white flowers bloom May to August in terminal clusters on erect stalks.

**How to use**   In rich, humusy, acid soil, pipsissewa makes a good ground cover under trees or in shady parts of a rock or wildflower garden; it also holds the soil on a bank. It can be found in dry, sandy woodlands throughout southern Canada and all but the most southerly United States.

The leaves have a peculiar flavor that is both sweet and pleasantly bitter. An infusion of the leaves has been used for many medicinal purposes, but the plant's main use has been as one of the flavoring ingredients of candy and soft drinks, particularly root beer.

**How to grow**   Plants can be started from seed or divisions taken in spring, or from cuttings, which root best in late summer to fall. The plant grows slowly. Pipsissewa needs dry, acidic, sandy soil rich in leaf mold and benefits from a mulch of oak leaves or pine needles.

## Potentilla, cinquefoil, tormentilla, goosewort, silverweed
*Potentilla* species
*po-ten-TIL-la*

▮ Zones 2–8
Full sun to light shade
Ornamental, cosmetic, dye

**How to identify**   The nearly 500 species of this genus include 3 listed in the USDA's Selected Weeds, 2 on its list of threatened plants, and various ornamental perennials and low shrubs. The leaves and the flowers resemble those of the strawberry, but the flowers, which bloom for several weeks in

**Top: Pipsissewa
Bottom: Potentilla**

summer, come in yellows and reds. The leaves are toothed and divided into 5 or 7 leaflets. Erect cinquefoil (*P. erecta*)—also called bloodroot or tormentilla—has star-shaped leaves divided into 5 parts. Silverweed (*P. anserina*) has leaves that are silvery underneath and pinnately divided, shaped somewhat like those of tansy. Bush cinquefoil (*P. fruticosa*) has small yewlike leaves although the plant is deciduous.

**How to use**   The plant's long blooming period makes it useful in shrub borders or as a low hedge. Many of the varieties are excellent for flower borders, rock gardens, or ground covers, or as small flow-

**Purple coneflower**

ering shrubs for borders or foundation plantings. Medicines from a decoction of the root were once considered a remedy for fever, toothache, and mouth sores. Pieces of the root of *P. rubra* were chewed to clean teeth. The astringent leaves make potentilla ideal for facial lotions and herbal baths. Potentilla contains enough tannin to tan leather. As a dye plant it turns wool red-brown or purple-red; it turns leather red.

**How to grow**   Potentilla spreads by runners and can be started by divisions or softwood cuttings. It adapts to almost any soil or exposure and grows easily; bloom starts the second year. Plants should be pruned in winter to keep the form compact and bushy; a third of the stems can be removed.

## Purple coneflower, black-sampson, red-sunflower
*Echinacea angustifolia*
*e-ki-NAY-see-a*

▌ Zones 3–9
Full sun to light shade
Ornamental, medicinal

**How to identify**   This lovely perennial wildflower found on the prairies and other dry, open places from Canada to Texas has slightly fragrant, large, daisylike blooms with rose-colored ray flowers, often recurving or cone shaped rather than flat. The centers can be purple to brownish orange. Leaves are long and hairy with 3 distinct veins along their length. The plants can grow from 1 to 5 feet tall, depending on climate and variety, and will give 2 months or more of mid- to late-summer bloom. This plant is distinct from coneflower, or black-eyed-susan (*Rudbeckia hirta*).

**How to use**   Both the wild and several improved varieties make excellent additions to the flower border or wildflower garden. The plants are hardy and long lived and can withstand drought, heat, and high humidity. The abundant blooms attract butterflies and are choice cut flowers; the dried seed heads can be used in dried bouquets or wreaths.

Native Americans prized purple coneflower most highly among all the native plants and used the thick roots for a panacea to help restore general health; to treat snakebites, stings, toothaches, and mumps; as a blood purifier; and to render their hands, feet, and mouths insensitive before holding, walking on, or swallowing hot coals. As late as the 1920s, purple coneflower was one of the plants used most by some drug companies, but it fell from favor with the coming of antibiotics. Some still consider the plant to be antiseptic, antibiotic, tumor inhibiting, and immune system enhancing.

To harvest the roots for medicinal use, it's best to wait until the mature plant begins to die back after several hard frosts. The roots should be cleaned and dried; the crown can be replanted.

**How to grow**   Seeds sprout in 5 to 20 days and more reliably if they are given a month of cold treatment and then sown on the surface of sandy soil enriched with humus and lime. Plants should be spaced 1½ to 2 feet apart. Winter mulch is beneficial. The plants should be divided and reset in new soil every 4 to 5 years.

### Ramp, wild leek
*Allium tricoccum*
*AL-ee-um*

▌Zones 6–7
Full sun to light shade
Culinary

**How to identify**   This perennial, found as an understory plant in moist woodlands, is about a foot

**Ramp**

tall, with wide, smooth leaves on petioles. The plant resembles lily-of-the-valley except it lacks the fragrance. The leaves die down in summer; in fall, flowering stems appear with rounded clusters of white or greenish white blooms followed by black seeds.

**How to use**   The slender underground stems can be pulled loose from the rhizomes, the leaves and outer skin can be used or discarded, and the little that is left can be used sparingly to flavor meats or greens. Ramp is known and grown mostly in the southern Appalachians, where it has long been used for flavoring gamey meats and waterfowl and steamed as a spring delicacy.

**How to grow**   Wildflower specialists offer seed and plants. Ramp should be planted in spring in shaded areas in rich, humusy soil and watered during dry spells. Acid soil and a mulch of leaf mold should be maintained around the plants. The plant spreads by seeds and underground rhizomes but is not invasive.

## Rose, damask rose, French rose, rose of Provins

*Rosa* species and hybrids
*RO-sa*

■ Zones 4–10
Full sun
Ornamental, culinary, cosmetic

**How to identify**   The hardy shrub damask and French roses had traditional herbal uses, but they are the ancestors of many modern hybrids, and any rose can be used today for herbal applications.

**How to use**   Volumes have been written about roses, and most people are familiar with their use. William Penn brought bushes to the American colonies in 1699 and John Adams first planted them around the White House.

Some people consider roses difficult; however, they need not be. New, improved types, including the remarkable landscape roses, bloom throughout the season with a minimum of care. There are roses for every garden use—accent, background, hedges, climbers, miniatures, and trailing types such as *R. wichuraiana,* which stops erosion on banks.

Rose hips, the fruit that forms if blooms are not removed, are rich in vitamin C, also in vitamins A, B, E, and K and in organic acids and pectin. Some roses are bred especially to produce many and large hips for easy gathering, but all rose hips are edible. Tea can be made by pouring 4 cups of boiling water over 1 cup of washed hips. It has a rather sharp, pleasant flavor with a hint of sweetness; it can be drunk as is or added to juices, fruits, and soups. Rose petals can be added to salads or fruit pies, or candied as a garnish.

Rose petals that are gathered, separated, and dried just before the flowers open often increase in perfume

**Rose 'MacGregor's Damask'**

as they dry. They are favorites for potpourris and sachets. Rose water, made from an infusion of the flower petals, adds fragrance and is astringent and cleansing for the skin. Rose oil can be used as perfume.

**How to grow**   Most roses are started from purchased plants; they can also be grown from seed, which takes 3 to 4 months to germinate, or from cuttings taken in fall. Bare-root stock should be planted when dormant, potted roses anytime of the year. The graft point, if there is such a slight swelling, should be 2 inches below the soil surface. After early spring planting and again for winter wherever temperatures drop below 10° F, it is best to mound soil over the crown of the plant in a cone 6 to 12 inches high. This should be removed gradually each spring about the time forsythia blooms. Where winters are severe, a 20 percent loss of

roses over the winter can be expected, though hilling up and the use of rose cones may keep this to a minimum. Roses taken for cut flowers should be snipped back to a 5-leaflet joint so that new flower buds will form.

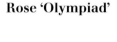

Rose 'Olympiad'

Rose
(*R. wichuraiana*)

**Rosemary**

Varieties with pink, white, or blue flowers are available. Where it thrives, it becomes an evergreen shrub with scaly gray bark.

**How to use**   Rosemary can be used as a shrub or an accent plant or set in a container, according to the climate. It thrives against hot, sunny walls. Prostrate forms make a good ground cover and are attractive in hanging baskets.

Rosemary is good fresh or dried with roasted meats, including game, and with vegetables, cheese, pizza, eggs, and dry beans. Flowers and leaves can be used as a garnish. Sprigs can be frozen.

Rosemary is one of the most ancient and beloved of all herbs. In folklore, it symbolizes remembrance; students in ancient Greece wore garlands in their hair while studying for exams to improve their memory. It is a fine strewing herb, adds scent to sachets, and can be used in a stimulating bath. A tea of rosemary will help clear the head if one has a cold. It makes a good hair rinse for brunettes. As a dye it gives shades of yellow-green.

**How to grow**   Seed is slow and difficult to germinate. More vigorous plants can be started from layering or cuttings; sprigs with a pair of growing tips are preferable. Rooting hormone helps, although cuttings still take up to 6 weeks to root. Lime or wood ashes should be applied to an acid soil. Wet soil inhibits growth, but in pots the soil should never dry out completely. Plants grown indoors should be misted to help them survive dry heat. The leaf tips can be harvested; not more than a fifth of the growth should be taken at any one time. Sprigs should be harvested when plants are brought indoors. Root-bound plants should be shifted to larger containers.

**Rosemary**
*Rosmarinus officinalis*
*ros-ma-RI-nis*

▐ Zones 8–10
Full sun to partial shade
Culinary, crafts

**How to identify**   Upright forms of this member of the mint family grow 5 to 6 feet tall outdoors and 2 to 4 feet as a potted plant. There are also prostrate forms, which are lovely cascading over walls. Both adapt well to bonsai and growing in special shapes. Tiny gray-green leaves can be from needle thin to the width of a pencil and have a strong, delightfully piney fragrance.

## Rue, herb-o'-grace

*Ruta graveolens*
*ROO-ta*

▮ Zones 4–10
Full sun
Ornamental

**How to identify**   Rue grows 2 to 3 feet tall with upright stems of finely cut, lacy blue-green foliage. It is evergreen in warm climates, a perennial subshrub with woody stems near the ground. In colder regions it dies back to the ground in winter. There are extra-blue, dwarf, variegated, and dark green varieties. The flowers come in clusters of mustard yellow, attractive against the blue-green foliage. They bloom from midsummer until fall and can be hung to dry for bouquets. Tiny glands over the entire plant release a volatile oil that has a musky fragrance and bitter flavor.

**How to use**   Rue is a decorative plant for the herb or flower garden and can be clipped for knot gardens. It is attractive in containers of mixed herbs. It is said that as a companion plant it should not be located near basil, sage, or cabbage.

Bunches of rue were once used in churches for sprinkling holy water. Both Michelangelo and Leonardo da Vinci claimed that rue helped their eyesight and creative inner vision. Rue was once planted near stables to repel flies or hung in rooms to keep them insect free. The roots produce a rosy red dye.

**Caution**   Touching the plant causes a rash much like poison ivy in some people, especially when the plant is wet or the sun is hot. Taken internally rue is toxic.

**How to grow**   The common variety can be started from seed; the named varieties should be started from plants, cuttings, or divisions. Plants should be set 2 feet apart in the garden when the soil warms. Moderate fertilization produces the most intense blue foliage. Root diseases can be a problem in hot, moist climates.

Rue

**Safflower**

## Safflower, saffron-thistle, false-saffron, dyer's-saffron

*Carthamus tinctorius*
*KAR-tham-mus*

▌Zones 2–10
Full sun
Ornamental, culinary, dye

**How to identify**    Often grown as an annual, safflower is 1 to 4 feet tall with smooth, erect whitish stems branching near the top. The shiny, oval dark green leaves are alternate on the stems. The leaf margins have sharp, prickly orange hairs. Safflower belongs to the daisy family and produces an abundance of yellow, purple, white, or, most commonly, yellow maturing to orange-red thistlelike flowers with leafy bracts in June and July. Seeds, which hide in thistly down, follow in August.

**Safflower**

**How to use** Clumps of safflower are attractive and colorful in the flower or herb garden or with wildflowers. The flowers are attractive in fresh or dried bouquets; the seed heads are also decorative.

Safflower is used as a saffron substitute to color and flavor foods, although the flavor is much more bland than that of saffron. The flowers can be cut and dried in late summer and the petals stored in an airtight container, then crushed or powdered (just before using) to add a red color to salad dressing, vinegars, pasta, sauces, marinades, cream soups, chicken gravy, rice, or curries. The flowers can also be used for or added to herbal teas.

Safflower has been used as a dye plant for centuries; some of the wrappings of the ancient Egyptian mummies were dyed with these flowers. The plants are raised commercially in California and in the Southwest for their seeds, which yield the vegetable oil of the same name. This oil is also used in paints and varnishes. The powdered petals have historically been used for rouge. The plant makes shades of yellow to red dyes for silk and wool.

**How to grow** Safflower prefers the dry climates of the West and average to poor soil. It grows easily from seed sown in place in early spring; seed germinates in 3 to 18 days depending on the temperature. Seedlings do not transplant well. They should be thinned to 6 inches apart and protected from rabbits until the tender young leaves develop their spiny self-defense. Blooms come in about 12 weeks. Where summers are very wet, safflower is prone to disease, and the seeds may sprout on the plant before they ripen. Plants often self-sow.

Saffron crocus

**Saffron crocus, true saffron, saffron**
*Crocus sativus*
*KRO-cus*

▮ Zones 5–10
Full sun to light shade
Ornamental, culinary, dye

**How to identify** Saffron crocus differs from other crocus in two ways. It blooms in fall and it has no true stem; instead the flower sits on the tubular portion of the corolla. The grasslike leaves, about 18 inches long, appear in late summer shortly before the lovely chalice-shaped buds open to starlike flowers up to 2½ inches across, each with 6 petals. Blooms come in white, lavender, and shades of reddish purple.

**How to use** Saffron crocus looks best planted in large drifts for a charming addition to the autumn flower border or rock garden, or among low ground covers or grass that need not be mowed until the following spring.

Saffron crocus has been prized since the beginning of civilization for its color, flavor, and aroma; it was a luxury usually reserved for royalty, heroes, and gods. The wealthy early Romans used it to perfume their homes and baths. The prominent stigmas, or female parts, of the crocuslike flower protrude like intense cinnamon red tongues, and it is these that must be gathered by hand from about 160,000 plants to produce perhaps 2 pounds of the slightly bitter herb per acre, at a cost of more than $4,500 per pound. Whole threads are the desired form to buy or harvest. After harvesting, they should be dried, then stored in an airtight glass container.

A few saffron crocus threads will go a long way when added to rice, noodles, chicken, bouillabaisse, paella, cakes, cookies, and breads. The herb gives a warm yellow color wherever it is used. Large amounts taken internally, ¼ ounce or more, are toxic. It yields an excellent but water-soluble yellow dye, impractical for most purposes today.

**How to grow**   Saffron crocus grows best in zones 5 to 7. It does not do well in the Deep South, and although it grows as far north as southern New England, it will probably not bloom freely enough in cool climates to produce many of the cinnamon red threads. Corms should be planted in spring or early summer in groups 2 to 6 inches apart and 2 to 4 inches deep in light, rich, well-drained soil. Where they thrive, they will multiply and can be divided every several years.

## Sage, common or garden, clary sage, muscatel sage, pineapple sage, Mexican sage
*Salvia* species
*SAL-vee-a*

▌Zones 3–10
Full sun to light shade
Ornamental, culinary, bee plant

**How to identify**   Common sage (*S. officinalis*) is a perennial of the mint family and is the hardiest member of the group. It has pebble-textured, fragrant gray-green leaves, long, narrow, and opposite on the square and sometimes woody stems. Spikes of purple or violet-blue flowers bloom in summer. Clary sage (*S. sclarea*) is a 3-foot biennial with large, velvety, oval leaves and pinkish purple spires of flowers from May to September. Pineapple sage (*S. elegans*) has 2-inch-long lanceolate leaves and small firecracker-like scarlet flowers that attract butterflies. Mexican sage (*S. leucantha*) has purple flowers and pointed leaves similar to those of common sage but less aromatic. Pineapple sage and Mexican sage are hardy only to zone 8 but can be grown as annuals or in containers farther north.

**How to use**   All of the sages are attractive garden plants with at least a few weeks of fairly showy flowers that bees make into delicious honey. There are many species, varieties, and cultivars, 500 or more, some only decorative, others useful as well. Three attractive forms of common sage for culinary use are tricolor sage (*S. officinalis* 'Tricolor'), golden sage (*S. officinalis* 'Aurea'), and purple sage (*S. officinalis* 'Purpurascens'); all are excellent for window box or garden accent. Others are ideal for edging, background, or low hedges. Sage is considered a good companion plant for cabbage, carrots, tomatoes, strawberries, and marjoram, but it should not be grown near onions.

Common sage is used mainly as a culinary herb; its leaves give poultry stuffing and many sausages their traditional flavor. Young fresh leaves are good in salads, soups, omelets, fritters, breads, marinades, meats, or vegetables. Dried leaves have a stronger but somewhat different flavor. The leaves can also be frozen.

Common sage has long been thought to increase wisdom and improve memory. A tea from the leaves was used for all manner of cures in the Middle Ages; it was even supposed to promote longevity. A natural preservative, it contains an antioxidant that improves the stability and shelf life of certain foods. Dried flowers can be added to herbal wreaths, especially culinary ones. The dried leaves of pineapple sage and the dried flowers of Mexican sage are good in potpourris. Common sage makes yellow-buff to green-gray dyes.

**How to grow**   Common sage grows easily from seed started indoors 8 to 10 weeks before the last frost date. Other types of sage are best started from divisions or cuttings. The seedlings should be thinned or transplanted to 2 feet apart, then well watered until established. After that they are drought resistant and will perish if overwatered. Plants may not bloom until August of the first year; leaves should not be cut after September because the plants need some foliage to get through the winter. In spring the plants can be cut back to within a few inches of the roots. The prunings are aromatic when added to a wood fire or charcoal grill. Plants should be replaced every few years or when they become too woody.

**Mexican sage**

**Opposite, top:
Santolina
Opposite, bottom:
Summer savory**

**St. John's wort**

## St. John's wort, amber touch-and-heal, goatweed

*Hypericum perforatum*
hy-PER-i-cum

■ Zones 2–7
Full sun to light shade
Ornamental, dye

**How to identify**   This and many related species are small shrubs or hardy but short-lived perennials growing about 3 feet tall with erect, bushy stems, each with 2 raised ridges along their length. The leaves are oblong-oval in opposite pairs, each pair at right angles to the pair above and below. Oil glands near the margins of the leaves look like small black dots. The plant smells of turpentine or balsam. All forms have 5-petaled bright yellow flowers in late summer. The plant grows wild in woods and dry meadows and along roadsides from Quebec to Nevada.

**How to use**   Choice varieties are attractive in the shrub or flower border and in rock gardens, and as a bright summer bloomer in the herb garden.

Although this plant was once used to cure many conditions, from tuberculosis and madness to bed wetting, it is unsafe in large or continual doses. No home remedies are recommended. The plant is being studied as a possible food preservative. Yellow and red dyes can be made from the flowering tops.

**How to grow**   The shrub varieties are usually started from seed, cuttings, or divisions in fall. Herbaceous types spread by runners but seldom become invasive in North America. Flowers grow on the current year's growth. Severe pruning in spring improves the plants. Old, weak wood should be removed and the remaining shoots cut to 9 to 12 inches.

## Santolina, lavender-cotton

*Santolina chamaecyparissus*
san-to-LYE-na

■ Zones 6–10
Full sun
Ornamental, insect repellent

**How to identify**   This shrubby perennial member of the daisy family has a woody base and grows up to 2 feet tall and as wide with aromatic, delicate silver gray or green leaves, ½ inch to 1½ inches long. The leaves are divided into tiny, comblike leaflets that resemble coral. The leaves feel sticky with oil, the fragrance of which can be intensified by crushing the leaves between your fingers. The flowers are bright yellow buttons, up to ¾ inch in diameter, that bloom singly at the tips of long, erect stems in June and July.

**How to use**   Santolina makes a fine outdoor shrub, or an aromatic winter houseplant if it receives at least 5 hours of sun a day. Its fragrance and compact habit make it ideal for formal and informal herb gardens; it became an important garden plant in Elizabethan England for its use in knot gardens. It is also attractive in rock gardens, as an accent plant, and for edging, texture, and color contrast in the border. It is an excellent seaside plant and indeed blooms best in that situation.

Dried sprigs repel moths. A tea made from the seeds and flowers was historically used to treat ringworm. The flowers and foliage are decorative in dried bouquets and herbal wreaths, and add scent to sachets and potpourris. The flowers should be hung upside down to dry. Santolina gives golds and yellows for dyeing wool.

**How to grow**  Santolina can be started from seed, cuttings, divisions, or layered pieces in spring. Seed and cuttings take up to 2 years to make plants of useful size. For quickest growth, the soil can be mounded around the plant in fall to encourage layering, then the sections pulled apart in spring. Dry, light, neutral-to-alkaline soil is best; good drainage, especially in cold winters, can be crucial. The plant is drought tolerant. It should be pruned in spring to encourage compact summer growth; it should never be pruned to the ground, for the new growth arises from the old wood. Mulching for winter protection is beneficial.

**Savory**
*Satureja* species
*sa-tu-REE-ja*

▮ Zones 5–10
Full sun
Culinary, ornamental

**How to identify**  Summer savory (*S. hortensis*) is grown as an annual in cold regions; it reaches about 2

feet tall and has white or pink flowers and linear gray leaves that turn purple in fall. Winter savory (*S. montana*), a perennial, grows 6 to 20 inches tall with stiff, upright, square stems that are woody at the base. Leaves are an inch long or less, narrow, glossy, and dark green. White to lavender mintlike flowers are borne in the leaf axils. Both savories bloom from July through mid-September. The entire plants are aromatic, with a peppery flavor similar to but milder than that of thyme. Summer savory is sweeter and more delicate; winter savory is a bit stronger.

**How to use**   Both savories make good potted plants as long as they receive at least 5 hours of direct sun each day. Growing more than one summer savory plant is recommended, because each plant gives only about ¼ cup of leaves per cutting.

Winter savory can be sheared for knot and ribbon gardens. Summer savory, preferred for cooking for its milder flavor and better leaf texture, is sometimes called bean herb and goes well with dried beans, lentils, peas, or fresh green beans. A good salt substitute, it brings out the flavors of foods as salt does. Savory cuts the strong flavor of cabbage, turnips, and brussels sprouts. Leaves can be chopped into salads, soups, stew, and anything with cheese. The leaves have more flavor if picked before the flowers bloom and can be frozen or dried for storage. Winter savory can be used after the frost has killed summer savory.

For hundreds of years, summer and winter savory were thought to regulate sexual desire—summer savory to increase it, winter savory to cool it. Both savories, but especially winter savory, were used to stimulate the appetite. The ancient Romans planted savory near beehives

for pleasant-tasting honey. Summer savory makes a tea for stomach problems, sore throats, or coughs. Crushed leaves rubbed on stings or insect bites may bring relief. Both leaves and flowers can be added to sachets and potpourris. The savories can be used as strewing herbs; they can also be added to facial steams or baths to cleanse oily skin.

**How to grow**   Summer savory can be seeded in place in early spring, then thinned to 4 to 6 inches apart. Mounding the soil around the stems gives additional support if plants become too floppy. Bushiness is encouraged by starting to harvest about 6 weeks after the seeds sprout.

Winter savory can be started from cuttings, root divisions, layering, or seed begun indoors 4 months before the last frost date. Seedlings should be spaced 12 inches apart outdoors. Bushiness is encouraged by starting to harvest about 6 weeks after transplanting.

Winter savory should be mulched for winter, especially in the northern part of its range. It is most subject to winterkill in wet places or seasons. Dead wood can be removed anytime. Winter savory should be replanted every few years or when plants become too woody. Container plants should be cut back at transplanting time; the soil should be allowed to dry out somewhat between waterings.

## Sesame, benne
*Sesamum indicum*
*SE-sa-mum*

▌Zones 7–10
Full sun
Culinary, crafts

**How to identify**   Sesame is a strong-smelling, tender annual with unbranching stems. In warm climates and rich soil, it will reach 6 feet with flower spikes 2 feet long, but a height of 2 to 3 feet is more common. It has close-set, glossy leaves, sometimes opposite at the bottom and alternate toward the top. Each leaf is 3 to 5 inches long, oval to lance shaped, with smooth or entire margins, pointed tips, and a granular feel to the underside. The entire plant is covered with short white hairs; the square stems are deeply grooved in the center of each side. Trumpet-shaped flowers are borne in the leaf axils, each trumpet 1 inch long and mostly white with pink, yellow, or lavender markings. The flowers bloom all summer. Felty, 4-grooved seedpods form inside the fading flowers and become closely packed on long, curving stems. They burst open suddenly when fully ripe—perhaps the reason behind the magic passwords "open sesame."

**How to use**   The plant itself is not especially attractive. It is grown commercially in its native Asia and Africa for the oily, nutty seeds that produce sesame oil, which is rich in vitamins and minerals and can be stored much longer than any other vegetable oil without turning rancid. The residue makes a good protein supplement for cattle and poultry. Each plant yields only a single tablespoon or less of seed.

Sweet, nutty-tasting sesame seed is widely used on hamburger buns and in breads, cakes, confections, and cookies. The seed is also ground into a paste called tahini, used in Middle Eastern cuisine. Seedpods explode and scatter seeds 4 to 5 weeks after the flowers open. To gather seeds for drying, the stems should be cut before the seedpods explode and hung upside down in a paper bag in a warm, airy location. After the pods split and curl back, the seeds fall to the bottom of the bag. They should be stored in an airtight container.

The seedpods make fascinating additions to dried arrangements.

**Sesame**

**How to grow**   Seed can be sown directly in the garden when the soil is warm or indoors 8 weeks before the last frost date. The seeds sprout in as little as 2 days; seedlings should be thinned or transplanted to 6 to 8 inches apart. The plants begin blooming while less than a foot tall. The roots are shallow, so staking may be needed. The longer and hotter the summer, the better, for the plants, though easy to grow, mature slowly, in about 120 days. Manure and lime in the soil are beneficial; too much nitrogen should be avoided.

## Soapwort, bouncing-bet, fuller's-herb, wild-sweet-william

*Saponaria officinalis*
*sa-po-NA-ree-a*

▮ Zones 2–8
Full sun to light shade
Ornamental, cosmetic

**How to identify**   This perennial grows wild along roadsides and in pastures and old gardens, usually in clumps. Its single upright stem reaches 1 to 2 feet tall. The leaves are opposite, lance shaped, and up to 3 inches long on short, broad stalks. Flowers on wild plants are pink or whitish, opening from a dense cluster of darker buds, each bloom an inch across with 5 petals.

**Soapwort**

Flowers bloom from July through September.

**How to use**   These are among the easiest plants to grow. Several types have been bred for garden use in colors from white to purple. Shorter varieties, such as the trailing *S. ocymoides*, are attractive in the rock garden. Taller forms, which make excellent cut flowers, thrive in a wildflower garden or in drifts along a hedgerow.

Early settlers brought this plant to North America from England, but it was also known to the medieval Arabs, Chinese, and Native Americans. It was used mostly for its saonins, which produce lather when the roots or leaves are crushed, soaked, or boiled in water. This natural soap can be used to clean and brighten anything from kid gloves to metal utensils. It was used to thicken and clean newly woven wool cloth in New England textile factories, thus the name fuller's-herb. It is still used to restore rare old fabrics in museums. The Pennsylvania Dutch used it to make beer foamy; commercially produced saponins are still used in brewing.

The plant was once used as a medicine, but it is a strong purgative and tastes like soap, so it is no longer recommended for internal consumption. Used externally, it is said to stop itching and irritation from acne and eczema. It also makes an effective natural shampoo.

**How to grow**   Soapwort can be started from divisions, or seed planted outdoors in September or from March to June for a succession of bloom. It prefers darkness to germinate and sprouts in 10 days. Plants should be thinned to 6 inches apart. It self-sows and can become invasive, although cutting the flowers before they go to seed should alleviate this situation.

## Sorrel, French, garden sorrel, dock, greensauce

*Rumex* species
*ROO-mex*

▮ Zones 3–10
Full sun to partial shade
Culinary, dye

**How to identify**   Sorrel is found in the wild in meadows and along roadsides. An erect stem grows from the basal rosette of leaves, arrow shaped on French sorrel (*R. scutatus*), lance shaped with small points at the base on other types, including broad-leaf sorrel (*R. acetosa*). The 2- to 2½-foot stem branches toward the top. Upper leaves are alternate and embrace the stem. Clusters of small reddish green to brown flowers bloom from June to September; round, flat seedpods follow. In the garden, French sorrel is prostrate, with bright yellow-green leaves up to 12 inches long. Wood sorrel (*Oxalis acetosella*), or oxalis, is a completely different plant, although its shamrocklike leaves contain oxalic acid, as do the leaves of French sorrel.

**How to use**   The seeds of French sorrel are greatly favored by goldfinches. A short row can be planted at the side of the vegetable garden where the plant can grow as a perennial, or a few plants can be included in an herb garden.

French sorrel was once grown regularly in vegetable gardens. A classic soup made from its leaves is its greatest claim to fame. The leaves were also mashed and mixed with vinegar and sugar as a popular green sauce with cold meat and fish. A perennial of the buckwheat family, sorrel contains oxalic acid and vitamin C, which give it a unique, tart, lemony flavor; however, the acid can be toxic to small children, the elderly, or persons in poor health. It is extremely poisonous in large amounts, but parboiling before cooking reduces the problem.

For culinary use, the leaves of French sorrel can be harvested starting about 4 to 6 weeks after sprouting, or when they are 4 to 6 inches tall. They can be cut down to ground level and will grow back vigorously. Small amounts can be added to salads. It is delicious with spinach or other cooked greens even though it turns an unappealing brownish green when cooked. Leaves do not dry well but can be frozen for winter soups.

Before commercial copper polishes were available, sorrel leaves, salt,

**French sorrel**

and vinegar were used to scour and shine copper pans. The branches with seeds are attractive in flower arrangements; they should be picked before the seeds spread through the garden. The leaves and flowering tops produce a greenish yellow dye.

**How to grow**   Sorrel can be treated as a biennial, the seed sown in fall or very early spring, since it tastes best before it flowers and tends to bolt in warm weather. It should be grown in rich, moist soil. It can also be started from root divisions. Plants should be thinned or transplanted to 4 to 8 inches apart. A mulch will help keep leaves from turning bitter in hot weather. The mild flavor will return in the fall crop of leaves. Harvests can continue several weeks past frost. Although the leaves may turn reddish in the cold, the flavor is unchanged. The roots are difficult to remove and can become invasive. This can be handled by digging up and dis-

carding the entire row when it first bolts in summer, then planting a new row for fall harvest. Otherwise, French sorrel should be planted where it can be contained, and the plants divided every 3 to 4 years. Container plants should be watered frequently and given at least 5 hours a day of direct sun. Potted plants will reach only 8 inches. Red spider mite infestations can be treated with a soapy spray.

## Stinging-nettle
*Urtica dioica*
*ur-TIE-ka* **or** *UR-ti-ka*

▮ Zones 3–8
Full sun to light shade
Culinary, tea

**How to identify**   This perennial can grow from 4 to 6 feet tall with erect, unbranched stems and opposite, heart-shaped dark green leaves with saw-toothed edges. The plant grows in waste and weedy places, often near water, from southern Canada through most of the United States. It looks bushy because it grows from underground roots in a dense cluster. The small, hollow hairs that cover the stems and undersides of the leaves are not obvious, but when brushed against they break off and inject a stinging chemical into the skin. Nettle flowers are inconspicuous, tiny and light green, and borne on slender branched spikes that hang from the axils of the leaves from June through September. An annual form—a 1-foot-tall dwarf nettle (*U. urens*)—is found almost worldwide.

**How to use**   Stinging-nettle is rich in nitrogen and is said to stimulate plant growth and to increase essential oils in herbs. The leaves can be made into a manure tea or added as an activator to the compost pile. Nettle tea is said to repel insects and is also supposed to help curdle

**Stinging-nettle**

milk in cheese making. Nettles are hosts and food for the caterpillars of many butterflies.

The leaves are rich in protein, iron, and vitamins A and C and make a nutritious tea. Rubber gloves should be worn when picking and washing the leaves. Experienced herb growers use young, not-yet-stingy shoots in salads; the leaves lose their sting if cooked or added to soup.

The fibers of this plant have been used to make strong cordage and cloth. The by-products of this once-large industry included sugar, protein, starch, and alcohol. The plant was once used medicinally to cure everything from baldness to tuberculosis. It was long an honored spring tonic. Touching the leaves of this plant results in stinging pain, with or without a rash. Because the sting draws blood to the area, people with gout and rheumatism once resorted to scourging with nettles to relieve their greater pains. Nettle is a commercial source of chlorophyll.

Today, some people use the leaves or the tea in herbal baths to stimulate the skin and improve circulation, or as a scalp massage to combat dandruff. Nettles have been used to make wine, beer, and pudding and can be dried for animal feed, and chicken feed that boosts the nutrition of eggs. The roots provide a yellow dye, the tops a green dye; the seeds yield an oil used for illumination.

**How to grow**   Seed and plants are commercially available. Nettle can also be started from divisions of wild clumps. Heavy clothing and gloves should be worn when handling it. Stings can be somewhat relieved by rubbing with the juice of curly or yellow dock, mullein, or the nettle's own juice.

**Sunflower**
*Helianthus annuus*
*hee-lee-AN-thus*

▌ Zones 3–10
Full sun
Ornamental, culinary, birdseed

**How to identify**   Usually grown as an annual, sunflowers can reach 20 feet in height with blooms 12 inches or more across. Leaves are alternate, light gray-green, and heart shaped with toothed edges. The stems are thick, hairy, and upright. Daisylike flowers, bright

**Sunflower 'Sunrise'**

yellow with yellow, brown, or amber centers, bloom from late summer until frost. The large, flat seed heads develop edible seeds in concentric patterns.

**How to use** The flowers are striking in the background of the garden and are best grown in masses as a windbreak or focal point. Smaller named varieties make excellent cut flowers. The seeds attract birds. Sunflowers should not be planted near potatoes; they can stunt the growth. The plants are good for absorbing moisture from the ground near a house and have been used to reclaim marshy land in the Netherlands.

To use the seeds, they should be boiled in salted water until the shells crack (about 5 minutes), then drained and dried. They can be eaten raw; they can also be roasted with oil or butter and salt for 20 minutes at 300° F. Seeds can be sprouted (just ¼-inch sprouts; beyond that they become bitter) for a nutritious addition to salads and sandwiches. Buds can be eaten raw or steamed like artichokes.

The Spanish explorers took the sunflower back with them to Europe. Commercial growing began in Russia; there the seeds were sold as snacks on street corners and in railway stations. All parts of the plant are usable. Its pith—one of the lightest of cellular structures, even lighter than cork—is used in scientific laboratories as well as for making rope, paper, life preservers, and textiles. The seeds are pressed for oil, which is used in cooking.

Sunflower seed is prized by birds and wildlife and increases egg production when fed to chickens. Dried stems have been used for fuel. The flowers make a yellow dye.

**How to grow** Sunflowers are easy to grow from seed sown outdoors after frost or indoors in pots. Seedlings should be thinned or transplanted to 12 to 18 inches apart. Once the heavy flower heads form, the plants may need staking. To save the seeds, the flower heads can be cut as they droop, then hung in bags or over newspapers until the seeds fall out. Growing them is a fine project for children because the plants gain height so quickly.

**Sweet cicely, myrrh, sweet-chervil, anise-fern, candyplant**
*Myrrhis odorata*
MIR-is

▮ Zones 3–10
Part sun with afternoon shade
Culinary, ornamental

**How to identify** A member of the parsley family, sweet cicely grows 3 to 5 feet tall with ferny fronds of leaves that are velvety on top,

**Sunflower 'Color Fashion'**

whitish and spotted on the undersides. The flowers are flat white umbels, similar to Queen-Anne's-lace, about 2 to 4 inches across, with the inner blooms male and the outer ones bisexual. The seedpods are decorative, like clusters of folded umbrellas, each up to an inch long; they ripen from green to dark brown or black.

**How to use**   Sweet cicely is ideal for the back of an herb or flower garden, for accent against a fence, or for a foundation planting.

Every part of the plant is edible and intensely aromatic, with an anise-like fragrance and sweet, lingering licorice flavor. Sweet cicely is a natural sweetener. A related species grows wild in some woodlands. Although sometimes called by the common name myrrh, sweet cicely is not the myrrh of the Bible, which is the aromatic gum of a tropical tree.

Leaves from established plants can be added to fresh salads or used as a garnish from early spring until snowfall, because this is one of the last plants to turn brown between fall frosts and winter freezes. Leaves are sweet and good in tea or in breads or pastries. Like French tarragon, it seems to take the fishiness out of fish and enhance the flavor. The licorice-flavored green seeds can be chopped and used for flavoring. The seed heads should be harvested before they mature, then hung in paper bags until dry. Each plant will yield about 4 cups of leaves and ½ cup of seeds per year. Seeds are good in confections, cakes, and in apple pie. The root can be harvested in late fall or when the plant is divided, then peeled and chopped. It can be eaten raw, or parboiled for use in salads or stir-fried dishes, or browned in butter and served like parsnips, or grated and added to quick breads.

The flowers and foliage are excellent additions to flower arrangements, and the seed clusters are decorative in dried bouquets or wreaths. The oily seeds can be mixed with melted beeswax for a scented furniture polish.

**How to grow**   Sweet cicely seems to need strong winter dormancy; seed sown in fall where winters are cold often germinates the following spring. Once started, sweet cicely is an easy, hardy, long-lived perennial and also self-sows. Seedlings should be thinned or transplanted to 2 feet apart in moist, rich, slightly acid soil with at least afternoon shade. Each plant will form 1 or 2 deep taproots, about 2 inches thick, that can be split. If the root is harvested, the top and eye can be replanted.

**Sweet cicely**

## Sweet woodruff

*Galium odoratum* (formerly *Asperula odorata*)
*GAL-ee-um*

∎ Zones 4–8
Light to moderate shade
Fragrance, flavoring, ornamental, strewing herb

**How to identify**  This square-stemmed perennial member of the Madder family sprawls to about 8 inches in height. The leaves are shiny, rough edged, and dark green, and are arranged like the spokes of a wheel around the stem in whorls of 6 to 8. The leaves have only a slight fragrance when fresh, but they dry with a scent of vanilla and new-mown hay that lasts for years.

**Sweet woodruff**

In spring sweet woodruff is smothered with loose clusters of tiny, star-shaped, 4-petaled white flowers. It grows wild in moist woodlands and along roads.

**How to use**  Sweet woodruff is an excellent ground cover for woodlands, under lawn trees, and in combination with flowering crab apples, shrubs, and roses. It spreads rapidly.

Sprigs of sweet woodruff are essential for flavoring May wine, the making of which is both a tonic and a celebration in Germany in spring. Sweet woodruff is used in punches and commercial beverages, is added to tobacco and snuff, and is a fixative for perfumes. In medieval times the leaves were hung in churches to scent them for holidays; in Elizabethan England the dried leaves were used in sachets, wreaths, and nosegays to ward off diseases and mask unpleasant odors. Sweet woodruff tea was said to soothe both nerves and stomach, among other ailments, and was added to other medicines to improve the flavor.

**Caution**  Large quantities can cause dizziness and vomiting. The Food and Drug Administration considers sweet woodruff safe for use only in alcoholic beverages.

Traditional May wine is made by adding a few sprigs of sweet woodruff to a bottle of Rhine wine for a day or so, then decanting the wine into a punch bowl and floating fresh strawberries on top. Used in moderation, sweet woodruff is delicious in fruit drinks and makes a soothing tea. The leaves freeze well.

As a strewing herb it is fragrant between linens and woolens, where it is said to repel moths, or folded in sofa beds. It can be harvested anytime, but just before or during bloom yields the most intense fragrance. Drying it in darkness will preserve some greenness. It should be stored in an airtight container until needed. Leaves add a long-lasting scent to sachets and herbal pillows. Stems and leaves make a tan dye, the roots a red one.

**How to grow**    Sweet woodruff is best started as nursery plants, divisions of creeping stems, or cuttings, which root quickly. They should be set 9 to 12 inches apart in rich, moist, acid soil, and weeded carefully so as not to disturb the spreading stems.

## Tansy, scented-fern, stinking-willie, bitter-buttons
*Tanacetum vulgare*
*ta-na-SEE-tum*

▌Zones 3–10
Full sun to light shade
Ornamental, dye, insect repellent

**How to identify**    Tansy is a hardy perennial that grows in a clump 2 to 5 feet tall. It is often found wild along the roadsides across the northern states. The leaves are feathery and dark green and alternate along the stems with many deeply cut leaflets. Buttonlike buttery yellow flowers bloom in clusters almost like yarrow from July to October.

**How to use**    Though once used as a tea, in cooking, and as a medicine, tansy is now known to contain a toxic oil and is unsafe to be taken internally.

Several varieties are available for the garden, including such choice ones as silver and curled or the variety 'Crispum'. All can be grown in containers or near paths where they will be brushed often to release their pleasant fragrance.

With its strong, camphorlike scent, tansy has long been favored as a natural insect repellent supposed to deter flies, lice, fleas, and ants.

**Top and bottom: Tansy**

**French tarragon**

### Tarragon, French
*Artemisia dracunculus*
*ar-te-MEEZ-ee-ah*

■ Zones 5–10
Full sun
Culinary

**How to identify**   This perennial grows up to 2 feet tall with simple, alternate, glossy, narrow leaves ¼ inch to 3 inches long that smell like anise when crushed. The aroma increases with drying or wilting. The lingering flavor is somewhat like a bittersweet licorice. Tiny gray-green flower heads appear from July to October; they are ⅛ inch across and neither showy nor capable of producing seed. This herb can easily be confused with Russian tarragon (*A. dracunculoides*), a more vigorous and aggressive plant with little flavor.

**How to use**   French tarragon is considered a good companion plant for most vegetables. It also grows well on a sunny windowsill for a year-round supply. Chewing a leaf of this herb gives a numb feeling to the tongue. Essential to French cuisine, French tarragon is one of the main ingredients of fines herbes, béarnaise sauce, and tartar sauce. It is slightly on the bitter side, so it should be used carefully. It enhances fish, meats, vegetables, mushrooms, rice, soups, cream sauces, cheeses, and eggs. It is excellent in herbed vinegars, mayonnaise, and butters. It keeps well in vinegar or can be frozen or dried.

**How to grow**   Genuine French tarragon must be started from cuttings or divisions. (Tarragon that is started from seed is Russian tarragon.) French tarragon requires some dormancy and does not do well where winters are mild or summers are long and hot. Plants take until the second year to become well established. They should

Colonial housewives spread tansy between sheets and the mattress and rubbed leaves on meat to preserve it and to discourage flies.

Lotions with tansy are very soothing and cleansing and effective for controlling acne. The flowers are excellent fresh or dried in bouquets, and the foliage is attractive in arrangements. The leaves make green dyes and the flowers yellow dyes.

**How to grow**   Most varieties of tansy are so easily grown from seed or divisions in spring or fall that they can become invasive. They spread by underground rhizomes and also self-sow freely. Plants should be spaced 12 to 24 inches apart. Clumps should be divided frequently or contained like mint.

be set 2 feet apart in well-drained soil. The soil should be kept free of grass or anything that will hold moisture around the roots; mildew can kill the plants.

French tarragon has serpentine roots that should be divided every 2 to 3 years. Flowers should be removed to keep the plants productive. The plant can be cut back nearly to the ground in fall.

### Thyme, common, mother-of-thyme, woolly thyme
*Thymus* species
*TI-mus*

∎ Zones 2–10
Full sun to light shade
Culinary, ornamental, crafts

**How to identify** Thymes are the third largest group of herbs (next to sage and mint), with almost 400 types. Some are creeping ground covers. Others are aromatic shrubs growing to a foot tall with variable foliage and fragrances that mimic many other herbs. Tiny gray-green leaves are usually ⅛ inch long and in opposite pairs; young leaves are dark red on the undersides. Mats of foliage are covered with white, pink, or lavender to purplish red flowers from April to July.

**How to use** Various thymes are ideal for ground covers, between paving stones, in rock gardens, as edgings, or cascading over walls. Mother-of-thyme (*T. serpyllum* and the similar *T. praecox*) can be used as a lawn substitute and mowed or walked upon or sat upon in a growing garden seat; brushing against them or walking on them releases the fragrance. Like woolly thyme (*T. pseudolanuginosus*), these are more decorative than flavorful. Upright types are attractive in flower or herb gardens or in the front of a foundation planting. In the vegetable garden thyme seems to

Top: Variegated lemon thyme
Bottom: Woolly thyme

enhance the growth of plants in the nightshade family, such as potatoes, tomatoes, peppers, and eggplant. It also repels cabbageworms and whiteflies. Thyme is an excellent bee plant and thus ideal around fruit trees. Thyme honey has an exquisite flavor.

There are few foods not improved by adding a bit of common thyme (*T. vulgaris*). With marjoram, parsley, and bay, it is bouquet garni. Alone or in combination with other herbs in tea, a teaspoon per cup of hot water, thyme is said to calm the nerves and soothe coughs. It is also used to flavor Benedictine® liqueur. An overuse of oil of thyme can be harmful.

Thyme can be used as a strewing herb, as protection against moths, and in sachets and potpourris. Thyme contains a powerful disinfectant, thymol, which is effective against bacteria and such fungal infections as athlete's foot. Thymol is used in many colognes, soaps, detergents, and shaving lotions. The leaves are good in herbal lo-

tions and baths and especially in herbal pillows.

**How to grow**   Common thyme is the easiest to grow. Mother-of-thyme will not thrive in warm climates. Plants take up to 2 years from seed to be usable, so buying plants or dividing existing clumps is recommended. A little bonemeal is beneficial when planting; otherwise thyme should be fed sparingly the first year. A mulch of stone chips is one of the best ways to keep the roots cool and the foliage dry. Winter mulching is recommended; thyme is not reliably hardy.

## Valerian, garden-heliotrope, allheal

*Valeriana officinalis*
*va-le-ree-AN-a*

▮ Zones 3–10
Full sun to partial shade
Ornamental, cosmetic

**How to identify**   Valerian is a somewhat weedy perennial that grows 5 feet tall. Opposite, almost ferny leaves have 5 to 12 pairs of leaflets. The tiny, fragrant, fluffy

**Valerian**

flowers are borne in terminal clusters from May to August and come in several colors, mostly white to pale pink. There is another garden heliotrope with dark blue flowers that belongs to the borage family, an unrelated plant with few if any similarities. The same is true of American valerian (*Cypripedium calceolus* var. *pubescens*), a name sometimes given to lady's-slipper, a wild orchid. When dried, true valerian root has an unpleasant odor. Greek-valerian, or Jacob's-ladder (*Polemonium caeruleum,* zones 3 to 7), is also similar, with drooping sky blue flowers with yellow stamens. It prefers moist ground.

**How to use**   This old-fashioned flower now comes in new cultivars of various colors and heights. It is attractive in the herb or flower garden and as a fragrant cut flower. The plant will naturalize in the northern states for a meadow or wildflower garden.

The root is sometimes used as rat bait. The dried root is used in many medicinal preparations in Europe, where the plant is grown as a cash crop in some places. It has been used historically as a natural tranquilizer.

The roots can be harvested in spring or fall, then washed, dried quickly at 120° F until brittle, and stored in an airtight container. The dried root can be used alone or with catnip to stuff cat toys. Large doses of valerian can cause vomiting and dizziness; long use may lead to depression. Valerian is used in soaps and makes a soothing bath. A decoction can be used as a facial wash to treat acne and skin rashes. The oil is added to tobacco and beverages.

**How to grow**   Valerian is easy to grow from crown or runner divisions or seed in rich, moist soil. Seed should not be covered, only

Valerian

pressed into the soil. Plants should be spaced 15 to 18 inches apart. Cutting the flowers after they bloom encourages root growth. Plants should be divided every 3 years and replanted in new soil.

## Vervain, blue vervain, herb-of-the-cross

*Verbena officinalis*
*ver-BEE-na*

▮ Zones 3–10
Full sun
Interesting weed

**How to identify**   A common weed in pastures and along roadsides, vervain has opposite, oblong, coarsely toothed lower leaves that look like elongated oak leaves. The upper leaves are more slender. The flowers are not showy; they are borne in rings on long, slender, erect stems up to 2 feet tall. Each lilac-hued flower has 5 petals and blooms from June to October.

**How to use**   There are many showy, blooming verbenas, but this plant is one to be tucked in a back corner of the herb garden. The American colonists brought this unassuming herb to North America and used it as a tonic and general cure-all. Some believed that it lifted depression, countered nervous exhaustion, and was effective in treating migraine. Chewing the plant or the root was once thought to strengthen gums and teeth. But even in moderate doses, vervain can cause vomiting. Pregnant women should not ingest any of the herb.

**How to grow**   Vervain grows easily from seed; although it is short lived, it reseeds itself readily. In the wild it is usually found in rich, moist soil in full sun.

**Vinca, periwinkle, Madagascar-periwinkle**
*Catharanthus roseus*
*kath-ar-ANN-thus*

▌Zones 7–10
Full sun to light shade
Ornamental

**How to identify**   This is a common bedding annual in the North, a ground cover in the South. It has opposite, glossy dark green leaves about 2 inches long, ½ inch wide, and rounded at the ends. It grows 1 to 2 feet tall and blooms in shades of white, pink, lavender, and rose, sometimes with a different color eye. Flowers are about an inch across with 5 petals. This tidy plant blooms neatly, with no unsightly faded flowers or seedpods, all summer long.

**How to use**   Shorter varieties are lovely in containers; all are excellent as bedding plants or ground covers on banks and in rough

**Vervain**

places or where other plants have trouble getting established.

The juice from vinca leaves has been used to ease the pain of wasp stings and as a gargle for sore throats; an extract of the flowers was once used as an eyewash. Vinca can have side effects, however, including vomiting and hair loss. Excessive home use is not recommended.

**How to grow** Vinca starts easily from seed sown indoors in March or outside after danger of frost. Barely covered seed takes 15 to 20 days to germinate. Seedlings that have developed their second pair of leaves should be transplanted to individual pots and hardened off before planting in the garden. Plants should be set 8 to 15 inches apart; they will withstand drought once established. Vinca will continue to bloom all year in the South, until frost in the North. When the old plants become shaggy they can be clipped back. New plants will keep coming up as they self-sow. Vinca also starts easily from cuttings.

### Violet, purple violet, florist's violet, johnny-jump-up, heart's-ease
*Viola* species
*vye-O-la*

▮ Zones 3–10
Sun to partial shade
Ornamental, fragrance

**How to identify** One of the most beloved heralds of spring, the purple violet (*V. odorata*) blooms wild in the woods in much of the United States. Basal rosettes of heart-shaped dark green leaves with scalloped edges grow from 2 to 12 inches tall. Each spring nodding lavender to deep purple flowers appear on delicate stems. A few white and yellow varieties can be found in some woods, but the purple violet is the most fragrant. The plants

Top: Vinca
Bottom: Violet

spread on creeping runners called stolons. Johnny-jump-up, or heart's-ease (*V. tricolor*), has pansylike leaves and purple, white, and yellow flowers ¼ to 1 inch long. Actually a biennial, it reseeds readily.

**How to use**   Purple violets make ideal woodland ground covers. All parts of the plant are edible and high in vitamin C. Leaves, buds, and flowers can be added to spring salads or greens or used to thicken soups. Dried flowers can color jams, fruit drinks, wines, and salads. Purple violets are one of the traditional flowers to candy with sugar (see page 98) and use to decorate cakes and pastries.

The dried petals of purple violets add color, though not long-lasting fragrance, to potpourris. Their fragrance varies and is so subtle and fleeting that many people are sur-

prised to learn that their fragrance was once so important. Violets are still used in the most expensive perfumes, although they've been replaced by synthetics in much of the industry. A decoction of flowers can be used for an eye bath and mouthwash; a decoction of leaves makes a facial steam. Crushed fresh leaves can be used on bruises and boils.

Johnny-jump-up was once used for love potions, its purple petals symbolizing memories, white symbolizing loving thoughts, and yellow symbolizing souvenir. None of its healing claims has been validated.

**How to grow**   Violets and johnny-jump-ups are easiest to start by divisions or runners set 1 foot apart in moist, humusy soil. Purple violets prefer partial shade; johnny-jump-ups prefer sun.

**Johnny-jump-up**

## Wintergreen, partridgeberry, mountain-tea, teaberry

*Gaultheria procumbens*
*gual-THEE-ree-a*

▌Zones 4–7
Partial shade
Culinary, decorative, cosmetic

**How to identify**   Wintergreen is a shrubby evergreen of the heath family that grows only 6 inches tall. It is found in acid soil in woods and on mountains from Canada to Georgia. The stems are half underground with upright tips. Shiny, ovate leaves are finely toothed, pale green or yellow-green when young, dark green and leathery when mature, reddish purple in winter. The leaves grow 2 inches long. Urn-shaped, ¼-inch white to pinkish flowers bloom in July and August; the red berries that follow provide food for deer, partridge, and other animals all winter long.

**How to use**   Wintergreen makes an interesting ground cover for shady places and is attractive in rock gardens or rock walls.

American colonists made tea from the leaves. Native Americans ate the berries raw or cooked with grease or dried for winter use. They also used poultices of the leaves to soothe muscle aches, swelling, wounds, rashes, toothaches, arthritis, and rheumatism.

The active constituent in wintergreen, methyl salicylate, is found in the oil, which was distilled from the dried plants. The oil is poisonous in large doses, and has caused fatalities in children who drank it. Although it can be safe in very small amounts for most people, it can also burn even when applied externally, so it is not recommended at all for home use. The oil is now synthesized for such products as wintergreen gum, candy, toothpaste, and birch beer.

**How to grow**   Plants can be started from seed sown on the surface; the seed needs light to germinate. Seed may also benefit from cold treatment. It takes 3 to 100 days to germinate. Plants are easier to start from cuttings, layering, divisions, or suckers. The soil should be acid and moist, and the plants should be mulched with pine needles.

**Wintergreen**

## Yarrow, milfoil, bloodwort, stanchgrass, thousand-leaf

*Achillea millefolium*
*a-KILL-ee-a*

▮ Zones 3–10
Full sun
Ornamental, medicine, dye

**How to identify**   Yarrow is a perennial plant growing from 8 inches to 3 feet tall with stems branching near the top, feathery gray or green foliage of finely divided, almost fernlike leaflets, and flat clusters of flowers. The species blooms from May to November with many tiny yellow-centered daisylike flowers, each with 5 petallike white ray flowers. Yarrow grows wild in fields, roadsides, and open places in most of the country except the Southwest.

**How to use**   Several related and improved varieties are outstanding for specimen planting or in flower borders and rock, herb, or cutting gardens. As a ground cover yarrow stops erosion on banks; woolly yarrow can be mowed and used as a fragrant lawn substitute. Some gardeners say that yarrow increases the essential oils in other herbs planted nearby. It attracts beneficial insects, such as predatory wasps.

Flowers of improved cultivars bloom from late spring through summer in white, lime green, pink to crimson, yellow, and gold. The foliage and flowers are used by florists in arrangements and dried for winter bouquets and wreaths.

Native Americans of at least 46 tribes have treated a number of ailments with yarrow. Yarrow contains salicylic acid (the active ingredient in aspirin). In Sweden and Africa, it has been used as a substitute for hops in brewing beer. Poultices can be applied to wounds or bruises. Yarrow is added to lotions as an astringent. The flowers make a yellow dye, the whole plant an olive-hued dye.

**Caution**   Ingesting yarrow can cause sensitivity to sunlight in some people.

**How to grow**   Yarrow is easy and quick to grow from seed. If seed is sown indoors in March, the plants will bloom the first year. Clumps can be divided in spring or fall. Yarrow adapts to many soils and withstands drought. The most difficult form to grow, creeping yarrow, requires excellent drainage or it may rot. For drying, flowers should be cut while in full bloom and hung upside down.

**Yarrow 'Summer Pastels'**

## MAIL-ORDER SOURCES

Here is a list of suppliers of fresh herbs, herb seeds, dried flowers, teas, essential oils, and craft supplies, as well as gardening accessories, soil amendments, and beneficial insects. If your garden center doesn't carry what you want, you can try these mail-order sources. Catalogs are free unless otherwise indicated. Note that some appreciate a stamped self-addressed envelope (SASE).

**Brundy's Exotics**
P.O. Box 820874
Houston, TX 77282-0874
Catalog $2
*Exotic gingers, butterfly-attracting plants*

**Companion Plants**
7247 North Coolville Ridge Road
Athens, OH 45701
614-592-4643
Catalog $2
*Extensive list of herb varieties*

**ECHO, Inc.**
(Educational Concerns for Hunger Organization)
1730 Durrance Road
North Fort Myers, FL 33917
Catalog $2, plus SASE
*Unusual seeds*

**Gardens Alive!**
5100 Schenley Place
Lawrenceburg, IN 47025
*Organic garden products, natural controls, soil amendments*

**Hartman's Herb Farm**
Old Dana Road
Barre, MA 01005
508-355-2015
Catalog $2
*Dried flowers, craft supplies, essential oils*

**Hearthstone House**
1600 Hilltop Road
Xenia, OH 45385
*Hand-painted slate markers, garden art, wholesale and retail*

**Herb Gathering, Inc.**
5742 Kenwood Avenue
Kansas City, MO 64110
SASE
*Fresh herbs, catnip toys*

**J. L. Hudson**
Star Route 2, Box 337
La Honda, CA 94020
Catalog $1
*Unusual seeds, information*

**Le Jardin du Gourmet**
Box 75C
St. Johnsbury Center, VT 05863
*Extensive list of vegetables and herbs, 25-cent packets*

**Johnny's Selected Seeds**
Foss Hill Road, Box 2580
Albion, ME 04910
*Cover crop seeds*

**Nichol's Garden Nursery**
1190 North Pacific Highway
Albany, OR 97321-4598
*Herbs, rare seeds, teas, essential oils*

**Richters**
357 Highway 47
Goodwood, Ontario L0C 1A0
Canada
905-640-6677
*Exceptional color catalog, many unusual varieties, gardening supplies, beneficial insects, herb books*

**Sandy Mush Herb Nursery**
316 Surrett Cove Road
Leicester, NC 28748-9622
*Catalog $6, plant list free*

**Territorial Seed Co.**
P.O. Box 157
Cottage Grove, OR 97424
*Herbs, essential oils, supplies, mortar and pestles*

**Thompson & Morgan, Inc.**
Box 1308
Jackson, NJ 08527
*Extensive color catalog of flowering plants*

**Urban Farmer's Source Book**
Worm's Way
3151 South Highway 446
Bloomington, IN 47401-9111
Catalog $3
*Beneficial insects, drip irrigation systems, gardening supplies, hydroponic equipment*

**Well-Sweep Herb Farm**
205 Mt. Bethel Road
Port Murray, NJ 07865
908-852-5390
Catalog $2
*Dried herbs, plants, seeds*

# GLOSSARY

**Acid soil**  Having a pH of less than 7 and containing no free lime.

**Alkaline soil**  Having a pH greater than 7. Some herbs thrive in alkaline soil but most prefer slightly acid to neutral soil.

**Alternate leaves**  Growing singly along the stem rather than opposite.

**Anesthetic**  Causing loss of feeling or consciousness.

**Annual**  Plant that completes its life cycle from seed to seed production in one growing season and then dies.

**Antibiotic**  Substance that destroys or stops the growth of disease-causing organisms.

**Antiseptic**  Substance that prevents sepsis, decay, or infection, inhibits the action of microorganisms, and kills germs.

**Aromatherapy**  Use of fragrant plants to enhance beauty, health, and well-being, usually involving essential oils and inhalation, massage, and relaxation.

**Aromatic**  Having a pleasant or spicy scent or flavor.

**Astringent**  Causes the skin to draw together, tighten. Can check minor bleeding.

**Balm**  Fragrant, soothing, healing ointment, derived from the word *balsam.*

**Basal**  Growing from the base of a stem or from the crown of the plant.

**Biennial**  Plant that takes two growing seasons to complete its life cycle, often making vegetative growth the first year and reproductive growth the second.

**Blender**  In perfume, a secondary, complementary fragrance that makes the other ingredients mingle well. In the kitchen, an appliance that mixes, chops, and purées.

**Botany**  Study of plant growth, form, function, and classification.

**Bract**  Modified leaf that often appears to be the flower, as in poinsettia and dogwood, sometimes found at the base of the flower stalk.

**Compound leaf**  Divided into two or more leaflets all arising from the same bud.

**Crown**  Base of an herbaceous perennial plant; the point at or near ground level from which the roots and leaves arise.

**Culpeper, Nicholas (1616–54)**  Noted English apothecary and author of *Herbal* and *The English Physician.*

**Cutting**  Bud, leaf, root, or shoot removed from one plant and induced to root and start a new plant.

**Deadhead**  To remove spent flowers both for neatness and to prevent the plant from going to seed.

**Deciduous**  Usually refers to trees and shrubs that lose their leaves all at once just before winter, as opposed to coniferous, or evergreen.

**Decoction**  Herbal preparation made by boiling bark, seeds, and roots or any plant part, usually a part that is hard and woody, in water in a covered container, then simmering for 15 minutes or longer.

**Dioscorides, Pedanius**  Greek physician who lived in the first century A.D., probably shortly after Christ. He wrote *Materia Medica,* which stood as the most authoritative herbal for the next 1,500 years. Considered the father of modern botany.

**Distillation**  Process of extracting an herbal essence by heating the herb in a liquid to separate the more volatile parts, and then condensing and collecting the vapor as it cools.

**Diuretic**  Substance that increases the flow of urine from the body.

**Essence**  Concentrated herbal medicine or cosmetic, usually a solution of 1 ounce of essential oil in 2 cups of alcohol.

**Essential oil**  Volatile and fragrant liquid produced in various parts of herbs. Used in cosmetics, medicines, and potpourris and sold by herb-craft suppliers and aromatherapists.

**Evergreen**  Plant whose leaves remain green all year and fall off a few at a time throughout the year rather than all at once in fall; coniferous.

**Extract**  Concentrated and potent part of a plant, often a strong decoction.

**Fixative**  Substance added to potpourri or perfume to absorb and preserve the fragrances.

**Floret**  Individual flower in a cluster, or a small flower.

**Flower head**  Entire cluster of flowers on a stem.

**Genus**  Group of closely related plants, the first word of the Latin botanical name.

**Gerard, John (1545–1612)**  English herbalist and author of *Gerard's Herbal,* published in 1597; perhaps the best known of the herbalists.

**Hardy**  Referring to a plant that can survive the winter outdoors.

**Herb**  Any part of any plant with potential uses—culinary, aromatic, therapeutic, medicinal, cosmetic, insecticidal, insect-attracting, or for natural dyes—beyond the conventional uses of plants for landscaping or food production.

**Herbaceous**  Any perennial plant whose stems are not woody and whose leaves and stems die to the ground in winter.

**Herbalist**  Person skilled in the identification and use of plants; originally, an apothecary or the author of an herbal.

**Hippocrates** Greek physician and herbalist who lived about 400 B.C. and is considered the father of modern medicine, hence the term *Hippocratic oath.*

**Infusion** Herbal preparation made by steeping herbs in just-boiled water. Made like tea but steeped longer and therefore stronger.

**Linnaeus, Carolus (1707–78)** Swedish botanist and physician whose classification system of naming plants is still largely used today.

**Macerate** Soak to soften or to extract by steeping in a solvent.

**Mordant** Substance used to fix the color in dyeing; as a verb, to treat with such a substance.

**Mortar and pestle** Bowl and clublike tool used to pound or grind seeds, leaves, or other material.

**Mulch** Material such as straw, leaves, grass clippings, or plastic used to cover the ground and protect plant roots. Keeps in moisture, evens soil temperatures, and blocks weed growth.

**Perennial** Plant, usually herbaceous, that lives from year to year.

**pH** Scale for measuring acidity and alkalinity. Neutral is 7; anything below is acid, anything above is alkaline.

**Pliny the Elder (A.D. 23–79)** Roman who wrote *Natural History* in 37 books, often quoted even today as an authority.

**Potpourri** French term referring to a mixture of herbs and spices used mostly for fragrance.

**Propagate** Increase and reproduce plants by seeds or asexual methods such as cuttings, layering, grafting.

**Rhizome** Thick, underground stem that stores food and produces roots and shoots.

**Runner** Stem that spreads along the ground and roots at various places as it goes. Most strawberries, thyme, and pennyroyal spread by runners.

**Self-seeding or self-sowing** Referring to plants whose dropped seeds produce a continuous succession of new plants.

**Simple** Medieval term for a medicinal plant or herb.

**Species** In the Latin botanical name of a plant, the second word. The classification below genus and above variety.

**Spice** Strongly flavored, aromatic substance, primarily from bark, root, berry, or pod and most often from vine, shrub, or tree grown in tropical regions of the Eastern Hemisphere.

**Theophrastus (c. 372–c. 287 B.C.)** Greek philosopher and history's first scientific botanist.

**Tincture** Extract made with herbs and alcohol, sometimes with vinegar, rather than water.

**Tisane** French word for tea.

**Topiary** System of pruning evergreen trees and shrubs to produce fanciful, geometric, or animal shapes.

**Umbel** Flat-topped flower head, characteristic of the carrot family.

**Variegated** Usually refers to leaves with more than one color, such as edges, spots, or strips of white, cream, or light green on a green background.

**Volatile** Quickly evaporating.

**Wort** Anglo-Saxon word or suffix originally meaning "root," then "herb" or "plant," occurring in names such as mugwort, liverwort, bloodwort.

*Nepeta*
  *cataria. See* catnip
  ×*faasenii*, 194
  *grandiflora*, 194
  *mussinii. See N.* ×
    *faasenii*
*Nerium oleander. See*
  oleander
New Jersey tea (redroot;
  wild-snowball)
  (*Ceanothus ameri-
  canus*), *244*, **244–45**
New York Botanical
  Garden, *20*
Nicandra (apple-of-Peru;
  shooflyplant)
  (*Nicandra physa-
  loides*), 6, 35, 125,
  *245*, **245–46**
*Nicandra physaloides. See*
  nicandra
*Nicotiana alata. See*
  nicotiana
Nicotiana (*Nicotiana
  alata*), uses for,
  potpourri, 112
*Nigella*
  *damascena. See* love-in-
    a-mist
  *sativa. See* cumin, black
Nightshade, deadly
  (*Atropa belladonna*),
  toxicity of, 44, 82
Nosegay, 160–61, *160*
Nutmeg, 6, 78, 110, 161
Nutmegflower. *See*
  cumin, black

**O**

Oak, 164
  Jerusalem. *See*
    ambrosia
Oakmoss, 115, 152
Oatmeal, 137, 142
*Ocimum* spp. *See* basil
Oil
  almond, 137, 138, 141,
    143, 145, 146, 149,
    151
  bitter, 139
    anise seed, 139
    antiseptic, 138
    astringent, 138
    avocado, 137, 138
    basil, 138, 139, 146
    bergamot, 125, 138,
      139, 146, 147,
      149, 151
    black pepper, 146
    calendula, 137, 138
    carrot, 137, 138
    castor. *See* red turkey
    cedar, 124, 139
    cinnamon bark, 139

Oil (*continued*)
  citrus, 139
  cloves, 125, 139
  corn, 138
  essential
    in cosmetics, 144–49
      *passim*, 151
    for massage, 138
    as moth repellent,
      124
    for perfume, 141
    for potpourri, 116
    in soap, 125
  evening primrose,
    137, 138
  fennel, 139
  geranium, 110, 138, 144
  herb, 88–89
  hyssop, 139
  insect-repellent, 124,
    138
  jasmine, 110, 116, 138
  jojoba, 137, 138, 141
  juniper, 125, 138, 139
  lemon, 124, 125, 138,
    146, 149
  lubicating, 138
  marjoram, 138, 139
  Massage, 137–39
  muscatel, 115
  myrrh, 139
  neroli. *See* oil, orange
    blossom
  olive, 88, 137, 138, 147
  orange
    blossom (neroli oil),
      116, 125, 138
    sweet, 116, 125, 149
  pennyroyal, 139
  peppermint, 124, 125,
    126, 138, 139, 149
  red turkey, 132, 137
  rose, 139, 144, 148, 149
  rosemary, 110, 125, 138,
    139, 149, 151
  safflower, 137, 144
  sage, 139
    clary, 139
  sesame, 137, 138, 147
  soy, 137, 138, 144
  sunflower, 137, 138,
    145, 151
  vanilla, 149
  wheat germ, 137,
    138, 143
  wintergreen, 139
Oil Treatment, Hair, 151
Oleander (*Nerium ole-
  ander*), toxicity of, 82
Olive oil, 137, 138, 147
Onion, wild (*Allium
  stellatum*), 19
Orange, mock. *See* mock
  orange

Orange (*Citrus* spp.), 112
  bergamot (*C. bergar-
    mia*), oil of, 125,
    138, 139, 146, 147,
    149, 151
  blossoms (flowers),
    104, 141, 151
  oil of (neroli oil), 116,
    125, 138
  oil of sweet, 116,
    125, 149
  zest. *See* zest, citrus
Orange flower water,
  143, 145
Oregano (*Origanum
  vulgare*), *246*, **246–47**
  to dry, 156
  growing, 23, 32, *73*
  recipes
    in oil, 89
    in pesto, 86
    in stuffing, 78
    in vinegar, 87
  uses for
    decoration, 161
    dye, 37
    potpourri, 112
    wild, 37
  *see also Origanum*
Oregon-grape. *See*
  mahonia
*Origanum*
  *heracleoticum*, 247
  *marjorana. See*
    marjoram
  *vulgare*
    *See* oregano
    ssp. *hirtum*, 247
Orrisroot (Florentine iris;
  German iris) (*Iris
  germanica* var.
  *florentina*, 248,
  **248–49**
  foot powder, 149
  in pillows, 152
  potpourri, 112, 114,
    115, 122, 123
  shampoo, 151
Osage-orange (bois d'arc;
  hedge-apple) (*Ma-
  clura pomifera*), *249*,
  **249–50**
  as insect repellent, 6,
    123–24
Oswego-tea. *See*
  bergamot
*Oxalis. See* wood sorrel
*Oxalis stricta. See* wood
  sorrel, yellow

**P**

*Paeonia* hybrids. *See*
  peony
Palm, 113

Pansy (*Viola cornuta*),
  82, 113
*Papaver*
  spp. *See* poppy
  *orientale. See* poppy,
    oriental
  *rhoeas. See* poppy, corn
Papaya, 136
Paraffin, 165, 167
Parkinson, John, 213
Parsley (*Petroselinum
  crispum*), 35, *53*, *73*,
  79, *79*, 164, *250*,
  **250–51**
  Chinese. *See* coriander
  'Dwarf Curled', *24*
  flatleaf Italian, 32, *73*
  freezing, 65
  gourmet. *See* chervil
  growing, 32, 47, 64, *73*
  horse-. *See* alexanders
  identifying, 19
  Italian. *See* parsley,
    flatleaf
  recipes
    in butter, 90
    for pesto, 86
    in stuffing, 78
    in vinegar, 87
  salting, 69
  uses for
    breath freshener, 6
    in cosmetics, 147, 149
    dye, 37
    hair, 151
Parsnip (*Pastinaca
  sativa*), 19
  wild. *See* angelica
Partridgeberry. *See*
  wintergreen
*Passiflora*
  spp. *See* passionflower
  *alatocaerulea*, 251
  *jamesonii*, 251
Passionflower
  (apricotvine; may-
  pop) (*Passiflora* spp.),
  22, 159, *251*, **251–52**
  *see also Passiflora*
Paste, hair coloring,
  151–52
*Pastinaca sativa. See*
  parsnip
Pastry, Herbed Quiche, 97
Patchouli (*Pogostemon
  cablin*), 112, 115, 148
  oil of, 138, 146, 148
  *P. patchouli*, as a
    fixative, 115, 152
Paths
  herbs for, 26
  to install, 30–31
Paving stones, herb-
  etched, 30

## U.S. MEASURE AND METRIC MEASURE CONVERSION CHART

| | | **Formulas for Exact Measures** | | | **Rounded Measures for Quick Reference** | | |
|---|---|---|---|---|---|---|---|
| | Symbol | When you know: | Multiply by: | To find: | | | |
| **Mass (weight)** | oz | ounces | 28.35 | grams | 1 oz | | = 30 g |
| | lb | pounds | 0.45 | kilograms | 4 oz | | = 115 g |
| | g | grams | 0.035 | ounces | 8 oz | | = 225 g |
| | kg | kilograms | 2.2 | pounds | 16 oz | = 1 lb | = 450 g |
| | | | | | 32 oz | = 2 lb | = 900 g |
| | | | | | 36 oz | = 2¼ lb | = 1000 g (1 kg) |
| **Volume** | pt | pints | 0.47 | liters | 1 c | = 8 oz | = 250 ml |
| | qt | quarts | 0.95 | liters | 2 c (1 pt) | = 16 oz | = 500 ml |
| | gal | gallons | 3.785 | liters | 4 c (1 qt) | = 32 oz | = 1 liter |
| | ml | milliliters | 0.034 | fluid ounces | 4 qt (1 gal) | = 128 oz | = 3¾ liter |
| **Length** | in. | inches | 2.54 | centimeters | ⅜ in. | | = 1.0 cm |
| | ft | feet | 30.48 | centimeters | 1 in. | | = 2.5 cm |
| | yd | yards | 0.9144 | meters | 2 in. | | = 5.0 cm |
| | mi | miles | 1.609 | kilometers | 2½ in. | | = 6.5 cm |
| | km | kilometers | 0.621 | miles | 12 in. (1 ft) | | = 30.0 cm |
| | m | meters | 1.094 | yards | 1 yd | | = 90.0 cm |
| | cm | centimeters | 0.39 | inches | 100 ft | | = 30.0 m |
| | | | | | 1 mi | | = 1.6 km |
| **Temperature** | °F | Fahrenheit | ⅝ (after subtracting 32) | Celsius | 32° F | | = 0° C |
| | °C | Celsius | ⅝ (then add 32) | Fahrenheit | 212° F | | = 100° C |
| **Area** | in.² | square inches | 6.452 | square centimeters | 1 in.² | | = 6.5 cm² |
| | ft² | square feet | 929.0 | square centimeters | 1 ft² | | = 930 cm² |
| | yd² | square yards | 8361.0 | square centimeters | 1 yd² | | = 8360 cm² |
| | a. | acres | 0.4047 | hectares | 1 a. | | = 4050 m² |